HOLLOW
GODS

HOLLOW
GODS

Why Liberalism Became
a Destructive Religion

DAVIDSON LOEHR

atmosphere press

TABLE OF CONTENTS

OPENING ARGUMENT 3

CHAPTER ONE: We Outgrew Traditional Religion 20

CHAPTER TWO: How We Replaced God and Heaven 40

CHAPTER THREE: Why only We can Envision This
Utopia. And What Kind of Government We Need 97

CHAPTER FOUR: How to Create the
(Socialist) Utopia..131

CHAPTER FIVE: Our Betrayal of Education..................... 155

CHAPTER SIX: Liberal Racism—Saving Whites,
Sacrificing Blacks 184

CHAPTER SEVEN: Some Distinctions.............................. 210

CLOSING ARGUMENT..222

BIBLIOGRAPHY 271

ANTAEUS:

Antaeus was the son of the sea god Poseidon and the Earth goddess Gaia in Greek mythology. He made all strangers who were passing by wrestle with him. Whenever Antaeus touched the Earth, his strength was renewed so that he was invincible, especially if thrown to the ground. Heracles encountered him in his 11th assigned Labor and was compelled to wrestle Antaeus to pass. Heracles figured out the source of his strength in combat and, lifting him from the Earth, crushed him to death.

It is the mark of an educated mind to entertain a thought without accepting it.

• Aristotle

Nothing is more annoying than a low man raised to a high place.

• (Roman proverb)

Imagine this game — I call it "tennis without a ball." The players move around on a tennis court just as in tennis, and they even have rackets, but no ball. Each one reacts to his partner's stroke as if, or more or less as if, a ball had caused his reaction. (Maneuvers.) The umpire, who must have an "eye" for the game, decides in questionable cases whether a ball has gone into the net, etc., etc. This game is obviously quite similar to tennis, and yet, on the other hand, it is **fundamentally different**."

• (Last Writings on the Philosophy of Psychology, vol. I, p. 110. ["The philosophy of psychology" was Wittgenstein's term for epistemology])

The most courageous act is still to think for yourself. Aloud.

• Coco Chanel

*Few men are willing to brave the disapproval of their fellows,
the censure of their colleagues, the wrath of their society.
Moral courage is a rarer commodity than bravery in battle or great
intelligence. Yet it is the one essential, vital quality for those who seek
to change the world which yields most painfully to change.*
• Robert F. Kennedy

*Let me never fall into the vulgar mistake of dreaming that
I am persecuted whenever I am disagreed with.*
• Ralph Waldo Emerson

*Reader! To whatever visible church, synagogue, or mosque you may
belong! See if you do not find more true religion among the host of the
excommunicated than among the far greater host who
excommunicated them.*
• Moses Mendelssohn

*Liberal institutions cease to be liberal as soon as they are attained:
later on, there are no worse nor more thorough injurers of freedom
than liberal institutions.*
• Friedrich Nietzsche

*If liberty means anything at all, it means the right to tell people
what they do not want to hear.*
• George Orwell

Our blight is ideologies—they are the long-expected Anti-Christ!
• Carl Jung, The Tibetan Book of the Great Liberation:
On the Method of Realizing Nirvana Through Knowing the Mind

OPENING ARGUMENT

This has been a painful book to write. I have been a liberal all my life and have believed some of the things in this book—not all, but some. My credentials look like the definition of an ultra-liberal. Consider:

1. My undergraduate degree in music theory is from the University of Michigan, which I attended from 1967-69, just after returning from my year in Vietnam. While there in the Army, I served first as the Vietnam Entertainment Officer. Then, when I felt cowardly and ashamed because all of my Officer Candidate School classmates were in the field, I transferred out to the field and served my final seven months as a combat photographer and press officer with the 11th Armored Cavalry Regiment in Xuan Loc. 1967 was also just five years after Tom Hayden wrote the Port Huron Statement on behalf of the SDS students. He had been editor of the Michigan Daily newspaper on campus, and his name was still in the air while I finished my final two years of undergraduate work.

2. I did my graduate work at the University of Chicago, where my M.A. was on "Methods of studying religion". My Ph.D. covers theology, the philosophy of religion, philosophy of science, and Wittgenstein's "Language Philosophy". My Ph.D. dissertation was "The Legitimate Heir to Theology: A Study of Ludwig Wittgenstein"—that's liberal, bordering on heretical.

3. I have been a Fellow in the liberal Jesus Seminar since 1992 and have presented one keynote address for them.

4. My first book was published in 2005: *America, Fascism & God: Sermons from a Heretical Preacher* (Chelsea Green Publishing Co.). The book had back cover endorsements from Robert F. Kennedy Jr., Chris Hedges, and George Lakoff. Later, RFK interviewed me on his radio show, I served on a panel with George Lakoff at a Unitarian General Assembly, and hosted Chris Hedges for a weekend visit to Austin. The book sold 10,000 copies. My most recent book is *Stories of Life: The Nature, Formation, and Consequences of Character* 2nd edition, (Palmetto Publishing, October 2021).

5. From 1986 to 2009, I served as a liberal minister in Unitarian Universalist churches. I also led more than 25 weekend workshops on science, religion, and the Jesus Seminar at churches and summer conferences around the country and wrote some articles for the denomination's monthly magazine.

6. Since 2014, I have been a presenter in the International Big History Association, presenting papers at our biennial meetings. I was also asked to write a chapter for our book, *Science, Religion and Deep Time* (Routledge Press, 2022). My chapter title is "The Nature of Humans, Science, and Religion." My 2021 presentation was on "Reclaiming Some of Religion's Insights," and I served on a panel with other presenters. The focus of my paper was on a personal story of claiming and owning the life-over-death psychological power of "faith healing" (available on YouTube in the 2021 International Big History Association meeting).

I love etymology, so let's start with some. My favorite definition of "liberal" is "a bigger helping". But during the past couple of decades, I've been increasingly uncomfortable with the ideology championed by the loudest voices of political, secular, and religious liberals. Not only does the ideology fail to be supported by empirical facts, but in the case of the "new" evangelical fundamentalist secular religion that appeals to many liberals—environmental activism—their beliefs and actions have led to tens of millions of innocent deaths, for which I wish the activists could be held accountable.[1]

Still, most of my liberal friends continue to be sure that only the liberal ideology is correct, that only it can be a gift to our society and world. The liberal-conservative political clashes feel like the war between Baptists and Catholics: the dynamics and passions are religion, not politics. At the beginning of 2019, I began writing some of these thoughts down. But the more I learned, the more extensive and more complex the picture became; it seemed to touch almost everything, and I couldn't put it together into a clear and coherent story. The quarantined seclusion of the Covid era in 2020 gave me more time to read, think, and make notes. Finally, in early 2021 this bigger picture began coming into focus. The final draft was completed in August 2022.

It's important to say at the beginning that this is *not* a condemnation of liberals! We are as decent and well-meaning as

---

[1] Dichlorodiphenyltrichloroethane is commonly known as DDT, developed in 1874 and still the most effective insecticide against the anopheles mosquito which carries malaria. Since the DDT ban in 1973, malaria has killed at least 96 million people. Famine, preventable through responsible government management and proper utilization of natural resources, kills millions more each year. Brian Sussman, *Climategate: A Veteran Meteorologist Exposes the Global Warming Scam*. WND Books, 2010, p. 8. Scientific studies have shown clearly that DDT is safe for humans, water, fish, birds, and plants, and it remains the best exterminator of the anopheles mosquitos that carry malaria—see Chapter Two.

conservatives or any other comparable group of people. Like almost all people, most liberals (and conservatives) don't know the connections between their beliefs and their deeper origin: the backstories. Humans are, above all, a *social species*: herd animals, easily turned into unthinking crowds chanting in one unreflective and uninformed voice. Think of the partisan crowds at sports or political events, passionate religious arguments, loaded social issues, and so on. We accept what we've been taught by the group and the people with whom our sense of identity is grounded. Every religion, all nationalisms, fraternities, sororities, and advertisers count on this.

And the deep origins and connections of our beliefs are a rough combination of accident, chance, insight, and ideological interpretation. No complex opinions are pure. Many, perhaps most, liberals will initially deny that they believe the things I'm sketching and may deny there could be any significant connection between them. And, since they are good people who mean well and are just as smart as I am, they will deny that they could do the depth and breadth of harm to the world I'm describing. But if my arguments are as clear and strong as I think I've made them, many readers may reconsider, and not happily.

What damage have we done? We have virtually destroyed education in the US—it's not ranked in the top quarter among developed world countries and has been ranked that low for two or three decades, with no sign that anyone knows how to fix it. This fraudulent education has now extended to our kindergartens—since the public school teachers were miseducated in the colleges that we liberals control (see Chapter Five). If anything, I am *understating* the depth and seriousness, as many good books have described in far greater detail.

Destroying the quality (or even the fact) of education was done only partly because the ratio of liberal to conservative faculty—then students—grew from around 3:2 in 1969 to

12.7:1 and more up to a mind-numbing 108:0 for communications and interdisciplinary studies, including journalism. In this same article, the author, Mitchell Langbert, makes this remarkable opening statement:

> The political registration of full-time, Ph.D.-holding professors in top-tier liberal arts colleges is overwhelmingly Democratic. Indeed, faculty political affiliations at 39 percent of the colleges in my sample are Republican free—having zero Republicans. The political registration in most of the remaining 61 percent, with a few important exceptions, is slightly more than zero percent but nevertheless absurdly skewed against Republican affiliation and in favor of Democratic affiliation. Thus, 78.2 percent of the academic departments in my sample have either zero Republicans, or so few as to make no difference.[2]

Langbert says his sample of 8,688 tenure track, Ph.D.-holding professors from 51 of the 66 top ranked liberal arts colleges in the *U.S. News* 2017 report consists of 5,197, or 59.8 percent, who are registered either Republican or Democrat. The mean Democratic-to-Republican ratio (D:R) across the sample is 10.4:1, but because of an anomaly in the definition of what constitutes a liberal arts college in the *U.S. News* survey, I include two military colleges, West Point and Annapolis. If these are excluded, the D:R ratio is a whopping 12.7:1.[3]

Langbert rates the faculty by academic area, and the areas differ in their D:R ratios, from a low of 1.6:1 in Engineering to

[2] "Homogenous: The Political Affiliations of Elite Liberal Arts College Faculty" by Mitchell Langbert, *National Association of Scholars*, Academic Questions Articles, Summer 2018. (https://www.nas.org/academic-questions/31/2/homogenous_the_political_affiliations_of_elite_liberal_arts_college_faculty)
[3] Ibid.

highs of 43.8:1 (Sociology), 48.3:1 (English), 70:1 (Religion) to the two major areas in which there were *no* Republican faculty, producing a ratio of 56:0 in Anthropology and 108:0 in "Communications", which includes journalism and interdisciplinary studies.[4] This helps explain why the media are so far left in their bias.

But the main reason was that we substituted indoctrination and activism for anything that could count as education or teaching young people how to question and think intelligently.

Why did we betray you? We did it because we didn't believe it was any kind of betrayal at all. We believed we had a nearly divine authority and duty to save our society as only we knew how. Though not many people know about the "two cultures", they're the easiest way to understand the deep difference between liberals and conservatives. There are many sources for this, because the two cultures have been noted many times and in many ways for over two millennia (See Chapter Three).

So now this book: **HOLLOW GODS: Why Liberalism Became a Destructive Religion.** Though I don't share all the beliefs here, I decided to write in the royal "We" because it took me so long to see and think clearly enough to write this, and because I feel guilty, on behalf of the smugness I have felt over the years, *so* glad that I was a liberal, and therefore shared in the kind of wisdom that the world needed, but that the "ignorant masses" lacked. I'll admit—defensively—that I knew Plato agreed with me—as did Confucius. We liberals were the Smart people, and our arrogance was just our taking seriously the

---

[4] Ibid.

job history had assigned us: leading the masses toward a utopian future that only we could envision. I think that serious critiques should begin in one's own ideology rather than just piling on "the enemy". I think a book like this should also be written about the betrayals of conservative ideology—but only if it is written by a conservative.

At first, it may not seem like all the parts I sketch could possibly be related; like maybe this is just a wild "conspiracy theory". I'm reminded that the phrase "conspiracy theory" was coined by our CIA back in 1967-68 as a clever way of dismissing—without having to engage—anyone who didn't accept the Warren Commission's theory of JFK's assassination. It was a brilliant phrase, though it makes denial very easy regarding any theories we don't share. "Oh, don't even listen to them. It's just those tinfoil-hat conspiracy theorists!"

In what follows, I confess the liberal beliefs that I and millions of others have had, and the serious, devastating, possibly permanent harm they have done and are doing to individuals, two generations of college students, our country, its politics, liberal religion, racism, sexism, and—through the Activism that has become about the only thing we can still count as Sacred—the unnecessary malaria deaths of over 100 million innocent people.

Some words on the plan of this book. While I have done a fair amount of research on these various subjects, this is *not* written like an academic paper. You don't need a Ph.D.—or any kind of diploma at all—to understand this. My philosophy here agrees with that of William F. Buckley Jr. when he famously quipped "I would rather be governed by the first 2,000 people in the Boston telephone directory than by the 2,000 people on the faculty of Harvard University."

I am trying to understand and be fair to both liberal and

conservative perspectives because I share some of each. I've divided each chapter into three sections:

VISION OF THE ANOINTED[5]: I'll try to explain our liberal beliefs so that any high school student can understand. The ideas are numerous and at times complex, but not hard to comprehend.

WHAT'S WRONG HERE?: Since I am of two minds about some of this, I've added these sections to every chapter to criticize what I've said in the **VISION OF THE ANOINTED** narrative. If you agree with the narrative, you may not agree with these sections. And vice versa.

EXCERPTS FOR A DEEPER UNDERSTANDING: These are excerpts and extended comments from some of the books I read while preparing this one. When we can see the bigger picture in more detail, most high school students can comprehend as clearly as most Ph.D.'s. (I learned this from my involvement in the International Big History Association. While telling the Big History from the Big Bang to today requires many disciplines, we ask all scientists to translate their work into ordinary language that average 18-year-olds can understand.) It would be ideal if all disciplines could translate their messages out of their jargon and into plain talk. If we can't put what we think in easily understood ordinary language, we really don't *know* what we're talking about.

How to read this book

First, read the **OPENING ARGUMENT** and the **CLOSING ARGUMENT.** They will give you an overview of what the book is about, with some idea of the research and reasoning behind it.

---

[5] In earlier drafts of this book, I had called these sections LIBERAL CERTAINTIES. I am indebted to Thomas Sowell for the more revealing description of our certainties as what our actions show we believe to be the VISION OF THE ANOINTED. See his book of the same name.

Second, read the **VISION OF THE ANOINTED** sections of each chapter to understand how we liberals think and why we're sure that we're right. Then read the **WHAT'S WRONG HERE?** sections for an uncensored critique of the ideology of the self-anointed—but dangerously wrong—liberals.

Third, to read other authors' perspectives, go back and spend a lot more time reading through the **EXCERPTS** and Footnotes. That will show you what I've used from the research I did. If your research was different, it will help you understand why and where we disagree. Perhaps it will help you either modify your position, or frame rebuttals to the positions sketched in the **VISION OF THE ANOINTED** or **WHAT'S WRONG HERE?** sections.

So here's the story

This book may look like it's about politics, education, the media, or race and gender, but *it is always about religion*. Specifically, it is about the secular religion liberals have used to fill the vacuum left by our sloughing off traditional Biblical supernatural religion during the past two centuries. Our new secular religion is made up of varieties of *utopianism*, and its evangelical fundamentalist wing, which is Activism—especially environmental activism. We need to feel that we're serving something like the God we no longer believe in and that we're participating in something that's somehow comparable to Heaven. Utopianism lets us believe we're helping build the perfect form of society here and now—socialism, or some form of one-party government under the control of liberals. That's a definition of "totalitarian" government, or as today's Democrats are putting it, "one-party rule". Only we know how to do this, which means that we have replaced God's omniscience with our own anointed wisdom. Since only we can create this perfect society for everyone, we need to control the government of our country—ideally, even the world.

A separate part of the big picture concerns just how we think we can control the US government and society. It seems unrelated, and really was when it first blossomed in 1962 in the SDS movement at the University of Michigan, headed by Tom Hayden.[6] But he had a plan for his socialist utopians to control the country. It sounded completely insane in 1962, when the national SDS membership was only about 200. But by 1968-69, through events nobody could see coming in 1962, SDS membership had grown two-hundredfold to 40,000, and their agenda suddenly became possible. Hayden's plan was that liberals should control the colleges and universities, and through them also control public K-12 education. That would also indoctrinate all the journalism majors who would staff the media outlets. This, Hayden believed, was the way—and the *only* way—that liberals could wind up controlling the US government, as well as the popular understanding of grand abstractions like Truth, Justice, and Utopia. This happened through liberals virtually taking over the K-12 public education, the colleges and universities, and the media during the past five decades. This should terrify every American. Readers over 50 may not realize or believe the virtually total control radical liberal activists now have over both education and the US media. It shocked me too. Check, especially, the excerpts from John M. Ellis's superb 2021 book *The Breakdown of Higher Education: How it Happened, the Damage it Does, and What Can Be Done.*

I have decided not to go into the "manmade" climate scam, which has been called the biggest hoax in human history. It

---

[6] Students for a Democratic Society. The actual form of government the SDS students wanted was a totalitarian socialism, but Tom Hayden and others knew the word "socialism" would feel like an unpatriotic turnoff to many, so they pretended they wanted democracy, while working to undermine it. It was, at least, clever!

has nothing to do with either climate or science, but is a plan to help effect the massive redistribution of wealth, removing power from citizens and making it easier for us—your liberal ruling class—to dissolve democracy and begin establishing the socialism which will let us control virtually everything. It's an important subject, and bigger than the subjects treated in this book, which are more like tactics to reach the ultimate world-wide socialist goal. I might make that a separate book, though there are already many good books on the subject.

We have betrayed you. The prognosis is not good. We will almost certainly destroy democracy, liberal religion, education, any hope of rising above liberal racism, and much more. We are aided by the media, which have become little more than bullhorns for our liberal biases (pun intended). This happened because of a liberal-to-conservative ratio of 8:1 to 12.7:1 and more in colleges and some industries—and a stunning ratio of 108:0 in communications, journalism, and interdisciplinary arts, as stated above. Almost all college majors have been indoctrinated into this ungrounded liberal ideology and see themselves as our culture's saviors.

While the story has many parts and operates on small to huge scales, it is not a hard story to understand. Everyone from high school on can understand it, without needing any diplomas to do so. If you can't understand some parts of this book, it's my fault, not yours.

WHAT'S WRONG HERE?

It will take more words to flesh out the huge, complicated, and interlocking pictures of how we betrayed you, and just what "betrayal" means here. Fortunately, more words are coming in the following chapters.

EXCERPTS

The Breakdown of Higher Education, by John M. Ellis[7]

Another study done by Gallup in June 2018 found that "No other institution has shown a larger drop in confidence over the past three years than higher education." (23)

Marxist ideas have such a hard time of it in the real world that those who espouse them have fled to the campuses for sanctuary. Campuses protect them from the merciless test of reality. (32)

Of the $4,681,192.76 in political contributions made by University of California employees in 2017-2018, no less than 97.46% went to Democratic candidates and causes. (36)

Making politics of any kind central to campus life must be damaging. First of all, political motives will always stunt intellectual curiosity.... Students will never learn to think for themselves if their thought processes must always conclude by fitting into a predetermined belief system. (39)

Radical faculty are making sure that students hear one side only and pressing them to accept it without hearing any other. This alone constitutes a stunning collapse of the quality and integrity of higher education. Democracy itself is damaged by this abuse of higher education. (42)

Courses in Western civilization were once required for all freshmen, but those requirements have now vanished almost everywhere. (97)

[Studies] all find that recent graduates have been very poorly educated. One study after another has found that they write badly, can't reason, can't read any reasonably complex material, have alarming gaps in their knowledge of the history and institutions of the society in which they live, and are in general poorly prepared for the workplace. (100)

---

[7] Encounter Books (August 10, 2021).

When you see high black unemployment, especially young black male unemployment, blame campus radicals. (111)

A study by two University of California economists, Philip S. Babcock of UC Santa Barbara and Mindy Marks of UC Riverside, found that whereas the average student in 1961 did 24 hours of academic work outside class every week, that figure had dropped to only 14 hours by 2010. Richard Arum and Josipa Roksa independently confirmed these findings; in fact, they found even fewer hours of study outside class. Students on average "report spending only 12 hours per week studying. 37% of students report spending less than five hours per week preparing for their courses." (138)

Arum and Roksa found that reading assignments were often so minimal that a third of students reported that they had not taken a single course in the prior semester that required at least 40 pages of reading.... The plain fact is that developing skill in reasoning is not what these teachers want. Making converts is. (139)

This is not education—it is propagandizing. (140)

One Nation, Two Cultures, by Gertrude Himmelfarb (1999)

In 1986, Senator Moynihan said "The central conservative truth is that it is culture, not politics, that determines the success of a society. The central liberal truth is that politics can change a culture and save it from itself. The primacy of culture for the conservatives, and of politics for the liberals, has not always been evident". (59)

Tocqueville believed it was religion in the service of virtue that made freedom possible. (87)

Left Turn: How Liberal Media Bias Distorts the American Mind, by Tim Groseclose (2011)

In at least one important way journalists are very different from the rest of us—they are more liberal. For instance, according to surveys, in a typical presidential election Washington correspondents vote about 93-7 for the Democrat, while the rest of America votes about 50-50. (vii)

What if we could magically remove the metaphoric glass and see, face-to-face, the average American, *once his political views were no longer distorted by media bias*? What would we see? The person whom we'd see would be anyone who has a political quotient near 25. A person's PQ indicates the degree to which he is liberal. [A PQ of 100 is a far left Democrat; a PQ of 0 is a far right Republican.] (viii)

As my results show, if we could magically eliminate media bias, then the average American would think and vote like people who have a PQ near 25. In such a world, American political values would mirror those of present-day regions where the average voter has a 25 PQ. Such regions include the states of Kansas, Texas, and South Dakota. They also include Orange County, California, and Salt Lake County, Utah. (viii)

Please Stop Helping Us: How Liberals Make It Harder for Blacks to Succeed, by Jason L. Riley (2015)

The notion that racism is holding back blacks as a group, or that better black outcomes cannot be expected until racism has been vanquished, is a dodge. And encouraging blacks to look to politicians to solve their problems does them a disservice. Having a black man in the Oval Office is less important than having one in the home. (33)

Today, more than 70% of black children are born to unwed mothers. Only 16% of black households are married couples with children, the lowest of any racial group in the US, while nearly 20% are female-headed with children, which is the highest of any group. (37-38)

Black cultural attitudes toward work, authority, dress, sex, and violence have also proven counterproductive, inhibiting the development of the kind of human capital that has led to socioeconomic advancement for other groups. ... A culture that takes pride in ignorance and mocks learnedness has a dim future. And those who attempt to make excuses for black social pathology rather than condemning these behaviors in no uncertain terms are part of the problem. (50)

Some 90% of black murder victims are killed by other blacks. (74)

Liberals don't help matters by making excuses for counterproductive behavior. Nor do the media by shying away from reporting the truth. (83)

Liberals who claim to care so much about underprivileged blacks not only relegate them to the worst performing schools, but also the most violent schools.... Liberals do no favors for black kids who are in school to learn by sympathizing with black kids who are in school to make trouble. (125)

Blacks as a group, and poor blacks in particular, have performed better in the *absence* of government schemes like affirmative action. (155)

The history of affirmative action in academia since the 1970s is a history of trying to justify holding blacks to lower standards in the name of helping them. (157)

White Guilt: How Blacks and Whites Together Destroyed the Promise of the Civil Rights Era, by Shelby Steele (2006)

One of the delights of Marxian-tinged ideas for the young is the unearned sense of superiority they grant. ... (46)

To up the ante on white guilt this new black consciousness led blacks into a great mistake: to talk ourselves out of the individual freedom we had just won for no purpose whatsoever except to trigger white obligation. (47)

Only in being responsible for one's life can one take agency over it. And agency—the sovereignty and will that we have over our individual lives—is what makes us fully human. (48)

So black militancy, for all its bluster of black pride and its rhetoric of self-determination, is a mask worn always and only for the benefit of whites. (59)

It must be acknowledged that blacks are no longer oppressed in America. (67)

Intellectuals and Society, by Thomas Sowell (2011)

George Orwell said that some ideas are so foolish that only an intellectual could believe them, for no ordinary man could be such a fool. The record of twentieth century intellectuals was especially appalling in this regard. (4)

The Madness of Crowds: Gender, Race and Identity, by Douglas Murray (2019)

At one recent conference on Content Moderation leading figures in both companies suggested that Google currently has around 10,000 and Facebook as many as 30,000 people employed to moderate content. And these figures are more likely to grow than to remain static. (111)

In the pursuit of anti-racism these people turn race from one of many important issues into something which is more important than anything else. At the very moment when the issue of race might at long last have been put to rest, they have decided once again to make it the most important issue of all. (122)

Candace Owens:

There is an ideological civil war happening [in the black community]. Black people that are focused on their past and shouting about slavery. And black people focused on their futures. What you're seeing is victim mentality versus victor mentality. (152)

... the question that the internet age has still not begun to contend with: how, if ever, is our age able to forgive? (176)

You cannot tell people simultaneously "You must understand me" and "You cannot understand me". (240)

Victimhood rather than stoicism or heroism has become something eagerly publicized, even sought after, in our culture. ... In fact, suffering in and of itself does not make someone a better person. A gay, female, black or trans person may be as dishonest, deceitful and rude as anybody else. (252)

To assume that sex, sexuality and skin color mean nothing would be ridiculous. But to assume that they mean everything will be fatal. (256)

A NOTE ON PUNCTUATION. I generally follow the Chicago Manual of Style, but follow the more sensible British rules regarding the placement of commas and periods "outside", rather than "inside," quotation "marks". The exception is when the entire sentence is in quotation marks, like this: "Here, the whole sentence is quoted, so the period belongs *inside* the quotation marks." You may prefer the US rules over the British, but at least you know why I did it my way.

CHAPTER ONE
We Outgrew Traditional Religion

THE VISION OF THE ANOINTED

Everything starts here. During the last two centuries, more and more liberals have grown beyond literal and supernatural religion. This was a positive move. "God" went from being a Guy in the Sky to being a symbol of what we thought of as Ultimacy. What are life's highest ideals, most demanding principles? How much courage does it take to do the right thing—especially when it isn't the popular choice of our community? What *must* we do, whether we like it or not? What must we *not* do? And what's the authority for all this?

Traditional Biblical religion has a ready answer: God. God demands decent and loving behaviors of us (except toward God's enemies—see I Samuel 15:3 and Ezekiel 35:1-9). And there are supernatural rewards and punishments, in Heaven or Hell. As students of religion know, that God of the Bible, Jahweh, was modeled on a tribal chief, so of course "He" would want to dictate rules of thought, belief, and behavior, and emphasize them through rewards and punishments. But as sciences, and scholarship in the history of religion developed in the 19th century, it became much harder to believe such things. God wasn't a Guy but a symbol and a metaphor. We don't need to obey the meanings given to that symbol by other people many centuries ago. Don't exalt ignorant belief.

What then should we do, and why should we do it? How should we live? Who should we be? Without that old father-figure tribal chief God, without Heaven and Hell, why should we even care? And unless we *are* serving God, and the highest ideals, what's the purpose and point of our life? Of what can we be proud? And if we can't answer these questions, why are we living? Merely for our own selfish, narcissistic, trivial wants? Is that all there is to us, just sociopaths? And without the supernatural rewards and punishments, why should we care? Is that really all there is to be to our lives—a pointless, unprincipled, temporary, and selfish existence? Are we to exist as no more than a curse or indifferent presence? And if we let the beliefs and ideologies of our various groups replace God, isn't that just too embarrassing even to contemplate? Are we then, by definition, just insignificantly transient and narcissistic irrelevancies?

These are among the existential questions that can condemn people to desperate and meaningless lives—and there are millions of such lives around. It's hard to overstate the depth, magnitude, or existential power of these questions. This is part of the vacuum left by the removal of God, Heaven, and Hell with no adequate replacements. We lost a vocabulary, and any clear and compelling way of framing the concerns, principles, rules of right and wrong, and the rest of it that had served as a foundation for believers for many centuries in Western civilization. Even that word "existential" is a vast, vague, dramatic, secular way of trying to frame our situation. Without an adequate way of framing these real-life situations, without a legitimate heir to God and "eternal life", we will struggle to get through life, or settle for dangerously superficial and arbitrary "rules": the rules of a club or ideology. Without a fulfilling way to frame who we are and how we should live, we can never believe there is much to our life that matters to anyone—even to us.

Still, the main point—and an extremely important one—is that we liberals, far more than conservatives, have outgrown the traditional Biblical religions of our culture. That's a good thing. And the new (alleged) Good News, as these **VISION OF THE ANOINTED** sections will show, is that we believe we have succeeded in finding a legitimate heir to both the non-existent Heaven and the old Biblical God. If we act proud of this, it's because we *are* proud of it.

WHAT'S WRONG HERE?

A lot. I have a Mennonite friend whose family goes back to the first generation of Mennonites in the early 16th century. I knew her in graduate school, where she was a first-class scholar of religion, as the University of Chicago Divinity School saw clearly: she was, at the time, the only M.A. student they put on a full-ride scholarship. But she too was expelled from the Garden of Eden.

These two elements collided during a Christmas vacation in 1981. In late December, we were sitting together in the coffee shop in the basement of the Divinity School when two other students from seminaries in the area joined us. They knew her by reputation; this was a woman who never made a "B" in her life, and probably set the curve in the majority of her classes. Wonderfully smart and tough. The seminary students, who were required by their seminary to get the academic M.A. in religion from the Divinity School, were whining about how expensive the school was when one of them unwisely turned to my friend and said, "It must be nice, getting your education at no cost!" A word to the wise: don't try to take on people a couple levels smarter, deeper, and quicker than you are. Without missing a beat, my friend said, "No cost? No cost? I have just been home with my family, four generations of Mennonites. They were filled with joy, celebrating the birth of their savior Jesus Christ, the son of God, and their assurance of eternal life together with each other, Jesus, and God in Heaven. Not me. I had lost all of that. What I was doing during that Christmas vacation was simply engaging in familial bonding activities centered on a primitive religious myth. That's what my education cost me." There is an impressive intellect in that insight, but not much comfort or warmth.

This hollowness, this vacuum, has been at the core of liberalism and of liberals for nearly two centuries. Everything that follows—our betrayal and destruction of education, journalism, politics, race relations, the meaning and purpose of life—it all has its roots in this self-anointed soil of empty godlessness. Our real problem is fundamentally and irreducibly a *religious* problem. What follows is about the secular *religion* of these proud and too-arrogant liberals. Understand: this isn't about God, and trying to return to the Biblical God would not be possible anyway. Our world has changed too much from the more naïve ancient world's vulnerability to superstition, beliefs in supernatural gods, heavens and hells, as well as vulnerability to the theological con games of the worst preachers and churches.

Etymology can help here. "Religion" (*re-ligare*) shares its root, *-lig*, with words like *ligament* and *ligature*. It refers to a kind of *connection*. Some have defined religion as a kind of "binding back"—as though once we were somehow "connected" but are no longer—you may recognize the feeling. Our religion, whether we recognize it as a religion or not, is what we most deeply "bind back to" and "connect to" in the most important sense. It grounds our most important identity: who we aspire to be at our best. A good religion can help make our lives meaningful, a blessing to others in our little worlds. A bad religion can damn us and make us a curse without whom the rest of the world might well have been better off. The fact that we haven't adequately filled that vacuum doesn't diminish its terrible power. Habitual denial helps, but it's not enough.

Traditional Biblical religions, at their best, give believers one of the most noble and comforting foundations imaginable. Believers served God: the highest source of good, love, and justice. And the rewards and punishments were dramatic and permanent: eternal life in Heaven, with God, Jesus, the angels and prophets, saints, and all the others on the "A-list" of notable, meaningful former people—or if we fail, in Hell.

The passage of time has made it easy for us liberals to make fun of these beliefs. A Guy in the Sky? Living above the clouds forever? Or burning down under the ground in molten lava forever? Come on, friends: wake up! Grow up! This is a children's comic book! These things aren't real, aren't true, aren't meant for intelligent grown-ups. It's why church attendance is under 20% and falling. Hardly anyone can take these literal pictures seriously any longer.

It's easy to blame this on the passage of time into our "modern" age, or the continuing growth of sciences. But that's too easy. These problems are psychological, theological, existential, **ontological** (one of the most important words in this book).

This is about language. Traditional Christianity's vocabulary gave priests and believers an imaginative world that worked at one level with children and literalists, at another with those who could understand it symbolically and metaphorically, and at still another level for those who could understand what it meant to "live sacred lives" rather than just mouthing sacred words.

Liberals lost that vocabulary. We (rightly) rejected the literalisms because they were supernatural, superstitious, and untrue to reality as revealed by the evolving sciences. Life wasn't created by God in the Garden of Eden. It *evolved* from lower forms of life over a period of hundreds of millions of years. And God never spoke to anyone about anything. The Bible's stories were all written by a bunch of people who didn't always agree and weren't always wise. And while the man Jesus qualifies as one of history's gifted prophets with insight into who we should be and how we should live, most of the sayings attributed to him weren't from him at all, but from sayings common at the time or from those who wrote the New Testament—none of whom actually *knew* the man Jesus.[8]

If there is one word at the heart of what serious religions are about, that word is *ontology*. Sounds like something from a sleep-inducing academic treatise, but its meaning is simple, profound, and challenging. It comes from the Greeks and has two parts. The first two syllables refer to what it means to *be*— to be, to exist, most meaningfully and significantly as a human being. And the last two syllables refer to understanding the first two syllables. At its most fundamental and important level, all religion is about ontology. Does our religion— whether traditional, supernatural, sacred, or secular—really do a good and challenging job of sketching an outline of the way we should be and live as a fulfillment of our best potential and a gift to our larger world, so that when we look back, we can be glad we lived that way? If not, it's a poor—and probably dangerous—fake religion. There are a lot of those around, you know.

But merely rejecting the ancient vocabulary without understanding how that vocabulary was used by some of the best minds at the time is a mistake made by far too many liberals. To choose just one thinker—a man who lived between the time Jesus lived and the time that Christianity was finally formalized in the 4th century, we can take the man Origen, who lived from about 183-185 to about 253-255 when he died in prison

---

[8] The information about Jesus and early Christianity comes from my association with the Jesus Seminar, in which I have been a Fellow since 1992.

after extended torture. Origen was one of the most brilliant minds in the history of any religion. He had one of those genius minds two or three levels above anything most of us could even imagine. I've known a few such gifted people in several areas: music, photography, philosophy, science, religion. And they're always wonderfully humbling. Origen was one of those. This third-century religious fanatic gave up his job, slept on the floor, ate no meat, drank no wine, fasted twice a week, owned no shoes, and reportedly castrated himself because his teenage hormones drew his attention away from the demands of his faith. Origen was the first Christian to write systematic theology. He was a prolific writer who wrote roughly 2,000 treatises in multiple branches of theology, including biblical exegesis, hermeneutics, textual criticism, homiletics, and spirituality.

Here is the three-level understanding Origen developed for the Bible, religion, and life. Remember, this was written in the early 3rd century—1,800 years ago:

"Divine things are communicated to men somewhat obscurely and are the more hidden in proportion to the unbelief or unworthiness of the inquirer.

"Moreover, some of the simpler folk believe such things about God that not even the most unjust and savage of men would believe. And the reason why they have a false apprehension of these things is that they don't understand scripture in its spiritual sense, but only in its literal sense.

"There are three layers of meaning in scripture, each suited to different degrees of intellectual development and spiritual maturity:

"**A.** The simplest folk may be edified by what we may call the **body** of the scriptures (for such is the name we may give to the common and literal interpretation);

"**B.** Those who have begun to make a little progress and are able to perceive something more than that may be edified by the **soul** of scripture;

*"**C.** Finally, those who are most advanced in both mind and spirit may be edified by the **spiritual** dimension of scripture: by those parts that may be said to have been written under the inspiration of the Holy Spirit. These are the believers who are led to live sacred lives, rather than merely understanding sacred words.*

"How then should you understand sacred scriptures? You should understand them by knowing that these mysteries were portrayed figuratively through the narration of what seemed to be human deeds and the handing down of certain legal ordinances and precepts. The aim was that not everyone who wished should have these mysteries laid before his feet to trample upon, but that they should be for the ones who had devoted themselves to studies of this kind with the utmost purity and sobriety and through nights of watching, by which means perchance they might be able to trace out the deeply hidden meaning of the Spirit of God, concealed under the language of an ordinary narrative which points in a different direction.

"In other words, we should try to discover in the scriptures which we believe to be inspired by God a meaning that is worthy of God. And here the Holy Spirit can guide us, for the Spirit calls the attention of the reader, by the impossibility of the literal sense, to an examination of the inner meanings.

*"In summary, all our reading of sacred scriptures must be guided by two considerations. **We are seeking, with honest minds and pure hearts, for those things which are both useful to us, and worthy of God.** If we keep these things in mind, we will not easily be misled." (From Origen's* On First Principles, Book IV, *adapted)*

Origen's three-level structure could make an excellent outline for a Christian religious education program going from kindergarten through adulthood. The many good stories from the Bible could easily become parts of young children's Sunday mornings. Then sometime during high school, the kids will become mentally able to begin understanding the far richer meanings those stories carry as symbols and metaphors. Finally, for adults, Origen's three stages can serve as the spirit of a lifelong religious education. Are churches doing this? Surely some are.

Flippant religious liberals often shrug off the literalism of the Biblical supernatural religion without being aware of the second and third levels of religion that Origen outlined so clearly 1800 years ago. Nor have most liberals come up with anything comparable to Origen's third level: that idea of living lives worthy of "God"—meaning the highest levels of awareness, compassion, love of self and others, a sense of duty to become a gift to our larger world: living a life that's a blessing rather than a curse or an indifferent presence to others. Doing this is not easy, but it is necessary if we are to pretend that we have really found a legitimate heir to religion. So, what's often wrong with liberal pronouncements about the nonsense of (literal) religion is that we have understood religion only at the literal level suitable for children, so our pronouncements mostly just show that we have no idea what religion at its best must be. This means that what we accept as "religion" is likely to be little more than an ideology, or the implicit rules of our club.

But for liberals who no longer read or know the Bible, it can be much harder to design an effective way to build a "legitimate heir" to a lifespan understanding of our place, our duty, our possibilities, and our limitations. Without a god, how can liberals develop a religious—ontological, existential—perspective to keep them from simply succumbing to the arrogant narcissism—and what author Roger L. Simon calls "moral narcissism"—that has spread through liberalism, and most of the Second Culture (see Chapter Three). Simon thinks this moral narcissism of liberals "is destroying our republic, if it hasn't already".[9] I also think it's that deep, that serious, and worth trying to remedy, if it's even possible now.

Why "Hollow Gods"?

For two centuries, liberals have been sloughing off traditional religion, its omniscient supernatural God, and eternal reward in Heaven. They often seem quite proud to have "outgrown" these concepts. So why frame liberalism in theistic terms? It is a central point of this book: understanding liberalism not primarily as a social or political ideology, but as a failed substitute for religion. Our often ungrounded ideals serve as and are treated as our gods. Our atheistic religion is treated as an orthodoxy in colleges, the media, and politics. People trying to cite the traditional God of the Bible are often jeered or shouted down on campuses across the country, just as heretics used to be. So yes, we have gods. But they're hollow. Grown-up religion should be *ontological*, concerned with the deepest and most commanding principles of what it means to be a responsible and compassionate human. When this is expressed in God-talk we call it *theology*. But it needn't be put into God-language, and can communicate with a broader audience if we learn how to express it simply in ordinary language. Below theology is mere *ideology*: far more popular. Now we're into politics and social customs rather than any really high and life-giving principles. As will become clear later, we have substituted our own alleged wisdom for the wisdom of an omniscient God. We're sure that only we have the wisdom needed to tell others what they should believe and how they should live. And how should they live? To replace the mythical eternal Heaven, we have sought, for two centuries, to create a perfect utopian society here and now. We have usually identified it as

---

[9] Roger L. Simon. *I Know Best: How Moral Narcissism is Destroying Our Republic, if It Hasn't Already*. Encounter Books, 2020.

socialism, but have also called it communism (until the fall of communist Russia three decades ago). But what socialism and communism have in common is the fact that they are *totalitarian* forms of government. We must have the absolute authority to inflict our dystopian utopia on everyone. It's not surprising to learn that the various socialist governments of the past century have murdered an estimated 170 million of their own citizens: those who see their self-appointed rulers as neither wise nor right. That's about as hollow as it gets: deadly, but hollow.

That doesn't mean we should return to the supernatural sort of God that Origen rightly identified as children's religion. But it does mean that we need a way to frame our deepest guiding principles as ontological ideals—rather than merely ideological, narcissistic, and sociopathic assumptions. The role played by the symbol and metaphor of God is to caution us that we don't have the wisdom to tell others how they must live. That would take "godly" wisdom, which we will never have. All we have are our various beliefs, orthodoxies, political ideologies, and personal and collective certainties. Each of them is, by definition, just partial and incomplete. Only by combining and merging all the various perspectives on life, politics, religion, and the rest could we hope to grasp a perspective adequate to rule without destroying others, society, and democracy. In theology, God symbolizes the wholeness that's always beyond us. When we don't know that, we exalt our idols, our ideologies, our theologies, etc. That's what liberals do (conservatives can, too). Without God or a decent religion, we grow up without seeing how partial, selfish, and destructive our certainties are—especially when forced on people who don't believe them: people just as smart, informed, and certain as we are, but who disagree with us. "God", at its best, is a symbol of, a metaphor for, the size of the kind of humans to which we aspire. We worship the symbol and idea of God because we know we can never become that pure, deep, broad, brilliant, or wise. That symbol is meant to give us an image of Infinity: an unbounded, unbridled, curious human, too big to be confined within any ideology or other idolatry. We're only as big as the number of boxes we can think outside of. So heretics may be tortured, burned, murdered by insecure but obedient masses, but all our advances in every field have come from the heretics who kept "choosing" when the ignorant but obedient masses declared the choices closed because only *they* had the wisdom to know the final answers. In retrospect, the distinction between Good and Evil is clear. And looking back, we can admire and respect the heretics, but the ignorant masses—including unquestioning liberals and conservatives— are simply laughable: clowns.

It is essential that developing humans have a way of internalizing an image of and invitation from unbounded questioning and choosing. No one will ever have enough wisdom to contain the Infinite, including all our conceptions of a god. We can't conceive of that Infinite kind of presence and command. The best we can do is devise symbols and metaphors to make the idea come alive in the developing minds, souls, and spirits of the young *Homo sapiens* who hope to grow into the most full and complete humans possible.

This is what's at stake when we toss around words like ontology vs. ideology vs. idolatry vs. mute and frightened obedience. Or gods, idols, apostasy, fools, and pitiful specimens, failures.

For liberals to mock conservatives shows an unflattering and crippling narcissism. So is thinking we have the wisdom of God. We cannot be wise enough to rule those who think we're wrong. We're not smarter and don't have wisdom (which can only be built by putting together all views, both parties, cultures). Without God, how would we find the rationale for humility? Without humility, we can't be fully human. The Stoics have two fertile metaphors that have helped millions of people over the past 2,300 years. The first is to imagine our lives as a huge set of concentric circles. The small circle in the center is us. Then as we move out into larger circles of which we are a part, we find our family, community, associations, nations, the world, and history. The second metaphor is to see ourselves as limbs on the body of Humanity. Both can help us find essential humility and connection. We seldom find much evidence of this Stoic wisdom in liberal actions.

(Yes, conservatives also need to be criticized, but that needs to be done by conservatives, not liberals.)

Who could *do* this? Who could teach us these things? Liberal churches like the Unitarian Universalist churches? The tiny Ethical Humanist groups? K-12 schools and colleges? Here's the sketch of a suggestion:

I. The great myths and stories of history are treasure chests for many of the stories that have been used for centuries to help us build better humans. Certainly, from the Biblical traditions—this is where many Christians are so far ahead of atheistic liberals. But there are lots of books telling and amplifying some of the great myths from other traditions. They all represent the projections of human imagination as we are trying to give form to deep insights and sensitivities that still feel like they're beyond words to express directly. These myths can be the atheists' successor to a single "Holy Book".

II. The Greeks have provided a rich collection, of which most of us are already at least a bit aware. And the Greek gods and goddesses are perhaps most accessible to those of us in Western Civilization because they were personifications of natural and psychological realities and have already been incorporated into so many Western stories and traditions. Also, of the Greeks' Olympian deities, seven were males and six were females (it was six and six in the original

Olympians, until a couple thousand years ago when they replaced quiet, invisible Hestia with the heavy-drinking party god Dionysus, whom the Romans called Bacchus). So even those whose thinking has been crippled by Politically Correct thinking can embrace the Olympian deities. And don't forget Hestia! The only one of the thirteen who was almost never drawn or sculpted, Hestia was the "spirit", the "presence", that made the difference between a church service and a worship service, or between a house and a home.

III. Why are these ancient gods so important to understand thousands of years after they were first imagined? Because the most important thing liberals must learn is *humility,* so we can stop exalting our certainties, stop imagining that our diplomas make us smarter than others, or give us the kind of wisdom that would give us any moral right to try and tell others how they should live, let alone getting the power to force them to live—in ways they think are wrong, even stupid.

Etymology again. "Humility" and "humble" have the same root as "human" and "humanity". We cannot be human in any deep or full way without humility—as any religion could teach us. The opposites of humility, like *hubris* and the self-absorption of *narcissism,* have always been identified as the most foolish enemies of the best gods. And calling a trait an enemy of the gods is a way of diagnosing it as too horribly myopic and insensitive to have the sort of character we mean by "human" at its most admirable quality. Who can have all the godliest traits? Who has the wisdom to simply lord it over others? No one. What humans are smart or wise enough to presume that they should be able to rule over others and tell them how they should or shouldn't live? No one. At our best, we have shown that we know this by creating gods as symbols and metaphors for the transcendental inclusive quality of knowledge and sensitivity which we know we don't and can't have but would be necessary for us to "play God" without simply becoming not only fools and clowns, but also an evil and dangerous presence, and a curse on all others. So much for socialism, communism, and all totalitarianisms.

As a college sophomore, I took a class in the New Testament taught by a very bright and blunt Jesuit. His take on the Bible was quite liberal—I'm sure he knew Origen's writings very well. He taught Religion as an orientation grounded in symbols, myths, metaphors, and existential wisdom. I loved it and had never heard religion taught so intelligently before. But the fundamentalist Baptist kid sitting next to me sure didn't like it! One day he finally exploded, accusing the Jesuit of insulting Jesus Christ our Holy Lord and Savior and only ticket into Heaven, and so on. The Jesuit quietly came over to the student's desk, leaned over a little, and said, "You *do* know these are *myths*, don't you?" The rest of the semester was great, even without that kid.

We have not found a legitimate heir, either to God or to religion. We have substituted a dangerously narcissistic ideology for ontology. We want to think like "liberals" do and vote only for "liberal" candidates. We have stopped thinking, stopped questioning, and are defining a human as little more than an ideological drone. This is as fundamental a betrayal of religion, and of people, as there is, and we have not shown any ability to get beyond it. If there's no more to us than this, we sound like sociopaths, as liberal psychiatrist Lyle H. Rossiter has diagnosed our actions.[10]

And we have no particular wisdom. Why would we think we did? Just our narcissism? Our diplomas?

There is no definitive date for the start of religious liberalism. Unitarianism began in Poland and Transylvania in the 1560s, but 1841 is a handy and more recent year. That's when the

---

[10] *The Liberal Mind*, p. 21.

book *The Essence of Christianity* was published, by German scholar Ludwig Feuerbach (1804-1872). It's still in print 181 years later, and still worth reading by anyone interested in this subject. The gist of Feuerbach's argument was that those living in the "modern times" of the 1840s were living in a world where the simplistic supernaturalism of traditional (Christian) religion had become unbelievable, even silly (though Origen had described the literalism as childish 1,600 years earlier). More: it was an insult to any serious consideration of the kinds of questions essential to religion. Those questions have always concerned two primary considerations. In my framing, these questions are:

- Who, at our best, are we?

- How should we live, so that when we look back we can be glad we lived that way?

But these aren't questions of *theology*. And Feuerbach argued that theology isn't the field we should be using to frame such questions. The proper field isn't the logical understanding of gods; it's the logical understanding of *humans*. And that field is called *anthropology*.[11]

Feuerbach was an important influence on all liberal Christian theologians since 1841. He was also a great influence on Karl Marx, Charles Darwin, Sigmund Freud, Friedrich Nietzsche, and many others. His notion that it was time to translate theology into anthropology was one of the most revolutionary ideas in the history of Christian theology.

In the century following 1841, several other thinkers expanded the bigger picture that Feuerbach had drawn,

---

[11] I prefer the word *ontology*, but don't think Feuerbach would disagree.

magnifying the size of reality and our own insignificance ex-
ponentially:

1859: Charles Darwin's *The Origin of Species* changed the
story from "special creation" by a supernatural God, to natural
evolution, where more complex forms of life—like ours—
evolved over hundreds of millions of years from simpler
forms. This discovery still acts like poison to much fundamentalist Christianity. But almost without exception, today's liberals accept evolution without hesitation.

December 30, 1924: Edwin Hubble discovered that the
Milky Way wasn't the universe. This sounds ridiculous a century later. But up until that time, most of our best astronomers
believed our Milky Way galaxy *was* the universe. Some of today's estimates say the Milky Way contains between 400 and
500 billion stars, so it easily *feels* like a universe. But until
1924, we thought ours was the *only* galaxy. Some current scientists estimate the entire universe contains between *6-20
trillion* galaxies, each containing hundreds of billions of stars.
This is beyond our ability even to imagine. Nor can we imagine
our—or our planet's—size and relevance compared to six to
twenty trillion galaxies, each containing hundreds of billions
of stars and many more planets—about half of which are older
than our solar system. Our own galaxy may contain over 300
million habitable planets; in the whole universe there may be
120 quintillion to 4 sextillion habitable planets (which would
represent only an estimated 2.5% of all planets—only one
planet out of every 40: pretty conservative figures). So much
for gods and local myths of how we were specially created.

Ethology (comparative animal behavior)—the most relevant
science for understanding the nature of our species—came
alive in the 1930s-1940s. In 1973, three early giants in this new

field were awarded the Nobel Prize: Karl von Frisch, Konrad Lorenz, and Nikolaas Tinbergen shared the award for discoveries in animal behavior patterns. We are related, genetically and behaviorally, to many other species. Since the discovery and exploration of DNA, we're now told we share about 99% of our DNA with chimpanzees and bonobos, and 98% of our DNA with gorillas. And we share much with them behaviorally—as we share with all "social species". It has been dramatically shown that a sense of fairness is innate in capuchin monkeys and a growing variety of other species (just do a search for "Monkeys and Fairness" to watch a three-minute scientific experiment showing this quite dramatically—and hilariously!). This ingenious experiment designed by Ph.D. Sarah Brosnan became an instant classic, has been replicated with several other species, and is one of the funniest and most persuasive scientific experiments you'll ever see.

All of this represents healthy intellectual growth, as we try to let our understanding keep up with the complexity of Reality. But the existential questions it raises are immense. Far from being the special creation and children of a God who, Biblical literalism teaches, created the universe, we have created many tens of thousands of gods in our history, each with its own version of a creation story, and each completely local, time-bounded, and looking a bit inadequate in the far grander scale of Reality. Six (or twenty) trillion galaxies?! Six hundred quintillion habitable planets? Three hundred million habitable planets just in our Milky Way Galaxy? So much for the Garden of Eden.

So, a great existential angst has accompanied our intellectual growth. Who are we, that matters at all in the greater scheme of things? What are we doing and serving with our lives that matters? For many centuries, we believed we were

the special creations, the children of the single God who created the entire universe. Our priests taught us that the highest
calling was to serve that singular God—as Origen summarized
it, we should seek those things that were "useful to us, and
worthy of God". Without the second part, the first part hardly
mattered, unless narcissism was the highest form of existence.
And we now have just this one life to do this—not any sort of
an "eternal" existence.

EXCERPTS

One Nation, Two Cultures, by Gertrude Himmelfarb (1999)

Tocqueville believed it was religion in the service of virtue that made freedom possible. (87)

The suspicion of the religious movement is especially conspicuous among journalists, who are generally liberal in politics and secular in belief. In 1993 a front-page story in the *Washington Post* described the "Gospel lobby" as "poor, uneducated, and easy to command". Protests from readers obliged the *Post* to retract that statement. (101)

The Madness of Crowds, by Douglas Murray (2019)

Hannah Arendt says only one tool exists to ameliorate the irreversibility of our actions. That is "the faculty of forgiving".

"Without being forgiven, released from the consequences of what we have done, our capacity to act would, as it were, be confined to one single deed from which we could never recover; we would remain the victim of its consequences forever, not unlike the sorcerer's apprentice who lacked the magic formula to break the spell." (178)

In some manner with which we still haven't even begun to wrestle, we have created a world in which forgiveness has become almost impossible, in which the sins of the father can certainly be visited upon the son. And we remain remarkably unconcerned to create any mechanisms or consensus over how to address the resulting conundrum. (182) [This feels like the mark of a civilization in decline, and beyond redemption.]

CHAPTER TWO

How We Replaced God and Heaven

THE VISION OF THE ANOINTED

As one of the consequences of the death of God, Fredrich Nietzsche foresaw that people could find themselves stuck in cy-
cles of Christian theology with no way out. Specifically, that
people would inherit the concepts of guilt, sin, and shame but
would be without the means of redemption which the Christian religion also offered.[12]

Considered heretically, many beliefs could replace traditional supernatural religion. Stoicism is probably the best ancient Western philosophical secular guide to personal awareness and behavior and has met the intellectual and emotional
needs of a wide range of people.[13] Stoicism is a personal philosophy, not aimed at shaping a political agenda: an ancient
Greek school of philosophy founded in Athens by Zeno of

---

[12] *The Madness of Crowds: Gender, Race and Identity*, Douglas Murray
(Bloomsbury Publishing Plc, 2019), p. 182.

[13] From rulers (Marcus Aurelius, George Washington, Thomas Jefferson
(also influenced by Epicurus), Theodore Roosevelt, Bill Clinton)—authors
like John Steinbeck, Ralph Waldo Emerson, JK Rowling, Ambrose Bierce,
to sports superstars including Tom Brady, Ben Roethlesberger, coach Bill
Belichick, to slaves (Epictetus) and people of every class in between for
2,300 years.

Citium (who lived from about 334 to 262 BC). The school taught that virtue, the highest good, is based on knowledge; the wise live in harmony with the divine Reason (also identified with Fate and Providence) that governs nature and are indifferent to the vicissitudes of fortune and to the easily misleading motivations of pleasure and pain.

But how do we replace Heaven? Two thousand years ago, the people who invented the Christian "Heaven" placed it up above the clouds—meaning it was symbolic and imaginative rather than an actual place—and decided it should last for ever and ever. In the world as we know it today, there is no "up there" of any kind, and the word "eternity" has a very different meaning. We are now told that the universe began about 13.8 billion years ago. Life has existed on this planet for several billion years, beginning as one-celled life and gradually evolving into more complex forms, including ours. And some scientists have estimated that in our Milky Way galaxy *alone* there are about 300,000,000 habitable planets. What is that other life like? Is it bigger, smarter, wiser, more established and stable than we are? If they have also created gods, how many and what kind of gods are there just in our galaxy? In the entire universe? We know that we are what's called a "social species", which explains a lot about us. It means we confer "Alpha" status on the men and women we have declared to be in charge: CEOs, priests, Queens, Kings, and of course the thousands of gods and goddesses we have invented along the way. We define those Alpha figures as able to make the rules we must follow, and we expect obedience from all under those Alpha figures (though Christians can't expect Buddhists or Muslims to obey the Christian rules and vice versa). And we're taught to take the word of those who convince us they are really speaking for these Alpha figures and rules. Seen this way, Yahweh is a projected super Alpha male charged with making up the rules we are to live by (though the priests and theologians have told us what those rules are, since this God doesn't speak in ways that we can hear, record, or record on video). We know that throughout human history, different cultures have created many tens of thousands of gods, though they always treat them as Alpha figures, as members of a social species would.

So, we are living in a very different world than the one in which these gods, heavens, and hells were first invented. We liberals seem to believe that the legitimate heir to the outdated eternal Heaven is a utopian society, here and now. To take this seriously, we have to believe that we have the insight and wisdom needed to construct this utopia—which would mean that the legitimate heir to the omniscient wisdom of the all-knowing God is ... us. Why only us? Why can only liberals envision this? (See Chapter Three.)

However, we have increasingly removed from our secular religion the human responsibilities that traditional religion had: our duty to do unto others as we would have them do unto us, and to love even our enemies: "Bless those who curse you, pray for those who mistreat you", as Luke 6:28 puts it. We have removed or ignored the duties of our personal behavior toward others who disagree with us; too often, we demonize them. This will—as it must—lead to the most fundamental and destructive failure of liberalism, especially in recent decades. We simply ignored humanistic guides to interpersonal behavior, like Stoicism or Aristotelianism. We just have not shown humility. Far from it.

Historically, these ideas of a here-and-now utopia go back at least to Karl Marx.[14] And the reason that it makes sense for

---

[14] But see William J. Murray's *Utopian Road to Hell: Enslaving America and the World with Central Planning.* WND Books, 2016. See his chapter 3: "Sparta and Plato's *REPUBLIC* inspire utopian tyrants", pp. 42ff. "Long before Karl Marx, Lycurgus was the ideal collectivist and central planner. He believed that Sparta's citizens were the property of the state and that they

modern liberals to be echoing Marxist thought is very simple. Karl Marx also sloughed off the traditional supernatural Biblical God and Eternity and realized it left us with the question of what could replace God and Heaven. To Marx's credit, he never claimed to know just how to do this.

But we do. American liberals have been drawn to communism and socialism since the 18th century, more strongly after the 1848 publication of Marx's classic book *The Communist Manifesto*. Many liberals idolized Communism since even before the 1917 Russian revolution, up until the Soviet Union fell apart in 1991. And Eugene V. Debs was the Socialist candidate for US President five times: in 1900, 1904, 1908, 1912, and 1920 (the final time from prison). And currently (2022), Bernie Sanders identifies as a "Democratic Socialist", and others at the far left are identifying simply as Socialists.

In Chapter Two of his Manifesto, Marx boldly states the goal of his envisioned new world order: "... the theory of the Communists may be summed up in a single sentence: Abolition of private property."[15] Property is to be owned by the State, which gives the State total power over its citizen-victims.

Engels died in 1895, twelve years after Marx's death. In the autumn of 1895, a double obituary was penned by a young, dedicated disciple of both, Vladimir Lenin. In it he wrote,

> ... *they were the first to explain that socialism is not the invention of dreamers but the final aim and necessary result of the development of the productive forces in modern society. All recorded history hitherto has been a history of class struggle. And this will continue until the foundations of class struggle and class domination—*

had no higher purpose than to obey the dictates of the rulers throughout their lives.", p. 43.

[15] *Climategate*, p. xiii.

private property and anarchic social production—disap-
pear. The interests of the proletariat demand the destruc-
tion of these foundations. And every class struggle is a
political struggle.

Lenin grasped the communist baton, ready to level the playing field and vaporize the ability of those who desired to move up the economic ladder, own property, and become economically self-sufficient. He articulated his concept of the end justifying the means: "We say that our morality is wholly subordinated to the interests of the class struggle of the proletariat." To destroy the foundations of property and a capitalistic economy, every option had to be on the table: lying, cheating—even murder—were necessary tools.[16]

WHAT'S WRONG HERE?

Don't forget the lesson of Antaeus, used as an Epigraph of this book:

> *In Greek mythology, Antaeus was the son of the sea god Poseidon and the Earth goddess Gaia. He made all strangers who were passing by to wrestle with him. Whenever Antaeus touched the Earth, his strength was renewed, so that—especially if thrown to the ground—he was invincible. Heracles encountered him on the way to his 11th assigned Labor and was compelled to wrestle Antaeus in order to pass. In combat with him, Heracles figured out the source of his strength and, lifting him up from the Earth, crushed him to death.*

These are ways of saying that ungrounded ideologies and utopian schemes cannot describe or prescribe to the real

---

[16] Ibid., p. xiv.

world without doing great harm to it; also, that no single ideology is adequate. Antaeus needs both feet on the ground. Both "Cultures" are necessary to balance each other: the two feet (see Chapter Three on the important understanding of the "Two Cultures").

It's also a way of saying that the most dangerous people on Earth are those who believe that they—and only those who think as they do—can tell everyone else how they must live. This is the soul of tyranny, totalitarianism, coercion—and ultimately, always evil, because no one has the wisdom and talent to dictate how all others should live. All religions warn of the destructive foolishness of those who try to play God.

There are two reasons why Communism and Socialism have garnered such attraction from American liberals. The first is above: proponents believe these Marxist-inspired forms of government can lead us toward the most perfect form of society imaginable: a here-and-now utopia to replace the mythical "eternal Heaven".

The second reason is almost never mentioned but is really the primary reason. Both communism and socialism require totalitarian forms of government: one-party rule. Words like Communism, Socialism, Marxism, Collectivism, and especially Totalitarianism are rude and unwise words to use for one's position. It's why the SDS student movement of the 1960s—about which much more later (Chapter Four)—called itself Students for a Democratic Society, though the form of government they envisioned was a totalitarian socialism.

But it's worth considering why, in fact, liberals believe they must have a totalitarian form of government to hope for the utopian society many liberals dream of as the legitimate successor to Heaven. The logic is clear, and as we'll see in more detail in the next chapter, thinkers going back to Plato 2,400 years ago saw the necessity of a totalitarian government. Plato disliked democracy because he believed—as we liberals tend to—that the "masses" are not capable of the wisdom or vision needed to picture this utopia. And if they can't see it, they should not be given political power, or they will just stand in the way of the elite few—today's liberals—who can see it. You don't hire a tone-deaf teacher to give you singing lessons, nor a mathematical imbecile to teach you your numbers. This is rude, but it's honest.

Not many will openly say they want totalitarian control of the US government, though you don't have to read between the lines much to see it. We're not pushing to admit hundreds of thousands of illegal aliens across our border because we care about them. If we did, we'd be advertising to countries all over the world just to get into the US any way they can, and our citizens will pay for their education, medical care (through emergency room visits), and the rest. We could attract billions of hungry, desperate, uneducated people. But we don't care about any of them. We just care about adding a few million more people who will feel obligated to vote for Democrats. (Liberals make up only around 24% of the US; conservatives, 37%. So it's easy to see why liberals want to open the borders.) And not many liberals will believe that our thinking has such clear ties to Karl Marx or his communism and socialism. Like most people, we're mostly not aware of the deep history and logic of the beliefs we would stumble trying to explain in much detail.

The purpose of this book is to explain how liberals betrayed you by identifying the depth and logical connections of our beliefs and explaining them to liberals as well as conservatives. For many liberals, it will seem just wrong to say our political and social beliefs should be seen not as politics but as the secular religion we have clung to, hoping and believing it can indeed be the legitimate heir to the old God-Heaven story. But it's about religion, all the way down. We're not looking for dialogue and compromise between equals who see things differently. We're looking for conversion, or coercion, as all utopians are.

While it's right to grow beyond the literalistic supernaturalism of our traditional religions, as all first-rate theologians have taught (remember that passage from the writings of Origen, who wrote 1,800 years ago), our rejection of religion was at the same literalistic level. It was as superficial—and anti-religious—as the outdated religions being rejected. There's an irony!

The purpose of religion is not to tell other people how they must live—that utopian dream. It's to help us see how *we* should live, so that when we look back, we can be glad we lived that way. This liberal pretense is just what it looks like: narcissistic arrogance that should be laughed off the stage before it does the serious and deadly harm it has done everywhere it's been tried. (In other words, the best informed of those who are trying to push us toward socialism know they are lying, and know their real motive is the power they think they can gain over the ignorant masses: both conservative and liberal.) As one liberal psychiatrist has put it:

> *Unfortunately, the history of radical liberalism's attempts to fulfill this [utopian] promise has been one of stunning failure. The radical agenda by any other name— communism, socialism, collectivism, progressivism, welfarism—has invariably resulted in large-scale social decline.*[17]

Remember that the word "utopia" means "nowhere". And the twenty or so times that socialism has been inflicted on countries during the past hundred years have all been

---

[17] Lyle H. Rossiter, Jr., M.D., *The Liberal Mind: The Psychological Causes of Political Madness*, p. 373.

disasters, including the murder of tens of millions of its own citizens.[18]

We're watching liberalism take a wrong and deadly turn, away from any grounded reality and down the road of being seduced by Grand Abstractions. Consider this wonderful metaphor from language philosopher Ludwig Wittgenstein:

*Imagine this game—I call it "tennis without a ball": The players move around on a tennis court just as in tennis, and they even have rackets, but no ball. Each one reacts to his partner's stroke as if, or more or less as if, a ball had caused his reaction. (Maneuvers.) The umpire, who must have an "eye" for the game, decides in questionable cases whether a ball has gone into the net, etc., etc. This game is obviously quite similar to tennis and yet, on the other hand, it is **fundamentally different.**"* [19]

Whether we realize it or not, we really can't claim intellectual supremacy. We may be more *articulate and fashionable* or believe that we are somehow *anointed*, but diplomas can't make us *smarter*. This is a religion; we're claiming theological—actually just *ideological*—supremacy. And we don't have that either. It's just that our ideology is lost in grand abstractions with no clear footing in the real world. But grand abstractions are seductive. Imagine thinking we are the only people serving all the capitalized abstractions: Truth, Beauty, Justice, Love … it's very much like thinking we're the only ones serving God, or that we *are* God, or His legitimate heir. But we're not wise. We're not right, we're just Certain, and Certainty is only an attitude. This anticipates a coming chapter

[18] R.J. Rummel, quoted in "Why is Anyone a Socialist?" by John C. Goodman in the October 1, *2018 Independent Institute.*
[19] *Last Writings on the Philosophy of Psychology*, vol. I, p. 110. ["The philosophy of psychology" was Wittgenstein's term for epistemology.]

(Six), but our sin is not "white supremacy"—it's the foolish and deadly claim of *ideological supremacy*, which feels a lot like narcissism and sociopathy.

Consider this "confession" by the liberal psychiatrist cited above for a feel of how gratifying the new secular liberal religion can be:

> *My discovery of modern collectivism was not just a revelation; it was a personal salvation. In discovering liberalism, I acquired an identity and even a life: I was no longer confused about who I was, how I would take care of myself, or what life should mean to me. All of that was resolved. I now belonged to an elite group of enlightened thinkers dedicated to freedom and justice. The rise of* **The Modern Parental State** *would provide everyone, including me, with economic security, social status and political significance. I could personally identify with the state's power over selfish villains whose greed and cruel indifference had so deeply hurt me and other victims of the world. Together we, the radical liberal minds, would oppose the villains, frustrate their goals, and deprive them just as they had deprived us. We, the world's new heroes, would be the dominant ones, not the villains. We would seize their authority and render them powerless, then punish them for their bad deeds and destroy their false sovereignty. We would overthrow the strict social taboos that inhibit self-expression. In the permissiveness of sexual liberation and moral relativism we would gratify ourselves without guilt or shame. As newly adopted children of The Modern Parental State we would not have to face the burdens of self-reliance or the risks of self-direction. The need to right old wrongs by violent protest would justify our aggression against an evil establishment. We would protect the environment from rapacious industry. Distributive justice would gratify our acquisitive impulses. Equal social status and political authority would create a classless, multicultural society. Equality for all would eliminate envy.*

As society's savior The Modern Parental State would finally guarantee the security that I and others like me had always longed for. The new State's benevolence directed to the noblest ends would abolish the torments that still haunted us. By projecting onto villains all that was bad and defective within us, we would deny our defects: only what was good and right and strong would remain within us. The villains would be the bad and defective ones. All of these ideas of radical liberalism resonated with my personal history and fortified my understanding of the human condition: it was now more apparent than ever that the world consists of victims, villains and heroes, and that survival in this world depends on seizing the levers of power. I found a home for this understanding in The Modern Parental State.[20]

Dr. Rossiter then adds this grown-up insight from Erik Erikson:

Adolescent man, in all his sensitivity to the ideal, is easily exploited by promises of counterfeit millennia, easily taken in by the promise of a new and arrogantly exclusive identity.[21]

But the cost of this delusion is paid by others: by the victims of this dystopian rationalization of seizing political power and forcing our self-serving visions on innocent others. One estimate is that the many failed socialisms of the 20th century have murdered around 170 million of their own citizens.[22] So much for The Modern Parental State.

---

[20] Lyle H. Rossiter, Jr., M.D., *The Liberal Mind: The Psychological Causes of Political Madness* (Free World Books, 2006), p. 370.

[21] Ibid., p.361.

[22] Gerald W. Scully, *The New York Times*, Section 4, Page 7, December 14, 1997, "Murder by the State". Also see footnote 15 where R.J. Rummel is quoted giving the same estimate of 170 million.

Environmental Activism: The (Secular) Evangelical Fundamentalist Religion of Liberalism

The worst dimension of liberalism's secular religion is its cult of Activism, especially environmental activism. For the True Believers, this is the activism that serves as liberal religion's secular *evangelicalism*, pushing (or dragging) all our liberal and conservative Ignorant Masses into the utopianism: the socialism under complete control of we enlightened liberals.

This cult has been responsible for the deaths of 50-100 million innocent people in the past 50 years, but the odds are you didn't even know it.[23] Environmental activists, from those in the 1960s to those exposed in Michael Moore's 2019 movie "Planet of the Humans", are often ignorant of the most relevant facts even in their own field, and are often willing and eager to lie about them (they believe they have strong authority to do this, as we'll see in the next chapter).

Fundamentalism, properly understood, is not about religion. It is a mindset, an attitude, about the inability to seriously entertain the possibility that we might be wrong. In individuals such fundamentalism is natural and, within reason, desirable. But when it becomes the foundation for an intellectual system, it is a threat to freedom of thought.[24] It's how and why utopianism always becomes coercive.

For example, the Environmental Defense Fund said it wanted air safe for people with cystic fibrosis, which affected

---

[23] The figures given by Brian Sussman in his 2010 book *Climategate*: "Since the DDT ban in 1973, malaria has killed 96 million people. Famine, preventable through responsible government management and proper utilization of natural resources, kills millions more each year." (p. 8) Since the figures are over a decade old, I've rounded up estimates that 40-50 million Africans died of malaria since the DDT ban and Sussman's estimate at a worldwide total of 96 million, to say the current figures are more likely over 50 million deaths in Africa, and over 100 million worldwide.

[24] Jonathan Rauch, *Kindly Inquisitors: The New Attacks on Free Thought, Expanded Edition* (1993), p. 28.

only .005% or .00005 of the population. One economist, calculating the price of similar standards to protect angina patients, suggested it would be cheaper to buy every victim of the disease a $200,000 condominium in the Florida Keys.[25]

As one environmentalist utopian put it, "It would be so easy to say, 'Let us regulate everything to zero exposure, and we have no more cancer.' The concept is so beautiful that it will overwhelm a mass of facts to the contrary." The findings of the National Cancer Institute's own National Cancer Survey have been treated like an "unwanted child" because they throw into question the assumptions of the regulatory programs. In the survey, seven cities were compared, four without any heavy industry and three—Detroit, Pittsburgh, and Birmingham—highly industrialized. The three dirty cities had an overall *lower* cancer rate, for white and black males, age-corrected, than the four clean cities.[26]

Other tactics could fairly be called treasonous.[27]

And the unnecessary deaths of 50-100 million innocent people can and should be laid directly at the feet of our environmental activists:

> *Inspired by Rachel Carson's* Silent Spring, *environmentalists moved to have DDT banned. Fake science was used to say it was harmful to all sorts of things. A 1977 book* Ecological Sanity *by George Claus and Karen Bolander exposed the studies as fake science, saying DDT did not cause cancer, or harm birds, freshwater fish, estuarine organisms or other wildlife. And considering its benefits, found that there is a present need for the essential uses of DDT. [It remains easily the most effective insecticide*

---

[25] *The Coercive Utopians*, p. 56.

[26] Ibid., p. 59.

[27] Ibid., p. 64. The political activists wanted to minimize energy production as a means to overturn the existing political and economic order, which they saw as incapable of continuing without abundant energy.

against the anopheles mosquitoes that carry malaria.] Nevertheless, it was banned by William Ruckelshaus, then administrator of the EPA—though he admitted later he had never read any of the reports. But it was a victory in the utopian campaign against modern technology. The pesticides, especially DDT, had enormously reduced parasitic and insect threats to food production and had permitted the expansion of agriculture in underdeveloped areas where plant infestation had been a major cause of malnutrition.[28]

It's hard to overestimate the deadly destruction brought about by ideological science and the activists and media that promote it. Sometimes the dishonesty simply screams:

If the value system that supports environmental degradation is changed, writes Robert Disch, editor of The Ecological Conscience, *"of necessity" we will eradicate "such seemingly unrelated problems" as "racism, poverty, health, aging, urban blight, and social injustice."*[29]

Even the rare honest admissions can seem infuriating:

In Entropy *Jeremy Rifkin admits that in the conserver society, Americans will live a "frugal or Spartan life-style" in which "production will center on goods required to maintain life." The desperately unattractive nature of the future that Rifkin sketches has led him to find more powerful levers. He has decided to use religion to declare that his vision would emphasize the fixed character of God's creation and the inadmissibility of tampering with any part of it. This would provide "a new set of governing*

---

[28] *The Coercive Utopians*, p. 70.
[29] Ibid., p. 77.

principles for how human beings should behave and act in the world."[30]

Utopian campaigns like these depend heavily on the cooperation of the unquestioning media for their success. The media do more than *believe* the utopians: they protect them. News that could prove embarrassing to the utopians is often simply not reported.[31] And of course narcissistic delusions like those of Disch, Rifkin, and other self-righteous and "anointed" activists depend for their success on being able to con and mislead the ignorant and gullible masses, both conservative and liberal.

These are the characteristics and mechanics of *religion*, and of True Believers. Once in the grip of a desire to believe, intellectuals dull their normally sharp critical faculties.[32]

What produced this utopian infection of our country? The assessment of the Isaacs has been echoed by others:

The single most important cause of the reemergence of utopianism [which was in disarray from the end of WWII to the 1960s] was probably the civil rights movement of the 1950s. ... The Vietnam War created new legions of converts to the notion of an evil America, again especially among college students feeling personally threatened by the draft. The emerging "New Left" on campus, energized by the war, could now argue that not only was the United States internally unjust, but it was an imperialist, expansionist, militarist state intent on subjugation of liberation

---

[30] Ibid., pp. 80-81.

[31] Ibid., p. 269. Reed Irvine has christened this "the Pinsky Principle" after North Carolina journalist Walter Pinsky, who described his approach in the *Columbia Journalism Review* in 1976. "If my research and journalistic instincts tell me one thing, my political instincts another ... I won't fudge it, I won't bend it, but I won't write it."

[32] Ibid., p. 285.

movements in faraway lands. The Watergate scandal became a final proof to many—not only were American institutions unjust, but American leaders were personally corrupt. More important, the Vietnam War and Watergate showed that the government could be defeated. The great imperialist juggernaut of the students' imagination was not invincible after all. It was vulnerable. Few but determined opponents could gather strength and eventually win against it.[33]

The coercive utopians are the vanguard of the New Class: those who produce and distribute knowledge rather than material goods. (This will also be called the Second Culture in the next chapter.)[34]

The utopians and environmental Activists have, for over half a century, found their home among Democrats.

The Isaacs include this summary at the end of their book:

The utopian rejects the question "Is it possible?" He asks only "Is it desirable?" And if he concludes that it is, assumes that it is necessarily possible. Utopian groups are not burdened by complexities. Holding out the promise of a perfect society and a new man, they are able to harness the emotional energies of a major segment of the New Class, whose suppressed religious cravings are satisfied by what are essentially millenarian ideologies. The utopian message revives in secular terms the religious opposites of death and life. ... The secular millenarianism of the utopians recovers for the bearers of a secular world view the transcendence craved—but lost—with the disappearance of their faith in traditional religion. Clergymen, under psychological stress in a secular world, may

---

[33] Ibid., p. 287.
[34] Ibid., p. 288.

experience the utopian drive as the rebirth of legitimate religious concern in a world where the old forms no longer awaken men's energies.[35]

Or, as Roy W. Spencer sees it:

The birth of the modern environmental movement is usually traced to the publication of Rachel Carson's Silent Spring. A biologist, Carson was passionate about the dangers of the insecticide DDT, which was in widespread use at the time. ... Governmental policies resulting from her work have caused the deaths of literally millions of people by allowing malaria to thrive in Africa. (Pressured by environmental activists, governments banned the use of the pesticide altogether.) That the most famous policy reaction to environmental concerns has caused so much human suffering should, by itself, make us wary of any sweeping efforts to "protect the environment".[36]

Spencer adds: "I believe that the environmentalists who have stood in the way of allowing the use of DDT in Africa are the real criminals." Rather than some theoretical future threat like global warming, the DDT ban is now known to have needlessly cost millions of lives in Africa. Where is the outrage over this very real tragedy? Is the silence because we don't really care about what happens to dark-skinned people in poor countries? The western world's adherence to our secular religion, environmentalism, is apparently more important to us than the unnecessary deaths of millions of black Africans.[37] The assurance that we are Saved is such an overpowering and

[35] Ibid., p. 311.
[36] Roy W. Spencer, *Climate Confusion: How global warming hysteria leads to bad science, pandering politicians and misguided policies that hurt the poor* (Encounter Books, New York/London, 2009), p. 3.
[37] Ibid., pp. 94-95.

wonderful feeling! To hell with the rest!

Novelist Michael Crichton also points to the example of the international bans on DDT, actions that were based more on emotion than sound science. DDT, by itself, would greatly alleviate the scourge of malaria in poor African countries, with almost no risk to humans or wildlife. Instead, millions of people, especially children, continue to die from this largely preventable disease. Might this be part of the environmentalists' religious rites? They offer sacrifices of children—but only children in some far-off land who have a skin color different from most of us.[38]

European countries have threatened trade restrictions on African countries if they use DDT, a relatively safe and extremely effective pesticide that the developed countries have already used to conquer malaria. As a result of this ban, nearly one million Africans die each year from malaria. Many more are permanently disabled. Forcing the environmental policies of wealthy countries on the poor countries has caused and continues to cause death and suffering. If environmentalists really are interested in helping the world's poor, let them demonstrate it by publicly supporting current efforts to reinstitute the residual spraying of homes with DDT in Africa. It is indefensible that the website of the Environmental Defense Fund brags about its role in banning the use of DDT. The situation is nothing less than a crime against humanity; it verges on genocide. For some strange reason, westerners seem to believe that the world's poor are better off living in poverty.[39]

Also: "When the search for truth is confused with political advocacy, the pursuit of knowledge is reduced to the quest for power." – Alston Chase

The practice of stealing government money and power for

---

[38] Ibid., p. 99.
[39] Ibid., p. 144.

one's own ideological scheme is not new. Nearly two centuries ago, French author Frederic Bastiat defined the phenomena of lobbying for political favors as "legal plunder".[40]

He also noted that "Whenever plunder is less burdensome than labor, it prevails",[41] and "The law has been perverted through the influence of two very different causes—naked greed and misconceived philanthropy."[42] He added, in 1850, that all the forms of plunder, when they become legal plunder, take the name of socialism. So linking "liberal" or "democrat" with "socialism" is not a new observation.[43]

Brian Sussman, author of *Climategate* (2010), relates the story of one of the many scientists who rejected Rachel Carson's unfounded claim that DDT was poison to humans, water, birds, and fish: "Dr. J. Gordon Edwards of San Jose State University began his talk by pouring a teaspoon of DDT into a glass of water and then drinking the glass empty. Besides being a bug doctor, he was also a famed mountaineer and well-known conservationist, who was making quite a name for himself by illustrating the lies of Carson's *Silent Spring*.

DDT, first created by a German scientist in 1874, was perfected in 1939 by Swiss scientist Paul Muller—who won the Nobel Prize for his work. In many ways, it was a miracle compound: inexpensive, nontoxic to humans, and extremely effective on targeted insects, while other forms of wildlife seemed to be immune to its effects. ... Edwards' extensive research completely debunked the primary pillars of Carson's book. For example, DDT is not a carcinogen and, in fact, might be a cancer-fighting drug. DDT does not thin bird eggshells. Thinned eggshells are caused by several natural factors including

---

[40] Frederic Bastiat, *The Law*, Creative Commons 2013 (originally published in 1850), p. vi.
[41] Ibid., p. 5.
[42] Ibid.
[43] Ibid., p. 14.

dehydration, old age, and extreme temperatures.[44]

"DDT does not kill wild birds. During the years DDT was used in the US there was a significant increase in the number of pheasants, quail, doves, turkeys, and other game species. Bald eagles were never threatened by DDT. Eagles were threatened with extinction as far back as 1921 due to reckless hunting, 25 years before the use of DDT here. From 1941 to 1960, there was a reported 25% increase in the bird's population. Likewise, the decline in the US peregrine falcon population occurred long before the DDT years. ... But in 1972, the pressure created by *Silent Spring* was the impetus for banning DDT domestically and internationally, eventually leading to the deaths of millions from malaria."[45]

There are many more works by real scientists showing the deadly DDT scam to be the hoax that it is. Just check bibliographies in these and other books—realizing that it is harder to get books published that tell the truth about the safety of DDT than those that echo the false but popular claim that it is deadly. That's part of the deathly power of the media, profits, academic grants and promotions, and—always—those ignorant masses.

In 1983 the husband-and-wife team of sociologists Rael Jean Isaac and Erich Isaac wrote a perceptive book on the emergence of Activism to take the place of theistic religion for liberals: *The Coercive Utopians*. Much of the message is in the title. Utopians dominated the leadership and professional staff of the mainline Protestant denominations and their related organizations, including the National Council of Churches. They were the leaders of almost all the peace groups, including the pacifist ones, like the War Resisters League and the American Friends Service Committee, and those who seek to reduce the

---

[44] Brian Sussman, *Climategate: A veteran meteorologist exposes the global warming scam* (WND Books, 2010).
[45] Ibid., p. 6.

risks of war, like SANE, Clergy and Laity Concerned, Physicians for Social Responsibility, and others. They are in the colleges and are particularly prominent in the law and social science faculties of elite universities. But those leaders don't represent the beliefs and feelings of the members in (especially) those churches and other organizations.

The Isaacs put it succinctly: "The problem is that utopianism, by its inherent logic, leads to coercion." The utopians are also attracted to the one teaching which provides a comprehensive secular explanation for all social ills, and prescribes an authoritarian, this-worldly, utopian solution: Marxism. As a form of secular messianism which assumes that perfect social arrangements will produce a new man, Marxism strikes a responsive chord in secular utopian hearts. And it fills the need that has driven liberalism even more since losing the ability to understand or communicate with the reality-based Scientific culture: a route toward totalitarian power.

Barry Commoner, Amory Lovins, and Jeremy Rifkin are among the most familiar figures foreseeing a society built around new energy technologies and new attitudes toward the use of energy. [They are against fossil fuels and all complex technology, including complex solar technology.][46]

Socialism as the new liberal religion

These perceptions aren't new. As long ago as 1850, French author Frederic Bastiat was warning that "We must make war against socialism."[47] By socialism, Bastiat meant *plunder*, whether extralegal or legal—and legal plunder, for Bastiat, meant socialism.[48]

---

[46] *The Coercive Utopians*, p. 6.
[47] Frederick Bastiat, *The Law*, p. 13.
[48] Ibid., p. 14.

"The socialists divide mankind into two parts. Men in general, except one, form the first; the politician himself forms the second, which is by far the most important."[49]

We are used to contemporary pronouncements about socialism like this, but it's instructive to hear the same observations made by Bastiat.

HERESY

To talk about religion is also to talk about heretics, for throughout history, the two go hand in hand. The people constituting and speaking for the orthodox beliefs of the time represent, for better and worse, the definition of the religion and the beliefs required of those claiming to be followers. The orthodox position, by definition, declares what choices are approved for believers, and declares that beyond those the choices are closed, for only the orthodox have the knowledge and wisdom to provide the final answers. Once those boundaries have been drawn by the orthodox, anyone who continues to make choices outside of those boundaries is, again by definition, a heretic. The word *heresy* itself comes from a Greek verb that simply means "to choose". But in religion, heretics are those who choose outside the box. Put another way, once the orthodox have closed off all further choices, the heretics are those people who say, "No, I'm not through choosing yet." Being a heretic can be, and often has been, a very dangerous, even life-threatening, choice.

---

[49] Ibid., p. 23.

A quick overview of what heretics are and how traditional religion has treated them

In the 13th century, heresy was listed first among the crimes against the state, because it directly undercut kingly power. In his *Summa Theologica*, Thomas Aquinas (1225-1274) put it bluntly: *Heretics have no right to life, because taking their teachings seriously would negate the believers' access to salvation.*[50] In 1022, people who were considered heretics were burned for the first time since antiquity. Heresy at the time meant believing or teaching religious ideas other than those of the Catholic Church. In the 12th and 13th centuries, the Inquisition was established by the church to combat heresy. Heretical sects condemned the Church's hypocrisy, undeserved wealth, and corruption as well as denying the legitimacy of the papacy, clergy, and even the sacraments. Estimates of the number killed by the Spanish Inquisition, which Pope Sixtus IV authorized in a papal bull in 1478, have ranged from 30,000 to 300,000. The last person burned to death at the stake for heresy was executed on 11 April, 1612.

True Believers screamed "heretic", "witch", or "demon" as they tortured and burned their victims alive. Today's True Believers shout "racist", "sexist", "white supremacist", and "hate speech".

But how did these new secular categories become the *religion* of liberals?

It's an important question because there is an answer, and the answer points to the real underlying agenda and plan, which is seldom acknowledged. Even the True Believers are mostly unaware of how these things became parts of our religion. Etymologically, "religion" stands for what we connect ourselves to for identity, our sense of worth and purpose.

What are we liberals after? Clearly, our writings and

---

[50] *Summa Theologica II:II, 11.3 corpus.*

actions show that we want to gain control of the culture and the government. Yes, we are focusing on the ignorant and gullible masses (luckily for us, they're always the great majority of both conservatives and liberals), as we must always do, because our focus is on power and control.

How can we influence and direct large mobs? To manipulate and steer the ignorant masses, you need to appeal to their emotions, not their sterile logical intellect—as we have done so well in redefining the whole educational system in the US. (See Chapter Four.)

So: what's emotional, and easy to turn into crowd-driving battle cries?

Douglas Murray offers some important clarification in his 2019 book *The Madness of Crowds: Gender, Race and Identity*.[51]

Ernesto Laclau (who died in 2014), along with his partner and co-author Chantal Mouffe, provided one of the earliest foundations for what would become identity politics. In their 1985 work *Hegemony and Socialist Strategy*, they start by nobly admitting that socialism has been challenged by "the emergence of new contradictions". The "traditional discourse of Marxism" has, they say, "been centered on the class struggle" and "the contradictions of capitalism". However, the notion of "class struggle" now needs to be modified. They ask:

> To what extent has it become necessary to modify the notion of class struggle, in order to be able to deal with the new political subject—women, national, racial and sexual minorities, anti-nuclear and anti-institutional movements etc.—of a clearly anti-capitalist character, but whose identity is not constructed around specific "class interests"?[52]

---

[51] *The Madness of Crowds: Gender, Race and Identity*, by Douglas Murray (2019), pp. 55ff.
[52] Ibid., pp. 55-56.

Google Scholar shows it to have been cited more than 16,000 times by groups including urban, ecological, anti-authoritarian, anti-institutional, feminist, anti-racist, ethnic, regional, or sexual minorities, giving purpose and drive to a socialist movement that needs new energy.[53]

It is necessary to bring all these movements under one umbrella: the umbrella of the socialist struggle. And this, whether the majority of liberals recognize it or not, has become the new spirit and soul of social and political liberalism.

In practice, these have been narrowed down to three main battle cries: Racism, Sexism, and White Supremacy. They have become cries to divide people, thereby weakening them and turning them against each other around words so powerful they don't even have to be true. This is part of the magical attraction of Grand Abstractions. Intelligent and informed people who are awake (rather than part of the WOKE-ing dead crowd) know the cries of white supremacy, racism, and sexism are lies. They don't describe the major problems in the real world today. They're just the newest mob-level con job by socialists trying to turn the ignorant liberal masses into an obedient and angry mob. It's a lie, but it's working.

Black people have never had it so good before in the US, in every field. At least since Sidney Poitier won the Best Actor Oscar in 1964, Martin Luther King Jr. inspired and instructed the majority of the country up until he was murdered in 1968. And we have been blessed by black thinkers like Malcolm X, Stokely Carmichael, Oprah Winfrey, writers like Shelby Steele, Thomas Sowell, Walter E. Williams, Jason L. Riley, John McWhorter, Candace Owens, and Neil DeGrasse Tyson. Then there's the fact that in 2008 for the first time in US history, we elected a black President—*twice*. The truth is, as Shelby Steele has written, "*It must be acknowledged that blacks are no*

---

[53] Ibid., p. 56.

longer oppressed in America."[54]

Add to that the overwhelming success—even domination— of black entertainers, basketball players, football players, and other athletes, and it's clear that, for black people with talent and gifts who are willing to work hard and get the proper education and preparation, they can succeed as often as white people (though in intellectual areas neither blacks nor whites can succeed as well or as often as Asians). Shelby Steele is right.

In serious, traditionally "white people's" music like opera, soprano Kathleen Battle made her opera debut in 1975 at the age of 27. In another traditionally "white" profession, ballet, Misty Copeland joined the American Ballet in 2001 at age 18, became a soloist in 2007 (at age 25), and was appointed a Principal Dancer in 2015. Neither Battle nor Copeland succeeded because they were black. They succeeded because they were better than all others in their field (Copeland won first prize in the ballet category of the Los Angeles Music Center Spotlight Awards in 1998 at age 15). It was not any concern with *diversity* that gave these exceptional people their success; it was the traditional concern with excellence, dedication, and hard work.

However, to be blunt, successful black people like these are of no use to us liberals. Their success could, if we focused on it, bring the country together by letting talent, dedication, and hard work completely trump liberals' desire to define people by their race: the very definition of racism. And it would define the USA, again, as the land of opportunity, rather than one still burdened by a past sin.

But back to our socialist ambitions. We have quite successfully programmed our ignorant and compliant masses—liberal, conservative, and independent—to scream that America is a

---

[54] *White Guilt*, p. 67.

horrible failure of a country because all white people are racists, holding black people down through their inherent and evil white supremacy—which, as Shelby Steele explains, equates to a belief in black inferiority. Yes, it's quite a stupid lie, but it serves our larger need to feel virtuous and move the country toward the one-party socialism that could finally exalt a few of us so we could inflict our utopian vision on the rest. And since we are superior to the ignorant masses, we have both the right and the necessity to lie to them when necessary. Plato would approve, as you'll see.

The goal, the necessity, is not to unite people. That would just make them peaceful and happy, for God's sake! The goal is to divide them, make them hate, and destroy any choice of unity except as the obedient servants of our socialist utopia. Yes, this is rough and naked language. I want to get your attention because these are some of the most important facets of our current reality.

But look how effective it has been to scream words like Racist! Sexist! Homophobe! White Supremacist! What we're doing when we shout those words should ring a big bell. We have made articles of faith out of the false idea that the US is hopelessly racist and sexist. Anyone who is aware and awake can see it isn't true. But these fake teachings are, for us, *holy*, and everyone must believe them. Those who don't—those who say the kinds of things I'm saying here—are today's *heretics*—choosing where we have forbidden choices. And we treat them exactly as the orthodox have always treated heretics.

I'm using religious terms because they fit better than any other vocabulary (politics, philosophy, ideology, etc.). This is, most deeply, about our religion. There is a mindlessness, a knee-jerk quality about the new orthodoxy, and a nearly hysterical lashing-out at non-believers that is unmistakable to anyone familiar with the history of religion.

And in this story, the most disruptive players are the

heretics. The hysteria of the orthodox shows how desperate we are to maintain the pretense that we have indeed found legitimate heirs to the omniscient Biblical God and the heavenly reward. It is the heretics who see that we do not have the wisdom to prescribe or build a utopia, that our orthodox liberal beliefs have no real-world merit, and that we have become not agents of godlike good, but of almost unmitigated evil. Some examples can make all this clearer.

SOME MODERN HERETICS

One such good heretic is Dr. Bruce Gilley, Professor of Political Science in the Mark O. Hatfield School of Government at Portland State University. He wrote a well-researched and clearly argued essay making the obvious point that colonialism had both good and bad effects. The paper, "The Case for Colonialism", went through double-blind peer review and was published in *Third World Quarterly* in 2017. It generated hysterical mob action from *ten thousand* academics, demanding that it be retracted and that whoever published it be fired. Serious threats of violence against the editor led the journal to withdraw the article, both in print and online. Gilley was also personally and professionally attacked and received death threats. No informed arguments were presented, and out of the mob of 10,000, it wasn't clear whether even a hundred of them had read the paper. These people were not acting like intelligent academics at all, but simply like a hysterical mob.

As Professor Gilley's paper said, "The case for Western colonialism is about rethinking the past as well as improving the future. It involves reaffirming the primacy of human lives, universal values, and shared responsibilities—the civilizing mission without scare quotes—that led to improvements in living conditions for most Third World peoples during most episodes of Western colonialism." He was clear that "Colonialism can return (either as a governance style or as an extension of Western authority) only with the consent of the colonized." Of course.

Many countries had been subjected to "forced sudden decolonization" because that word, "colonialism", had been declared evil. The grand abstraction of "colonialism" had been declared evil, and "self-rule"—including by incompetent, violent local forces who were destroying their countries—was declared sacred. This was Second Culture[55] myopia at its worst: seduced by grand abstractions but completely indifferent to the actual and deadly organizational harm done to millions of humans at the hands of incompetent, sociopathic local leadership.

Gilley had already won more awards and respect than over 99% of his 10,000 critics. His research made it clear that colonialism had improved many lives, whereas "a century of anticolonial regimes and policies" had taken "a grave human toll". Do you care about the millions of actual human beings who had been impoverished and killed, or only about the orthodox sacred status of the hated word "colonialism" and the ignorantly worshiped term "self-rule"? The answer, as Chapter Three explains more fully, depends on whether you are in the grounded and reality-based First Culture, or the abstract intellectual and unrealistic Second Culture. But liberal academics—a near-tautology—acting like an unthinking mob, collected 10,000 signatures demanding the article be withdrawn. No arguments, no data to refute Professor Gilley's heavily footnoted and double-blind peer-reviewed academic article. Unorthodox thoughts must not be permitted and unorthodox thinkers must not be allowed, because only *we* know the truth.

---

[55] The Two Cultures will be explained in Chapter Three.

No serious concern for facts or truth works this way.

This was not intellectual, not academic, not about any principles of education; it was not even grown-up. This was a fundamentalist mob gathering to condemn a heretic whose work exposed their knee-jerk biases to be ignorant, destructive, and dead wrong. Gilley was not attacked as a scholar. He was attacked as a *heretic*. This is always about *religion*.

What has made this censorship feasible is a systematic pattern of one-party appointments to college faculties over several decades. When the great majority of the faculty speak in only one key—that of the agenda of liberal orthodoxy—an ever-smaller minority becomes increasingly unwilling to speak in opposition.[56]

Heather Lynn Mac Donald is an American political commentator, essayist, attorney, and author. She is a Thomas W. Smith Fellow of the Manhattan Institute and a contributing editor of the institute's City Journal. Just the title of her 2018 book, *The Diversity Delusion: How Race and Gender Pandering Corrupt the University and Undermine Our Culture,* shows her sin: she is a conservative First Culture thinker. David Brooks, the *New York Times* thinker and author, has said that "If there were any justice in the world, Mac Donald would be knee-deep in Pulitzer Prizes and National Magazine Awards for her pioneering work." But Brooks has the freedom to think clearly because he is not restricted by any college:

> *"America is in crisis, from the university to the workplace. Toxic ideas first spread by higher education have undermined humanistic values, fueled intolerance, and widened divisions in our larger culture. Chaucer, Shakespeare and Milton? Oppressive. American history? Tyranny. Professors correcting grammar and spelling, or*

---

[56] *The Breakdown of Higher Education*, pp. 14-15.

employers hiring by merit? Racist and sexist. Students emerge into the working world believing that human beings are defined by their skin color, gender, and sexual preference, and that oppression based on these characteristics is the American experience. Speech that challenges these campus orthodoxies may be silenced with brute force."[57]

And so, naturally, an independent and courageous thinker like Mac Donald will trigger the fury of the mindless mob, just as heretics have always done. Mac Donald's sin? Doing enough research to find that "if there is a bias in police shootings, it works in favor of blacks and against whites. Officers' use of lethal force following an arrest for a violent felony is more than twice the rate for white as for black arrestees...."[58] Yes, there are the rare cases of unarmed people being shot by police. But that's what they are: rare.

Like other heretics, Mac Donald exposes the delusion of liberal orthodoxy as no more than ignorant narcissism, drowning in grand abstractions but ungrounded in the real world—a world to which those in the Second Culture often seem incapable of connecting.

She had already announced herself as a heretic in her 2000 book *The Burden of Bad Ideas: How Modern Intellectuals Misshape Our Society.* This is a credentialed heretic who has also attacked Black Lives Matter and accused President Barack Obama of "attacking the very foundation of civilization" by giving credibility to the movement.[59]

Steven Pinker, Charles Murray, and Shelby Steele were featured in blurbs for Mac Donald's 2018 book *The Diversity*

---

[57] https://www.manhattan-institute.org/diversity-delusion?gclid=Cj0KC QjwvO2IBhCzARIsALw3ASrw7Y3DLNU_cst9-ZQsjgSOABHrnOI4PdcnXxl Xp_zxGRn8A3lPShcaAno4EALw_wcB)

[58] Ibid.

[59] https://en.wikipedia.org/wiki/Heather_Mac_Donald

Delusion. Pinker, professor of psychology at Harvard University, wrote that "with her spitfire writing and scorn for nonsense she is forcing universities to live up to their own principles". Murray, an American Enterprise Institute scholar, said the book was "crammed with facts and numbers that universities go to great lengths to hide". Shelby Steele, a conservative author, wrote, "Not since Allan Bloom's *The Closing of the American Mind* has a book so thoroughly exposed the damage done to American institutions—particularly universities—by modern liberalism's glib commitment to diversity."

Writing in *The New York Times* in 2000, Robin Finn described Mac Donald as an "influential institute thinker who risks being stereotyped as a right-leaning academic curmudgeon". Columnist George F. Will wrote a blurb for Mac Donald's book, *The Burden of Bad Ideas* (2000), that praised her thinking about urban problems. In the *New York Times*, Allen D. Boyer wrote a positive brief review of *The Burden of Bad Ideas*, concluding that "among discussions of urban malaise, where so much hot air has been recycled, this book has the freshness of a stiff, changing breeze".[60]

But the praise of conservative thinkers just condemns heretics further in the eyes of today's college and university "elites". In spring 2017, a protest group announced plans to "shut down" Mac Donald's speech on the Black Lives Matter movement at a college campus in California, calling her racist, fascist, and anti-black. On April 7, around 250 protesters surrounded audience members and prevented them from entering the building where she was speaking at Claremont McKenna College. Mac Donald ultimately gave the talk to a small audience in the Marian Miner Cook Athenaeum that was live-streamed on Claremont McKenna's website. So the effort to silence her voice effectively amplified it to a much larger

---

[60] Ibid.

audience. The college subsequently suspended seven students.[61]

Why do we liberals do this? Why do we so desperately copy some of history's most mindless and violent persecutors? It's because we have nothing else; we have no choice.

Christina Hoff Sommers is another good heretic. Heretics needn't be conservatives. Even a self-described libertarian member of the Democratic Party like Christina Hoff Sommers can be attacked by the liberal mob for failing to endorse every ungrounded bias of the new Left orthodoxy. She is an American author and philosopher. Specializing in ethics, she is a resident scholar at the American Enterprise Institute. Sommers is known for her critique of contemporary feminism. Her work includes the books *Who Stole Feminism?* (1994) and *The War Against Boys* (2000). She also hosts a video blog called *The Factual Feminist*.

Her sin was suggesting that men and women are irreducibly *different*! Well, if you're grounded in First Culture reality, of course they are! Genetics and DNA show it so clearly even a rudimentary education makes it clear. But again, this heretic has exposed another delusion of the new Second Culture orthodoxy, which now controls the culture of US colleges and public schools and is working on controlling the whole US culture and laws. And so, for having the ability to think and the courage to do it out loud, her lecture at Lewis and Clark College on May 5, 2018, was shut down with the claim that she was a "known *fascist*" because she said that "personal preference, not sexist discrimination, plays a role in women's career choices", and that "not only do women favor fields like biology, psychology, and veterinary medicine over physics and

---

[61] Ibid.

mathematics, but they also seek out more family-friendly careers".[62]

Sommers has responded to the mob criticisms quite perceptively and accurately as "excommunication from a religion I didn't know existed".[63] Seduction of liberals by ungrounded grand abstractions blurs the line between academic subtleties and intellectual diarrhea.

The Liberal Betrayal of Religion

Other authors who have exposed the destructive hollowness of the liberal ideology that now defines and controls the culture of almost all colleges, universities, and public education systems in the US are Greg Lukianoff and Jonathan Haidt, authors of *The Coddling of the American Mind* (2018). Their book was named the best book of 2018 by *Bloomberg*. *The New York Times, The Financial Times, Inc. Magazine, The London Evening Standard,* and *The New Statesman* all named it one of the year's best books.

First Amendment expert Greg Lukianoff and social psychologist Jonathan Haidt show how the new problems on campus have their origins in three ignorant and destructive ideas that have become increasingly woven into American childhood and education:

- What doesn't kill you makes you weaker.
- Always trust your feelings over your intellect.
- Life is a battle between good people and evil people.

These Great Untruths contradict basic psychological principles about well-being and ancient wisdom from many

---

[62] *The Breakdown of Higher Education*, p. 16.
[63] https://en.wikipedia.org/wiki/Christina_Hoff_Sommers

cultures. Embracing these self-destructive untruths interferes with young people's social, emotional, and intellectual development. The resulting "safetyism", insisting that students shouldn't be exposed to ideas that make them uncomfortable, makes it harder for them to become autonomous adults who navigate life well. This misinformation is preached to them during the first 25 years of their lives, when their permanent adult character is forming. The betrayal of our young people—and our entire culture—could hardly be greater.

I counted 27 grateful endorsements inside the cover of *The Coddling of the American Mind* from authors, intellectuals, politicians, and others. Among the many praises being sung for the book, this one by Edward Luce of *Financial Times* resonated with its wonderfully poetic and illuminating analogy:

> *"The authors, both of whom are liberal academics—almost a tautology on today's campuses—do a great job of showing how 'safetyism' is cramping young minds. Students are treated like candles, which can be extinguished by a puff of wind. The goal of a Socratic education should be to turn them into fires, which thrive on the wind. Instead, they are sheltered from anything that could cause offense. ... Their advice is sound. Their book is excellent. Liberal parents, in particular, should read it."*

Somewhat surprisingly, this book hasn't evoked the anti-heretical hysteria of the works by Gilley, Mac Donald, Sommers, and others.

The effects even went beyond just education. One of the most hysterical and ominous reactions to the insights in the book has come not from academics, but from ministers in America's most liberal religion: the numerically insignificant fringe religion called Unitarian Universalism.[64] One of their heretical ministers, the Rev. Todd Eklof, minister of the Unitarian Universalist Church of Spokane, WA, read *The Coddling of the American Mind*. Rev. Eklof saw the same patronizing dehumanization happening within the churches and administration of Unitarian Universalism, with the same destructive and mind-numbing effects. Eklof wrote three essays to carry the message of the book to the ministers and congregants of the Unitarian Universalist Association.

Coincidentally, the UUA was holding its annual General Assembly in Spokane in June 2019. His church members paid to have Rev. Eklof's essays published, and they gave copies to about 200 ministers and ministerial students on June 21, 2019. In less than twelve hours, 300 self-identified "White ministers" filed a protest demanding that the book be withdrawn. And within 24 hours, 200 more ministers joined them, for a total of more than 500 Unitarian Universalist ministers. They called Rev. Eklof a racist, white supremacist, and the rest of the names reflexively hurled at the new heretics. The "White

---

[64] When the Unitarians and Universalists merged in 1961, their combined membership was 151,557. It is now 148,232. US population in 1961 was 183.7 million, so Unitarian Universalists constituted .0008 of the US population. In 2021, the US population is 335,030,503 (as of 1 August 2022), so now the UUs constitute just .0004 of the population: a loss of half their presence in the United States. https://www.google.com/search?q=US+POPULATION+IN+2021&sxsrf=ALeKk03RiQqmWeyBo7vaHhN4it xC0-GvRw%3A1629233012033&ei=dB8cYbrEAbuMwbkPlbiimAU&oq=US+POPULATION+IN+2021&gs_lcp=Cgdnd3Mtd2l6EAMyBQgAEIAEMgUI ABCABDIGCAAQFhAeMgYIABAWEB4yBggAEBYQHjIGCAAQFhAeMgYIAB AWEB4yBggAEBYQHjIGCAAQFhAeMgYIABAWEB46BAgjECc6BQguEJEC OgsIABCABBCxAxCDAToICAAQgAQQsQM6DgguEIAEELEDEMcBEKMCO gUIABCRAjoECC4QQzoECAAQQzoQCC4QsQMQgwEQxwEQ0QMQQzoHC AAQsQMQQzoKCAAQsQMQgwEQQzoICAAQgAQQyQM6BQgAEJIDOg0IL hCxAxDHARCjAhBDSgQIQRgAUMhMWLllYM1maABwAngAgAGbAYgBiR CSAQQxNS43mAEAoAEBwAEB&sclient=gws-wiz&ved=0ahUKEwi6zsD3 9bjyAhU7RjABHRWcCFMQ4dUDCA4&uact=5

Ministers' Letter" contains this mind-numbing statement:

> "We recognize that a zealous commitment to "logic" and
> "reason" over all other forms of knowing is one of the
> foundational stones of White Supremacy Culture."[65]

For their authority, they cited the UU Ministers Association Guidelines. These 500 ministers, very few of whom even read Rev. Eklof's essays, are, remember, actually ministers—*with diplomas*—in the most liberal religion in the United States. Unfortunately, liberal ideology—rather than theology or ontology—has become the Association's sacred orthodoxy. The betrayal and disgrace could hardly be bigger. Granted, when only four in ten thousand Americans are affiliated with this tiny denomination, this isn't a fact with many broad implications.

Our liberal ideology has done the deepest and probably the most permanent damage to liberal religion. Like most liberals, those who continue attending churches have outgrown the tribal chief God of the Bible and the supernatural trimmings (Heaven, Hell, angels, and the rest). So, while they can still sing the songs and take part in the rituals and sacraments, the deeper questions remain, as they do for all liberals. What do we really believe that matters? What healthy difference are we making? What are we serving that's admirable?

But the Unitarian Universalist answers don't come from the Bible. They're the same shallow, hypocritical, and patronizing answers other liberals have adopted. And they have enshrined the view that authors like Shelby Steele say turns blacks into our pets and Sambo dolls.[66]

These include the notion that people need to be protected from any ideas that make them uncomfortable (so they can never grow bigger than their small, frightened selves).

---

[65] *The Gadfly Affair*, by Todd Eklof, p. 21.
[66] *White Guilt*, pp. 132, 134.

Linked with this is the logical but insane notion that informed logical thinking (the kind that can expose their delusions) is prohibited because that kind of reasonable, logical, and grounded thinking is a symptom of "white supremacy"—implying that only white people can think in an intelligent, informed, logical manner.

This is beyond incredible! Such racism, dehumanization, and infantilization prohibit any possibility of honest ontological religion. It is a fundamental betrayal of any authentic religious calling: here done by 500 ministers, and the UU Ministers Association, which removed Rev. Eklof from fellowship for violating a "covenant". Yes, a covenant, but not a *religious* covenant: merely an ideological covenant chosen by the ministers' association. I served churches in this denomination for 23 years, and never encountered or even heard of standards this low or this insultingly racist.

A Personal Note: This issue has obviously hooked me! When I felt the strength and depth of my emotional response here, I became aware of the events in my own life that made these issues so very powerful and commanding. So at the likely risk of giving you Too Much Information, I'll tell you the story about serving high ideals that helped shape my own character many years ago. From age 21-25, I served with pride and gratitude in the US Army, including a year in Vietnam from 1966-67. Before enlisting, Dr. Jones, a psychologist and mentor, gave me one of the wisest and most influential paragraphs of advice I ever received. "The Army is a microcosm of life. You will get out of it what you put into it, and you need to put everything you have into it. At this stage of your life, you need powerful, principled, and formative experiences to get you out of your head and help you develop a grounded character. Get the best experiences and the most out of those experiences that you can, while making sure that the Army is getting the most for its money from you." I wound up (sometimes belatedly) following his advice to the letter. Enlisting for Germany, I attended the Army's best NCO Academy (held in the building that had been Gen. Patton's headquarters in Bad Tolz, Germany), spent six memorable months in the Artillery Officer Candidate School at Ft. Sill, Oklahoma, and had three quite memorable jobs as an officer. Out of OCS, I was assigned as the Assistant Brigade Adjutant for a 4,500-man training brigade at Fort Leonard Wood, Missouri—because in the pro forma interview with the commanding officer I persuaded him that's where I could do the best job for the Brigade. Call it ambitious arrogance. Sent to Vietnam nine months later, I didn't want to be a forward observer (I can't read a map and still have no sense of direction), so I arranged for an interview after arriving in the country. I became The Vietnam Entertainment Officer, with an air-conditioned office in Saigon, working for the small office that handled all the USO shows that toured that war zone (except the Bob Hope Show). I worked and had dinners with famous entertainers and spent many evenings on Tu Do Street (aka Sin Alley) in the bars and steam baths/massages. I thought I had really beaten the game! That lasted for five months, until I learned that an OCS classmate had just been given a Purple Heart and a Silver Star—the third-highest award for bravery under fire. Then my cocky little world came crashing down, and I realized I had forgotten Dr. Jones' wise advice. War is an archetypal experience, and this would be my only chance to experience it. I knew then that if I returned from Vietnam without having experienced war, I would not want to live with myself.

This wasn't about patriotism or bravery. It was about giving the most to and getting the most out of life; this was the essence of religion, as I would later understand. The Army—and Dr. Jones—taught me that it must always involve seeking and serving the highest values and most demanding experiences. So again, I arranged for an interview, and after five months in Saigon was transferred to the field, where I finished my final seven months in the Army as a combat photographer and press officer assigned to the 11th Armored Cavalry Regiment. Through powerful and unforgettable experiences in those final seven months, I was never wounded; I was lucky (though I still have the live bullet that was aimed at my head when the North Vietnamese Army 1ˢᵗ Lieutenant who pointed his AK-47 at me was killed by the two soldiers beside me). Nor was I ever heroic or particularly courageous; I just did my job, like all soldiers try to do. But looking back, I still rank the decision to leave Saigon and go into the war as the most important and proudest decision of my life. It let me serve higher ideals and earn a nobler character than my comfortable cowardice in Saigon ever could have given me. It doesn't take military or heroic courage to serve the highest ideals. But it *does* require *moral courage*, always. And moral courage is life-giving and life-enhancing in ways that clever cowardice, going-along-to-get-along and all the other mob and herd behaviors can never begin to touch. To put that decision in the context of my life, the *second* most important and proud decision in my life was earning an M.A. and Ph.D. from the University of Chicago. With that background, watching 10,000 academics or 500 ministers display such low ideals and such professional cowardice was absolutely repulsive to me, generating the level of outrage that my rhetoric here has given away. I recognize and respect your right to disagree.

More than any other religion, Unitarian Universalism shows how deeply our worst liberal ideology can destroy ontological religion. Without the old God, too many liberals have found no ontological authority to steer life along a path of humility, recognizing others by their common humanity instead of their more superficial differences: like race, and above all, no sign of anything resembling the Golden Rule. That should be easy, instinctive, and automatic. Yet—and perhaps this is the most brutal truth of our age—it seems that low standards can cripple a person's character so deeply that some may never be able to outgrow it. Then indeed, and tragically, we can seem like members of a different, and frightening, species.

The new names—"racist", "homophobe", "ableist", and "white supremacist"—are now used instead of "heretic", "witch", and "demon", but serve exactly the same purpose. Like "conspiracy theorist" they think that calling your enemies names means you don't have to deal with their arguments or data.

Treating any group of people as categorically incapable of logical reasoning is hateful, infantilizing, and dehumanizing. It's saying that these inferior people can't understand the standards that all grown-up people should know. So we pat them on the head, say, "There, there little people, we superior white liberals will protect you!" And it feels just marvelous!

How desperate! Yes, it's dishonest and hypocritical. Yes, it shows people either incredibly ignorant or sinfully dishonest and cowardly, without the integrity required to be anywhere near fully human.

In 2021, Rev. Eklof published his book *The Gadfly Affair*, to tell this whole story and reflect on it from the perspective of true, healthy, courageous, and ontological religion. He shows how Unitarianism was founded on, and for two centuries had proudly proclaimed its allegiance to, principles of the Enlightenment. These include ideas like the following:

> "*Enlightenment is man's emergence from his self-imposed immaturity. This immaturity is self-imposed when its cause lies not in lack of understanding, but in lack of resolve and courage to use it without guidance from another. Sapere Aude! Have courage to use your own understanding!—that is the motto of the Enlightenment.*"[67]

---

[67] Ibid., p. 4.

Religious humanism, born in 1911 in the church where, ironically, Rev. Eklof would eventually serve, defines itself like this:

"The authority of its belief is reason, the method of finding its beliefs is scientific. Its aim is to crush superstition and establish facts of religion." (And its) "First principle is freedom of opinion and is subject to no censure for heresy."[68]

These beliefs were central to the Unitarianism I knew and identified with back in Tulsa in 1962-63, in graduate school (1979-1986), and in 23 years of ministry to UU churches (1986-2009), when I identified myself as a religious liberal and a Unitarian, though never as a Unitarian Universalist.[69]

Few men are willing to brave the disapproval of their fellows, the censure of their colleagues, the wrath of their society. Moral courage is a rarer commodity than bravery in battle or great intelligence. Yet it is the one essential, vital quality for those who seek to change the world which yields most painfully to change. - Robert F.

---

[68] Ibid., p. 5.

[69] The new religion of "Unitarian Universalism" was really born after 1985, when seven "Principles" were adopted in that year's General Assembly, which have become known as "what UUs believe": in other words, a de facto creed. For its core, it adopted/echoed/parroted the new liberal embrace of PC thinking, including a self-righteous endorsement of hating white supremacy, logic and reason, and accusing heretics who exposed the shallowness, dishonesty, hypocrisy and patronizing minorities (especially blacks) of this new narcissistic cult—explosively and reflexively—as white supremacists, racists, homophobes and the rest. The hysteria helps us understand what's really going on—here and in the examples of Gilley, Wax et al from academia. These are all precisely cases of the unquestioning orthodox liberals accusing those who have the knowledge and courage to expose them as heretics. It's about our religion.

Kennedy[70]

Reader! To whatever visible church, synagogue, or mosque you may belong! See if you do not find more true religion among the host of the excommunicated than among the far greater host who excommunicated them.
– *Moses Mendelssohn*[71]

Liberal institutions cease to be liberal as soon as they are attained; later on, there are no worse and no more thorough injurers of freedom than liberal institutions. – *Friedrich Nietzsche* [72]

George Orwell famously gave these examples of double-speak from his novel *1984*:

WAR IS PEACE
FREEDOM IS SLAVERY
IGNORANCE IS STRENGTH

Today, as Rev. Eklof notes, we are seeing the same kind of doublethink demonstrated by the Unitarian Universalist Association and Unitarian Universalist Ministers Association with statements he similarly sloganized as:

LOGIC IS RACISM
FREE SPEECH IS OPPRESSION
THINKING IS HARMFUL[73]

And yet, over 500 liberal ministers followed in lockstep,

---

[70] *The Gadfly Affair*, p. 25.
[71] Ibid., p. 56.
[72] Ibid., p. 76.
[73] Ibid., p. 77.

like a mindless mob.

Worse: these new commandments create an atmosphere within which no honest or healthy religion, education, politics, or human relations are even *possible*. If teachers, preachers, or politicians claim to serve the highest ontological values, to help build the biggest, fullest, most admirable humans, they must be held to those highest ideals as a sacred covenant.[74] Today's heretics expose the dishonesty and hypocrisy of the new radical liberal orthodoxy.

But if the heretics are taken seriously—their arguments addressed and adopted as logical and reasonable rather than merely shouted down and condemned—it means the whole liberal agenda, our underlying religion, is completely bankrupt. Then we have *nothing*: nothing worth believing, nothing worth serving, nothing honest or healthy to offer to the real world.

That's why the responses to intelligent, mature, and courageous heretics are so completely mindless, hysterical, and desperate every time. Our salvation is at stake,[75] and our modern heretics are doing what the best heretics have always done: exposed the fallacies, the hypocrisy, and the deep

---

[74] These are the ideals held highest by almost all religions. They include things like honesty, integrity, the Golden Rule, loving your neighbor as yourself (which presumed a healthy self-regard), the kind of healthy and courageous character. Moral courage is a fundamental part of these high ideals. I'm reminded of Jesus' saying that the "kingdom of God" isn't supernatural and won't be established by God, but will only come to be when we can treat one another as brothers and sisters and children of God. It requires high ideals and the courage to serve them.

[75] I'm using the word "salvation" existentially, related to the root of the word "salve", referring to a healthy kind of wholeness. For me, as for many liberals, there is nothing otherworldly about salvation. But that healthy kind of wholeness is one of the most important qualities we can aspire to, and it will always require the awareness of the highest ideals and principles and the courage to follow them.

destruction that the prevailing orthodoxy is wreaking.

This makes it easy to view liberals as bankrupt, desperate, and dangerous. We want respect but can't earn it. So we are determined to get power and to inflict our spiritual and mental darkness on everyone while silencing critics (look at Russia, China, Cuba, and all other totalitarian socialisms. Such coercion is necessary when you lack the wisdom to construct a utopia but must silence your critics by all means necessary). Then we dress up, stage a parade or two and proclaim our special worth.

Yes, we seem that bankrupt, that desperate, and that dangerous.

EXCERPTS

The Liberal Mind: The Psychological Causes of Political Madness, by Lyle H. Rossiter, Jr., M.D. (Free World Books, 2011)

The Vagueness of Liberal Principles ["Grand abstractions"]

One of the most striking characteristics of modern liberalism is the vagueness of its social policies despite their apparent nobility of purpose. A typical "progressive" liberal platform, for example, will announce its goals to be the eradication of hunger, poverty, ignorance, disease, faulty childcare, material inequality and political oppression. The platform will dedicate itself to the provision of adequate jobs, housing, nutrition, education, social harmony and medical care. But in the real world, attempting to reach even one of these goals is a colossal undertaking, whose difficulties the liberal agenda never adequately spells out for review.

Radical Liberal Themes

Certain neurotic themes are dominant in the radical liberal mind's perceptions of the world. All of them portray the citizen as a suffering child who is victimized, helpless and in need of rescue. All are evident in various liberal platforms. They represent the liberal mind's transference of childhood dynamics into the world of adult relationships.[76] As expressed in his most passionate political pronouncements, the radical liberal mind believes that:

---

[76] I disagree with Dr. Rossiter's opinion of the etiology of these liberal longings. As a psychiatrist, he assumes liberals must have had a dysfunctional childhood. Instead, I argue that it all comes from our losing a loving God and eternal heavenly reward, removing a substantial part of the foundation of our sense of worth and purpose. The neurotic themes Dr. Rossiter lists reveal the deeply religious (or at least *faux*-religious) nature of the liberal belief that it's our sacred duty to save our world, as only we know how.

• A very large portion of the population is suffering; they are suffering because they are deprived, neglected, exploited or abused.

• They are suffering because of certain injustices inflicted upon them.

• They are helpless to stop their suffering.

• Bad people, such as capitalists and the rich, cause the victims to suffer by depriving, neglecting, exploiting and abusing them.

• These bad people are villains who must be stopped from preying on their victims.

• The villains are ruthless, powerful, selfish, cruel and mean spirited.

• The bad institutions supported by the villains are economic, social and political in nature; they include free market capitalism, basic property rights, strict moral and ethical accountability, reasonable social decorum, personal and financial responsibility, individual sovereignty, and just based on merit and desert.

• These bad institutions promote economic enslavement, social discrimination, political disenfranchisement, exploitation of minorities, forced pregnancies, and coercive advertising, among other things.

• The people are innocent victims; they have no important role in causing their suffering.

• Modern liberals are heroes whose mission is to rescue the victims from the villains.

• Modern liberals are compassionate, wise, empathetic and nurturing.

• Modern liberals are devoted to saving the victims from the villains just as nurturing parents protect their children from harm by others.

• Like children, most citizens cannot adequately direct or manage their own lives. Most citizens need a powerful liberal government to direct and manage their lives.

• Because the villains and their institutions are ruthless and powerful, the people need a powerful liberal government, The Modern Parental State, to protect them from the villains and the institutions supported by the villains.

• The Modern Parental State is the answer to problems created by the villains.

• The Modern Parental State will rescue the people and protect them from the villains and from other misfortunes.

• The Modern Parental State will nurture the people by providing for all their needs and desires.

• The Modern Parental State will blame and punish the villains for their deprivation, neglect, abuse and exploitation of the victims.

• Much of the suffering of the victims comes from too much freedom in economic markets, which allows the villains to exploit the victims for unjust gain.

• Proper controls instituted by The Modern Parental State to regulate the markets will prevent the villains from economically exploiting the victims.

• The Modern Parental State will cure the deprivation, neglect, exploitation and abuse of the victims by taking the wealth, power and status of the villains away from them and redistributing it to the victims.

• Some of the suffering of the victims comes from too little social freedom and too many restrictions on behavior in social situations.

• The Modern Parental State will lower the standards of social conduct in order to free the victimized citizen from guilt and from adverse legal consequences when he acts criminally, irresponsibly or offensively.

• By remaking the institutions of society, The Modern Parental State will liberate the victims from exploitation and oppression by the villains.

• The libertarian structure of ordered liberty grounded in basic property and contract rights allows the villains to exploit the victims.

• The Modern Parental State will eliminate these individual rights and create a new political architecture for a secure society modeled on the loving nurturing family. (334-335)

These and related themes of deprivation and neglect, exploitation and abuse, domination and control, blaming and punishing, caring and caretaking, protection and security, rescuing and nurturing—all are the radical liberal mind's unconscious projections of early childhood dynamics transferred into the political arenas of adult life.[77]

These projections define the transference neurosis of the radical liberal mind:

• They are the liberal's projections of a painful neurotic disorder; they are the legacy of his childhood.

• They represent his desperate longings for attachment, attention, affection, empathy, significance, esteem, adoration, recognition, indulgence, relatedness, guidance, direction, belonging and love.

• They represent his desperate efforts to heal real emotional wounds that he suffered when he was, in fact, significantly deprived, neglected, exploited or abused.

• They are his efforts to defend against his suffering by constructing an idealized world of loving care and exemption from responsibility; he seeks a world that will compensate him for the traumas of his childhood, relieve his neediness, indulge his impulses and heal the enduring wounds to his soul.

• They are distorted perceptions of the real world of economic, social and political processes; the liberal agenda is based on these transference perceptions. (336)

Unfortunately, all of the radical liberal's efforts based on these perceptions are badly misguided.[78]

Based on his conviction that the people are incompetent; it is

---

[77] Again, I believe that understanding liberal beliefs and actions against our background of losing belief in a loving God and eternal reward for living a good life is a much better and more defensible cause of our perverse, almost comical, "religion" of narcissism and sociopathy, as he describes it.
[78] Ibid., p. 336.

obvious to the modern liberal that someone must direct their affairs. The Modern Parental State staffed by an elite core of parent/leaders is what is needed to solve the problem. ... And because most people have to be made to do what is good for them, the new leaders are prepared to use whatever force is needed for that purpose. By this route, the world can be made safe enough for the radical liberal to trust it.[79]

Indeed, the radical liberal now feels driven to create a new world that will eliminate everyone's misery. In this new world the people will be coerced into living lives that are good for them.[80]

The defects in this plan are fatal to any rational social order. The institutions the radical liberal would overthrow are precisely those that protect ordered liberty. In particular, they are the institutions that prevent him from gaining control over the lives of others and taking what he wants from them without their consent. The radical liberal would overthrow the rules that protect self-ownership and property rights and prevent the citizen from being indentured to collectivist programs. The radical liberal would violate the integrity of contracts and overthrow equal protection laws in the name of social justice. The radical liberal would encourage litigation with laws that invite the perception of injustice where there is none. The radical liberal would establish a society of adult children who are incompetent to manage their own lives, dependent on the state's welfare programs, and subservient to its ruling elite. These and other defects inherent in radical liberal goals doom its agenda on the hard realities of the human condition.[81]

The liberal attitude is also not empathetic, despite its claims. The pseudo-empathy of modern liberalism is actually a perversion of the deep and wide-ranging insight that defines authentic empathy. Most of what the liberal mind calls empathy is a maudlin pity that is wholly inappropriate to distressed adults precisely because it discourages initiative, invites regression and fosters helplessness.

---

[79] Ibid., p. 341.
[80] Ibid., p. 342.
[81] Ibid., p. 347.

Liberalism's pseudo-empathy is, in fact, a passive substitute for active caretaking; one can easily watch from a distance while government bureaucrats make indiscriminate transfers to recipients. In this and many other effects, collectivism is the opiate of modern liberals.[82]

The liberal mind is an angry mind determined to force people into its stereotyped categories but unable to acknowledge that its own political coercion is a form of criminal violence. A similar mechanism operates in the liberal mind to deny the extent and nature of evil. So the standard liberal theory of the social origins of evil is simply wrong and contrary to the evidence. In fact, the most important variable in the control of human evil is the presence of positive relationships at critical periods in the child's life.[83]

In the radical liberal mind, the victim/villain paradigm is omnipotent against reality.[84]

Liberals believe that much, if not most, property should be government owned because only governments will protect it for the common good.[85]

In its childlike demands, the liberal mind seeks a world of cost-free benefits.[86]

The Coercive Utopians, by Rael Jean Isaac and Erich Isaac (Regnery Gateway, Inc., 1983)

In 1983, sociologists Rael Jean Isaac and Erich Isaac published their book *The Coercive Utopians*. It's an excellent book, partly because they saw the philosophical and political movements developing as *sociological* events. This offers fresh and still fertile insights. As I've said, I want my book here to be easily accessible without pretending that it requires a diploma to understand it. When the many pieces

---

[82] Ibid., p. 384.
[83] Ibid., p. 385.
[84] Ibid., p. 386.
[85] Ibid., p. 387.
[86] Ibid., p. 388.

of the overall picture are made clear, they are easy for any of us to understand (unless our ideology blinds us). I'll draw freely from this book and recommend it to anyone who would like to pursue some of these themes in more breadth and depth. I'll summarize and put the authors' text in the footnotes below.

Seen as sociological phenomena, they look different. Besides being ungrounded in the real world, the utopians reject our society, our economic system, our way of life and our technology, especially the parts that generate our power. The unstated, secret goal is no less than the destruction of our economy and our country.[87]

"Utopian" can sound like such an optimistic and positive term that it easily masks motives and objectives that are destructive, aimed primarily at making the utopians seem virtuous and righteous.[88]

---

[87] Most of the diverse groups we will describe are utopian because they assume that man is perfectible and the evils that exist are the product of a corrupt social system. They believe that an ideal social order can be created in which man's potentialities can flower freely. They are "coercive" because in their zeal for attaining an ideal order they seek to impose their blueprints in ways that go beyond legitimate persuasion. If they believe that society is perfectible, the utopians also believe that the society in which they live is deeply flawed, indeed hateful. And if one has to identify the single aspect of American life that they find most repugnant, it is our economic system. The reason for the abhorrence of capitalism varies among utopian groups. Churchmen, who have adopted a utopian perspective, believe that it fosters competition rather than the cooperation they define as a religious ideal. The militant wing of environmentalism believes capitalism is inherently wasteful, compelled to produce ever more products which people do not need to satisfy basic wants, and thus destructive of the environment. Consumerists believe capitalism produces ever more unsafe, shoddy and unnecessary goods in the pursuit of profit. The utopians do more than reject our economic institutions: ultimately, their attack is directed against modern technology and science itself. In a very real sense, the coercive utopians are 20th century Luddites. (Isaacs, p. 2)

[88] The efforts of the present-day utopians are two-pronged. Where public fear can be mobilized, the utopians work to stop the technology cold, as in the case of nuclear energy and genetic engineering. More fundamentally, the utopians seek to reorganize the economic system in such a way that

Utopians in any one facet of this larger movement may honestly say they are not aware of other facets, or of any larger movement. Many aren't. But we all need to see the bigger picture. In 1983, the authors wrote that "Utopians dominate the leadership and professional staff of the mainline Protestant denominations and their related organizations, including the National Council of Churches. They are the leaders of almost all the peace groups, including the pacifist ones, like the War Resisters League and the American Friends Service Committee and those who seek to reduce the risks of war, like SANE, Clergy and Laity Concerned, Physicians for Social Responsibility, etc." [89, 90]

---

complex technology can be eliminated. If there is one shibboleth which almost all the utopians invoke it is "appropriate technology". ... What is meant by appropriate technology is a technology appropriate to the human condition, as the utopians define that condition. In the words of E.F. Schumacher, who coined the term "appropriate technology", "Man is small, and, therefore, small is beautiful." Large coal-fired plants, nuclear plants, leave the individual, as utopian philosopher Amory Lovins points out, "humiliated" every time he turns on the light. ... What the utopians reject is market-controlled large-scale industrial civilization. Since that civilization runs on energy, it is through transforming the energy system that the utopians believe they can transform society. The US, as the most successful producer of goods and food, is seen by many of the utopians as literally the worst society in the world. In so far as the utopians have real life models, they are places like Cuba, Vietnam, Nicaragua and China (at least until it moved toward the West). The glorification of socialized Third World poverty reflects the romanticism of the utopians. (Isaacs, p. 3)

[89] Ibid., p. 4.

[90] They lead the consumer organizations established by Ralph Nader. They are in the colleges and are particularly prominent in the law and social science faculties of elite universities. [They are smart enough to keep their organizations' deep agenda hidden.] Most who contribute to the multi-million-dollar war-chest of Nader's Public Citizen do not feel themselves part of a movement to transform the basic structure of the corporation. Similarly, few who rally to the cause of the nuclear freeze know that the groups who created the freeze movement seek unilateral US disarmament and see the US as the greatest force for evil in the world. But once an individual becomes part of one of these movements, the leadership has an

Their intent to cripple and destroy the cheap energy that has made the US the economic leader of the world is everywhere, and can be quite vicious—while always secret:

Amory Lovins, for example, has said: *"It would be little short of disastrous for us to discover a source of clean, cheap abundant energy because of what we might do with it." Professor Paul Ehrlich, a guru of the zero population growth movement, puts it even more sharply: "Giving society cheap abundant energy ... would be the equivalent of giving an idiot child a machine gun."*[91]

The problem is that utopianism, by its inherent logic, leads to coercion. The utopian begins with a belief that the world is perfectible: a world of clean air and water, no nuclear weapons or energy, and a job for everyone. Racism and sexism would be eliminated; there would be no rich or poor nations because resources would be equitably divided; and decision-making would be so decentralized that people would participate in all the decisions that affect their lives. But if the vision can be realized, and all that stands in the way is greedy and/or corrupt economic and political institutions, it follows that the utopian has the responsibility to work to abolish the institutions that stand in the way of realizing an ideal order, in which no one is hungry and everyone is materially and spiritually nourished. Of course, where utopians have abolished existing institutions, they rapidly discover that human nature is not as malleable as they had assumed and that people must be transformed to fit their imagination. And so utopians become coercive, sometimes concluding that one generation must be sacrificed to create an ideal system for a future one.[92]

These utopians have had an enormous impact on the way we think. They write many of the articles we read in opinion-setting maga-

---

opportunity to "educate" him. As they become active, they are caught up in a web of social and political activity which as much as more formal educational devices commits them to goals they earlier did not think deeply about. (Isaacs, p. 5)

[91] Ibid., p. 7.

[92] Ibid., pp. 8-9.

zines, on the Op-Ed pages of the *New York Times* and *Washington Post*. We watch them on the panels that interpret current events for us on television. We hear them from the pulpit, and our children listen to them in college classrooms. They have largely set the fashions in thought, and fashion is every bit as tyrannical in ideas as in clothes. Publishers churn out their books, but do not churn out many books written by better-informed sources who disagree with the utopians' imaginative positions.[93]

While they seem to want anarchy, anarchy becomes totalitarian, because getting all the citizens to agree requires propaganda, force, suppression, etc.—as Russia, China, Cuba and other totalitarian societies have shown.[94]

Although the public has not been aware of the role of the utopians (echoed and championed by most of our media), the Republican victories of Reagan, Bush 43 and Trump were in part a repudiation of the utopians' manipulations of our press and our government.

Another dimension of this dichotomy between our "leaders" and the strong majority of our citizens is shown by the fact that although the National Council of Churches passed a resolution against the death penalty in 1976, 68.1% of members of Council-affiliated denominations favored the death penalty.[95] And although the NCC had passed a policy accusing the criminal justice system of undue

---

[93] Ibid., p. 10.

[94] The utopians are also attracted to the one teaching which provides a comprehensive secular explanation for all social ills—namely Marxism. As a form of secular messianism which assumes that perfect social arrangements will produce a new man, Marxism strikes a responsive chord in utopian hearts. Church bureaucracies and peace movement leaders have been especially prominent in providing support for third world Marxist liberation movements, whose victory, they believe, is essential for the creation of a global, just, peaceful, social order. The utopians are not open/honest with us. Their goals are put forward in such a way as to evoke a broad favorable consensus. Because much of the agenda of the new utopians is known only to the initiated, the public is in effect coerced into courses of action that a majority would reject if it were aware of their full implications. (Isaacs., p. 11)

[95] Ibid., p. 15.

severity, by an overwhelming 81.5%, members of Council-affiliated denominations considered the courts insufficiently harsh in handling criminals. Busing, supported by the NCC, was opposed by 82.3% of members of Council-affiliate denominations.[96]

Over 40 groups receiving Methodist funds were identified. What they all had in common was promotion of the view that America is an evil society.[97] But the countries the NCC leadership found to serve as positive ideals, were Marxist third-world countries that had either severely restricted or all but eliminated religion.[98]

The belief that violence is an appropriate means for achieving social change underlies both communism and liberation theology or, to bring this up to date, consider the violence of the BLM and Antifa riots and murders of 2020, applauded by Democrats and most media outlets.[99]

The Breakdown of Higher Education, by John Ellis (2021)

Few people are less intellectually open, flexible, and curious than a radical leftist. (27)

By 1999 it was clear that radicals ... were hellbent on hiring fellow radicals. (27)

"The Noble Delusion of Mass Activism" by Jeffrey P. Colin (2013)

Essentially then, "activism" centers around the idea of populist power. If one believes that the masses as a group can be moved to stand up to "injustices" or "inequality", then one tends to believe in the efficacy of "activism". History does not support such ideas [without specific, charismatic, powerful leaders].

The need for "movements" is largely overstated. Efforts to educate

---

[96] Ibid., p. 16.
[97] Ibid., p. 22.
[98] Ibid., p. 26.
[99] Ibid., p. 40.

and organize are necessary, but much of what is done by movements such as Occupy Wall Street has proven to be superfluous nonsense. As individuals, we really need to focus our efforts on things that yield clear and tangible results, and leave meaningless ideologies for dreamers, ideologues, and malicious obstructionists.

"Activist Delusions, Stranger than Fiction," The Center for Consumer Freedom Team, 9-23-2008.

They are on a messianic mission. It is almost a religion where there isn't any science base to it: "Mindless activists". Activists are types who, by some quirk of personality, enjoy long meetings, shouting slogans, and spending a night or two in jail.

CHAPTER THREE

Why only We Liberals can Envision This Utopia. And What Kind of Government We Need.

THE VISION OF THE ANOINTED

Though it may sound narcissistic, this is really the easiest question to answer, and the answer is quite logical, ancient, and persuasive.

Let's be honest about this. What we're talking about is establishing a form of government that can let us build our utopian vision.

So why us? Why do we believe that we alone are the people who can envision Utopia and construct a government system to realize it? Well, we know we are, and we're relying on an understanding of society going back over 2,400 years. This isn't imagination or fantasy; it's established history.

We humans often think in terms of two opposing groups, forces, or ideas: the haves and the have-nots, saints and sinners, true believers and heretics, the ignorant masses and the intellectual elites. This has been observed and commented on by many people throughout history.

While this could be its own book, I'll deal with it here using only a few sources. It concerns what have been called the Two

Cultures. This is fundamental to our new liberal religion, and a deep reality seen by great thinkers as far back as Plato, as seen in his Republic. Today, we too often act like we believe that only modern college-graduate liberals have the wisdom and the vision to see how to work toward the utopian society that can replace the mythical Heaven. So, we need to invest a little time in understanding what's so important and unique about liberalism.

The Two Cultures

1956 – This was the year that British scientist and writer C. P. Snow wrote his essay "The Two Cultures", which he begins like this: "By training I was a scientist; by vocation I was a writer." He was deeply grounded in both cultures. He called the first culture the Scientific Culture: fact-based, empirical, the concrete culture of people who make the world work. These include doctors, nurses, dentists, lawyers, engineers, construction workers, police, firemen, gardeners, and hundreds of other professions relying on technical knowledge of how parts of our world work, and the ability to apply that knowledge in the real world.

Snow called the second culture the Humanities or Liberal Arts Culture, but also called it the Traditional Culture—because the birth of the sciences in the late 18th and 19th centuries was "new" and was not understood by those who were then "traditionally" educated in the liberal arts and humanities. But that's changed. Science has come to define our most widely respected knowledge, but science courses are not significant parts of our liberal arts or humanities education. Yet without understanding these grounded sciences, the grand abstractions so attractive to liberals are ungrounded. Now, to understand the world and how it works in a hundred ways, students need to learn the First Culture well. The more abstract, less grounded Second Culture of Humanities and the

Liberal Arts are important too, but no longer fundamental, and no longer with a solid empirical grasp on just how the world really works. Their larger imaginative pictures are important, but only if they're grounded in reality. This is Antaeus again: we need *both* feet on the ground, including the humanities/liberal arts foot.

Though this is ungrounded, this more fashionable "thinking class" has usually seen ourselves as superior to the others, the "masses". We're sure we are smarter and wiser. This goes back at least 2,400 years to the time of Plato in the West and 2,500 years to Confucius in the East. To Plato they were "philosopher rulers"; Confucius called them "Princelings".

Plato took the idea of philosopher rulers from Socrates, who defined a philosopher as one who loved wisdom, had a passion for knowledge, and was always curious and eager to learn. Socrates underlined the abstract idea that a philosopher was one who loved truth. By his grasp of the Idea of Good, he was best fit to rule, implying that knowledge could be obtained only by a select few who had the leisure and the material comforts to absorb it. Plato dismissed the opinion of the average person and denied their participation in politics and decision-making processes. He also rejected democracy and any "majoritarianism" on the grounds that ordinary people—the masses—did not have the capacity to understand absolute truth and the abstract Idea of Good. Ironically and disturbingly, Plato's arguments were similar to those who advocate military rule today.[100]

We have come to believe that we are meant to be rulers, lawgivers, the smarter people whose duty it is to tell all others how they must live, believe, behave. We are not smarter and are not wise. But giving power to people whose minds are not grounded in reality—which include almost everyone in the

---

[100] "Plato's Theory of the Philosopher King," by Nitish Yadav.

Second Culture—is a formula for disaster and an invitation to totalitarian socialism, as history shows. John Stuart Mill put this clearly nearly two centuries ago:

> *In politics, again, it is almost a commonplace, that a party of order or stability, and a party of progress or reform, are both necessary elements of a healthy state of political life. ... Each of these modes of thinking derives its utility from the deficiencies of the other.*[101]
>
> *He who knows only his own side of the case, knows little of that.*[102]
>
> *It is in a great measure the opposition of the other that keeps each within the limits of reason and sanity. Where there are no right-of-center voices to keep the left healthy, the result will inevitably be a much more extreme and self-indulgent political culture.*[103]
>
> *When there is no opposition, leadership will flow to the most extreme and exciting positions of the left—that is, to its least defensible versions. Wishful thinking can then proceed without check.*[104]
>
> *This explains why all political monocultures will sooner or later degenerate into incoherence. ... The exclusion of their intellectual opponents dooms them to incompetence. ... A kind of intellectual laziness can set in when everyone agrees. Scholarship becomes unreflective and imprecise.*[105]

Our basic problem is still that the two cultures can't even communicate. They each live in different worldviews, concepts, facts, and vocabularies. And now (2023), 67 years after

---

[101] *The Breakdown of Higher Education*, p. 31.
[102] Ibid., p. 37.
[103] Ibid., p. 38.
[104] Ibid.
[105] Ibid.

Snow wrote his influential 1956 essay, the problem is far worse.

The irony is that we may be the wrong—even the *worst*—people to rule, because we *aren't* grounded in the real world. We can't make the world work; we can't create, build, or fix things. We live in our heads, our ideas, our style of talking, our language games. "Tennis without a ball", in Wittgenstein's fertile metaphor. But you don't find many liberals in the military, as farmers, meat producers, police, firemen, engineers, construction workers, etc.

EARLIER RECOGNITIONS OF THE TWO CULTURES

In his 1979 book *The Revolt of the Elites and Betrayal of Democracy*, Christopher Lasch described the Second Culture as "The Elites" and "The thinking classes", and as ungrounded in the real world. A few quotes should suffice:

> *"Elites, who define the issues, have lost touch with the people."*[106]

> *"Theirs is essentially a tourist's view of the world."*[107]

> *"They live in a world of abstractions and images, a simulated world that consists of computerized models of reality, as distinguished from the palpable, immediate, physical reality inhabited by ordinary men and women. The thinking classes have seceded not just from the common world around them but from reality itself."*[108]

---

[106] Christopher Lasch, *The Revolt of the Elites and Betrayal of Democracy*, p. 3.
[107] Ibid., p. 6.
[108] Ibid., p. 20.

"The culture wars that have convulsed America since the sixties are best understood as a form of class warfare, in which an enlightened elite (as it thinks of itself) seeks not so much to impose its values on the majority (perceived as racist, sexist, provincial, and xenophobic), much less to persuade them by rational public debate, as to create parallel or alternative institutions in which it will no longer be necessary to confront the unenlightened at all."[109]

"This new class maintains the fiction that its power rests on intelligence alone. It thinks of itself as a self-made elite owing its privileges exclusively to its own efforts."[110]

And looking back a century, Lasch says, *"In the 19th century, some held that 'labor and education are incompatible' and condemned the education of working people as 'useless' and 'dangerous'. It was a 'misfortune', in their view, that workers 'should have heads at all'".[111]*

He also believes that the emergence of a permanent class of wage earners after the Civil War was a profoundly disturbing development, as the thinking class and the working class became the two major classes (cultures) in America, and each tended to become hereditary.[112]

And back in 1850, Bastiat also saw the two cultures in similar ways:

"The socialists divide mankind into two parts. Men in general, except one, form the first; the politician himself forms the second, which is by far the most important."[113]

---

[109] Ibid., pp. 20-21.
[110] Ibid., p. 39.
[111] Ibid., p. 69.
[112] Ibid., pp. 75 and 81.
[113] *The Law*, p. 23.

"Think of the difference between the gardener and his trees, between the inventor and his machine, between the chemist and his substances, between the agriculturist and his seed. The Socialist thinks, in all sincerity, that there is the same difference between himself and mankind."[114]

"No wonder the politicians of the 19th century look upon society as an artificial production of the legislator's genius. This idea, the result of a classical education [today we call it a liberal arts or humanities education], has taken possession of all the thinkers and great writers of our country. To all these persons, the relations between mankind and the legislator appear to be the same as those that exist between the clay and the potter."[115]

And in ancient Greece, 2,400 years ago, the Greek playwright Aristophanes, in his play "The Clouds", called the Second Culture the Think Culture, headed by Socrates. It was these abstract questions of Socrates that, Aristophanes said, had corrupted the youth of Athens by making them question the assumptions, rules, and laws that held their society together. And it was this play, several decades later, Socrates said, that led to his trial, conviction, and the death sentence which made Socrates—who taught Plato, who in turn taught Aristotle—drink the hemlock and die. The threat of an ungrounded Second Culture cannot be overestimated, thought Aristophanes—and many of today's First Culture citizens agree.

Since Snow's essay and lecture have influenced so many later thinkers, here are some other things he said about the Two Cultures:

- *As a group, the scientists ... are impatient to see if something can be done; and inclined to think that it can be*

---

[114] Ibid., p. 24.
[115] Ibid., p. 24.

done, until it's proved otherwise. That is their real optimism, and it's an optimism that the rest of us badly need.

- *If I were to risk a piece of shorthand, I should say that naturally [the scientists] had the future in their bones.*

- *[And yet] It is the [humanities/liberal arts] culture, to an extent remarkably little diminished by the emergence of the scientific one, which manages the western world.*

- *They [the Second Culture] dismiss scientists who don't know the great works of literature as ignorant specialists. Yet their own ignorance and their own specialization is just as startling. Once or twice I have been provoked and have asked the company how many of them could describe the Second Law of Thermodynamics. The response was cold: it was also negative. Yet I was asking something which is about the scientific equivalent of: "Have you read a work of Shakespeare's?" I now believe that if I had asked an even simpler question—such as, What do you mean by mass, or acceleration, which is the scientific equivalent of saying, "Can you read?"— not more than one in ten of the highly educated would have felt that I was speaking the same language. So the great edifice of modern physics goes up, and the majority of the cleverest people in the western world have about as much insight into it as their Neolithic ancestors would have had.*

- *The young scientists know that with an indifferent degree they'll get a comfortable job, while their contemporaries and counterparts in English or History will be lucky to earn 60% as much. No young scientist of any talent would feel that he isn't wanted or that his work is ridiculous.*

- *There is only one way out of all this: it is, of course, by rethinking our education.*

In short accompanying essays ("Intellectuals as Natural Luddites", "The Scientific Revolution", "The Rich and the Poor"), Snow added some other relevant thoughts:

- *If we forget the scientific culture, then the rest of western intellectuals have never tried, wanted, or been able to understand the industrial revolution, much less accept it. Intellectually, in particular literary intellectuals, are natural Luddites.*
- *The Industrial Revolution ... was by far the biggest transformation in society since the discovery of agriculture.*
- *One truth is straightforward. Industrialization is the only hope of the poor. The gains of that revolution ... are the base of our social hope.*
- *Most pure [i.e., merely intellectual, academic] scientists have themselves been devastatingly ignorant of productive industry, and many still are. Pure scientists have by and large been dim-witted about engineers and applied science. They couldn't get interested. They wouldn't recognize that many of the problems were as intellectually exciting as pure [i.e., abstract intellectual] problems, and that many of the solutions were as satisfying and beautiful.*

It's important to have a good sense of the difference between these two cultures. Here are some of the other sets of terms various writers use to refer to them:

The First Culture	The Second Culture
Scientists	Liberal Arts/Humanities
Conservatives	Liberals
Factual	Abstract
Down-to-Earth	Above-the-Earth
Facts	Fancies/fantasies
Grounded	Ungrounded
Reality	Imagination

Tennis with a ball	Tennis without a ball
Democracy	Tyranny
The majority	The Anointed
The people	The elites
The working class	The Think Culture (Aristophanes)
The many	The few
The doers	The thinkers/talkers
The masses	The chattering class
The ignorant masses	The best and brightest
Civil society	The ruling class
Residents	Tourists

Many of us heard politician Hillary Clinton refer to Republicans in the "flyover" states as "Deplorables" and cringed at the cheap narcissism and low character it seemed to imply.

Speaking at a fundraiser in New York City on Friday, Clinton said,

> "You know, to just be grossly generalist, you could put half of Trump's supporters into what I call the basket of deplorables. Right?" Clinton said. "The racist, sexist, homophobic, xenophobic, Islamophobic, you name it. And unfortunately there are people like that. And he has lifted them up." (TIME, September 10, 2016)

Nor was Obama above this insulting depiction of working-class people (presumably Republicans):

Referring to working-class voters in old industrial towns decimated by job losses, the presidential hopeful said, "They get bitter, they cling to guns or religion or antipathy to people who aren't like them or anti-immigrant sentiment or anti-trade sentiment as a way to explain their frustrations". Talk about antipathy to people who aren't like them![116]

And this piece about a Hillary Clinton campaign speech to a black audience reveals her racist attitudes toward them:

"I don't feel no ways tired. I come too far from where I started from. Nobody told me that the road would be easy. I don't believe He brought me this far," drawled presidential aspirant Hillary Clinton, mimicking black voice to a black audience, at the First Baptist Church of Selma, Alabama. I'm wondering if Mrs. Clinton visits an Indian reservation, she might cozy up to them saying, "How! Me not tired. Me come heap long way. Road might rough. Sky Spirit no bring me this far." Or, seeking the Asian vote she might say, "I no wray tired. Come too far I started flum. Road berry clooked. Number one Dragon King take me far."[117]

But that is characteristic of the Second Culture's attitude toward the First. For an older example, Gertrude Himmelfarb wrote about author Virginia Woolf (1882-1941) opining, two days after the armistice ended WWI: "The London poor, half drunk and very sentimental or completely stolid with their hideous voices and clothes and bad teeth, make one doubt whether any decent life will ever be possible."[118]

We'll come back to the Two Cultures. They provide a fundamental concept for understanding today's conservatives (overwhelmingly the First Culture) and liberals (overwhelmingly the Second Culture). But just what are the Liberal Arts

---

[116] Ed Pilkington in *The Guardian*, New York @edpilkington Mon 14 Apr 2008.

[117] *Liberty Versus the Tyranny of Socialism: Controversial Essays*, by Walter E. Williams (2008), p. 322.

[118] Himmelfarb, Gertrude, *One Nation, Two Cultures* (Alfred A. Knopf, 1999), p. 6.

and the Humanities that make up the Second Culture?
The 7 "liberal arts" are:

- Trivium: grammar, dialectic (logic), rhetoric
- Quadrivium: arithmetic, geometry, astronomy, music

The humanities have been variously defined as "the disciplines that investigate the expressions of the human mind" (as opposed, for example, to empirical disciplines investigating the actual components of our world). They include ancient and modern languages, literature, philosophy, religion, and visual and performing arts such as music and theater. Areas that are sometimes regarded as social sciences and sometimes as humanities include history, archaeology, anthropology, area studies, communication studies, classical studies, law, and linguistics. Other sources add fields like languages, linguistics, jurisprudence, archaeology, comparative religion, and ethics. The *National Foundation on the Arts and Humanities Act* of 1965 also defines the humanities as "disciplines of memory and imagination, telling us where we have been and helping us envision where we are going". Before the rise of our sciences in the 19th and 20th centuries, "traditional education" meant the Second Culture. For liberals, it still does.

The source of our authority

Where do we liberals get our authority and influence? For some, it's wealth or class. But overwhelmingly, we cite our *education*: the fact that we have more *diplomas*.

This is especially true today, when the ratio of liberals to conservatives in colleges and universities overwhelmingly favors liberals. College today has been described as a process of baptism into liberal ideology. That's not education; it's indoctrination.

For Plato, who today would be considered Liberal Arts and Humanities extraordinaire, it was only the intellectual culture (today's Second Culture) that was fit to rule. Modern sciences were over two thousand years in the future, and abstract philosophical thinking was considered the mark of the superior thinkers. (Plato began as a playwright, turning later to philosophy, but his stories, metaphors, etc. show the expert touch of a good fiction writer.) Ironically, thinking of the ancient Greek myth of Antaeus, Plato was also regarded as a good *wrestler*. Plato's student Aristotle was grounded in sciences, as the online *Britannica* biography shows:

> *Aristotle's intellectual range was vast, covering most of the sciences and many of the arts, including biology, botany, chemistry, ethics, history, logic, metaphysics, rhetoric, philosophy of mind, philosophy of science, physics, poetics, political theory, psychology, and zoology. Aristotle (384-322 BC) was the founder of formal logic, devising for it a finished system that for centuries was regarded as the sum of the discipline; and he pioneered the study of zoology, both observational and theoretical, in which some of his work remained unsurpassed until the 19th century. But he is, of course, most outstanding as a philosopher. His writings in ethics and political theory as well as in metaphysics and the philosophy of science continue to be studied, and his work remains a powerful current in contemporary philosophical debate.*[119]

But for Plato the philosopher, only the "big picture" philosophers were capable of imagining a utopian society that had (and has) never existed, but which, in the imagination of ungrounded intellectuals, *sounded* like it must be far superior to all the actual societies of history.

---

[119] https://www.britannica.com/biography/Aristotle

So we in the Second Culture are reclaiming Plato's vision of creating a utopia here and now. And for this task, only Plato's philosopher-rulers can possibly hope to succeed.[120]

Plato denied the participation of the average person in politics and decision-making processes. Think of those "deplorables" in the "flyover states". By discounting the opinion of the average person, Plato tried to play safe and prevent any opposition, criticism, dissent, or even disobedience. He justified it on the grounds that these lead to factionalism and particularism, whereas a good society should promote the common good. Plato rejected majoritarianism and popular participation on the grounds that the ordinary person did not have the capacity to comprehend absolute truth and the Idea of Good. Plato's arguments were similar to those who advocate military rule in contemporary times. He strongly disliked democracy. He also didn't mince words about the power and freedom his philosopher rulers could and should exercise over the masses:

"Our rulers will have to make considerable use of falsehood and deception for the benefit of their subjects" (459c). A ruler may lie as necessary, but if he "catches anybody else in the city lying ... he will chastise him for introducing a practice as subversive and destructive of a state as it is of a ship". (389d). At the top, ruling over all, is the wise philosopher, whose love of wisdom "is impossible for the multitude" (494a).[121]

---

[120] A century before Plato, Confucius had some similar opinions. The more "educated" people whom Plato called "philosopher rulers" Confucius referred to as "Princelings".

[121] *Kindly Inquisitors: The New Attacks on Free Thought*, by Jonathan Rauch (2014), p. 33. (The quotes are from Plato's *The Republic*.)

PROPAGANDA: Plato's method, brought up to date

During World War I, Freud's nephew Edward Bernays and journalist Walter Lippman worked for our government's efforts to sell the war to a public that was against it. They used what we today recognize as advertising techniques, selling the war as a war "to make the world safe for democracy". But the word for what they were doing was PROPAGANDA. And after the war, Bernays, the father of modern public relations, wrote rhapsodically about the word, trying to give it a positive and healthy meaning (which the German use of propaganda during the war made impossible). Some of Bernays' rhetoric is mind-numbing:

> Calling these propagandists "invisible governors", he says, *It is not usually realized how necessary these invisible governors are to the orderly functioning of our group life. (38) It has been found possible to so mold the mind of the masses that they will throw their newly gained strength in the desired direction. (47) Propaganda is the executive arm of the invisible government. (48) The extent to which propaganda shapes the progress of affairs about us may surprise even well-informed persons. (51) Modern propaganda is a consistent, enduring effort to create or shape events to influence the relations of the public to an enterprise, idea or group. (52) Propaganda is here to stay. (54)*

And in words Plato could have written, this 20th-century genius of propaganda declares, *It is the intelligent minorities which need to make use of propaganda continuously and systematically in the active proselytizing of minorities in whom selfish interests and public interests coincide which lie the progress and development of America. Only through the active energy of the intelligent few can the public at large become aware of and act upon new ideas. Small groups of persons can, and do, make the rest of us think what they please about a given subject. (57) Men are rarely aware of the real reasons which motivate their actions. (74) Fortunately, the sincere and gifted politician is able, by the instrument of propaganda, to mold and form the will of the people. (109)*

WHAT'S WRONG HERE?

A lot of important things are wrong here.

Frederic Bastiat from 1850, again, quoting Rousseau:

If it is true that a great prince is a rare thing, how much more so must a great lawgiver be? The former has only to follow the pattern proposed to him by the latter. This latter is the engineer who invents the machine; the former is merely the workman who sets it in motion.

"And what part have men to act in all this? That of the machine. Or rather, are they not merely the brute matter of which the machine is made? So between the legislator ... and the people, there are the same relations as those that exist between the agricultural writer and the farmer, and between the farmer and the clod. At what a vast height, then, is the politician placed, who rules over legislators themselves and teaches them their trade..."[122]

Rousseau again: *"He (the legislator) ought to feel that he can transform every individual, that he can change the constitution of man, to fortify it, and substitute a social and moral existence for the physical and independent one that we have all received from nature. In a word, he must deprive man of his own powers, to give him others that are foreign to him."[123]*

---

[122] *The Law*, p. 31.
[123] Ibid., p. 33.

But this would require the omniscience of God, wouldn't it? So for that nonexistent God, liberals have substituted our *own* imagined omniscience. It's hard to imagine greater narcissism! Yet this attitude toward members of the two cultures—ordinary people and the self-anointed, elite Thinking Class—was already present in Plato.

Plato wanted the city to be ruled by *knowledge*, which he thought only philosophers have, rather than *power*, which (a) they don't have, and (b) is how the city is *really* ruled. Plato deserves great respect, but he could not be more wrong on these points. This is the fundamental fantasy in the idea of philosopher kings. It's a fantasy coming from ungrounded thought seduced by grand abstractions, with no historical or actual grounding in the real world. Socrates had originally described these "philosopher kings" as "those who love the sight of truth". Plato thought of the philosopher king as a ruler who possesses both a love of wisdom as well as intelligence, reliability, and a willingness to live a simple life. Such are the rulers of his utopian city *Kallipolis*, or "beautiful city". However, what percentage of actual politicians—or philosophers—can really be described this way?

But criticisms of ungrounded grand abstractions threaten the very foundation of our secular liberal religion. We still want to serve the highest values, want our presence to be a gift to our larger world rather than a curse or an indifferent blot. Who could live with themselves knowing their presence, the values they serve, their major deeds in the service of high ideals *harmed* the world and killed innocents? Only sociopaths or toxic narcissists; we are a social species, and much of our identity must be grounded in our value to the larger world.

What we finally settled on as our secular religion came from a combination of things thrown together by chance occurrences that took an increasingly solid form in the 1960s.

Still, we liberals *do* have the diplomas, the advanced education, so we think we *are* smarter, wiser, the only "culture" to be trusted with the future.

In the phrase used by Rael Jean Isaac and Erich Isaac, the "coercive utopians" serve as the vanguard of the New Class. Although the term "The New Class" was first coined by Milan Djilas to describe the Communist elite, in the US it has been used to refer to those who produce and distribute knowledge rather than material goods. Figuring prominently in the New Class are intellectual scientists and teachers, print and broadcast journalists, social scientists, planners, social workers, salaried professionals, and government bureaucrats. There has been a corresponding explosion in higher education to prepare people to fill the new positions. The number of students enrolled in degree credit programs in colleges and universities has multiplied sevenfold from 1940 to 1983—and doubled again since 1983. One out of three Americans has now completed four years of college. Both what these students learned—and what they did not learn—in college and later in New Class positions made them responsive to utopian appeals.[124]

But as C. P. Snow's essay described it, only the *first* culture is grounded in reality. He called it the "scientific" culture. It helps to remember that "science"—*scientia*—means *knowledge*. Here, it means the kind of empirical knowledge grounded in reality, not imagination. That's not the kind of knowledge that liberalism values or generally possesses. Since they are seduced by Grand Abstractions, liberals tend to think it is superior to mere facts. After all, we even *capitalize* most of these grand abstractions: Truth, Beauty, Justice, Fairness, Love, and the rest. Of course, our country should have open borders. Of course, we should allow and invite all foreigners into our country! Even calling them "foreigners" or "aliens" is an insult to grand abstractions. The ignorant masses may not

---

[124] *The Coercive Utopians*, p. 288.

be able to see this, but we certainly can.

Living only in these ungrounded abstractions means we are content to offer an implicit invitation to all people in the world: Just get into our country, legally or illegally, and our citizens will be glad to give you free medical care at any emergency room, free education, freebies beyond measure. This is the kind of insanity that ungrounded abstractions inflict on the world. It's easy to see that the real motive here isn't with helping our country or really wanting several billion poor people to come freeload off of us. The real motive is to attract several million people—mostly from Mexico and South America— to come, *assuming they will vote Democratic*. That's the same motive behind the talk of admitting Washington D.C. and Puerto Rico as new states—and maybe dividing California into three or four states and admitting them—all heavily Democrat-leaning communities. Don't assign noble motives to ignoble schemes.

And think about this business of equating diplomas with intelligence. First, when the ratio of liberals to conservatives in our colleges is so insanely high, then "education" is no longer happening; rather, it's *indoctrination*, like a religious conversion to liberal ideology.

The classic film *The Wizard of Oz* identified today's liberal intellectual delusion back in 1939. The lion, tin man, and scarecrow each lacked something which they hoped and believed the Wizard would give them. The lion needed courage, the tin man needed a heart, and the scarecrow needed a brain. But when the scarecrow finally met the Wizard (who wasn't really a wizard at all), the Wizard handed the scarecrow a *diploma*. The idea that college diplomas can make you smart, can qualify you to dictate to anyone else how they should live, is the Scarecrow's Delusion.

So, the problem with these narcissistic liberal assumptions is that they're wrong on almost every level. And these delusions can bring only harm to the real world unless they are re-strained by a well-grounded understanding of the real world. It takes a balance between the two cultures, not the rule of abstractions over reality. The Scarecrows should be laughed off the stage—and if they're teachers, they should be fired before they can betray and defraud more of our young people.

Liberals, including liberal professors, have no particular wisdom. They may be certain, but they're not right; they're just liberal. Look at the individual lives of our politicians, our screaming professors and students. They don't even have the wisdom to construct *one* ideal life. They certainly couldn't do it for 333 million others, most of whom think they're nuts.

Do you think the politicians actually work for us? Then ask why they have their own health care—far superior to ours—or why they have a retirement plan that pays them a full salary for the rest of their lives after just one year in Congress. There is shrewdness, but there is neither wisdom, honesty, nor integrity evident here. But most of them do have diplomas ... and delusions.

Yes, Plato endorsed almost everything they're doing. But Plato hated democracy. And between the two major forms of government—democracy and tyranny—both Plato and our current liberals easily choose the tyranny of one-party rule that will give them the power to command the ignorant masses and lead them all into the dystopian government that gives the liberals complete power over the rest of us. There aren't enough diplomas to make that look smart.

The scarecrow needed a brain, not a diploma

The most relevant meaning of "smart" here is a kind of over-view grounded in the details of the real world, not a haze of grand abstractions floating above the clouds. Here's a list of 113 *very* smart people who have reshaped our world in big ways. *Not one of these people graduated from college.* You've never heard of many of these people, but look a few of them up. They were very successful and interesting:

Steve Jobs

Bill Gates

Mark Zuckerberg

James Cameron

Oprah Winfrey

Ellen DeGeneres

Kanye West

Lady Gaga

Frank Lloyd Wright

Henry Ford

Larry Ellison (Oracle)

Michael Dell

Paul Allen

Kirk Kerkorian (Tracinda)

Dustin Moskovitz (Facebook)

Ralph Lauren

Walt Disney

David Green (Hobby Lobby)

Richard Branson (Virgin)

Sean Parker (Facebook)

Evan Williams (Twitter)

Jack Dorsey (Twitter)

Hiroshi Yamauchi (Nintendo)

Pat Farrah (The Home Depot)

Mark Rich

John Paul DeJoria

Frederick "Freddy" Laker

Leslie Wexner

Dean Kamen

Wolfgang Puck

Russell Simmons

Jan Koum

Travis Kalanick

Orji Uzor Kalu

Warren Buffett

Mo Ibrahim

Mike Adenuga

George Soros

Sam Walton

Jerry Yang

David Filo

Anita Roddick

Sergey Brin

Billy Joe (Red) McCombs

Craig McCaw

Mickey Jagtiani

Theodore Waitt

Y. C. Wang

Larry Page

Jeff Bezos

Martha Stewart

Henry Ross Perot

Aliko Dangote

Li Ka Shing

Cosmos Maduka

Sir Philip Green

Madame C. J. Walker

Ted Turner

Cornelius Vanderbilt

Mayer Amischel Rothschild

Ty Warner

Howard Hughes

Asa Candler

Jenny Craig

David Geffen

Dhirubhai Ambani

John Mackey

Joyce C. Hall

Kemmons Wilson

Leandro Rizzuto

Thomas Edison

Vidal Sassoon

Jay Van Andel

John D. Rockefeller Sr.

Jimmy Dean
Marcus Loew
Mary Kay Ash
Milton Hershey
Ray Kroc
Richard Devos
Richard Schulze
Rush Limbaugh
S. Daniel Abraham
Simon Cowell
Gary Sinise
Steve Wozniak
W. T. Grant
Wally "Famous" Amos

Isaac Merritt Singer
Jack Crawford Taylor
Dave Thomas
Kevin Rose
Rachael Ray
Abraham Lincoln
Andrew Carnegie
Andrew Jackson
Anne Beiler
Ansel Adams
Barry Diller
Henry J. Kaiser
Hyman Golden
Ingvar Kamprad

Ben Franklin
Carl Lindner
Coco Chanel
Col. Harlan Sanders
Debbi Fields
Dewitt Wallace
Frederick Henry Royce
George Eastman
H. Wayne Huizenga
Wilbur Wright
Orville Wright

These people are examples of what "Smart" means in the real world. They may be politically liberal or conservative, but not one of them finished college: many didn't even finish high school. The only diplomas they received were honorary, given by colleges and universities acknowledging their professional superiority to virtually *all* of the college graduates in the country. Today, college diplomas merely make students more articulate and fashionable, not smart.

Intellectuals haven't acted smart in their utopian dreams— quite the opposite, in many cases. But if you have a diploma, especially a graduate degree or Ph.D., you don't *need* a brain! Just start calling yourself "Dr." (or "Reverend" or "Professor"); that'll fool a lot of people—maybe including you.

What the New Class did *not* learn was much more important than what it learned. It learned very little about how the economy of the US actually worked. This was true even for those who took courses in economics, the least "soft" (and least popular) of the social sciences. The New Class also learned very little about other societies, obtaining no perspective from which to judge the virtues, as well as the defects, of its own society. Anthropology was an exception among the social sciences in this respect, teaching a diffuse cultural relativism, asserting that our standards were not intrinsically better or "higher" than those of any primitive culture. Since the New Class, for the most part, never entered business, experience did not compensate for educational failures. To be sure, a considerable number did enter profit-making corporations—journalists are a soft example—but their activities were detached from the economic aspects of running a business. The New Class could maintain its sense that it represented the "solution" part of the social order, the service sector, while the production sector, at least those at its helm, who made "profits" rather than salaries, were the source of its problems.[125]

The point wasn't that there was no merit to specific criticisms. Science and technology *did* have harmful side effects, which had to be addressed. But the movements lacked all perspective, emphasizing only risks and dangers, never the benefits of technology. The New Class was oblivious to this failure because it took the achievements of technology for granted. Thus, for example, the achievements of the modern pharmaceutical and chemical industry, which gave modern medicine powerful weapons against disease and revolutionized nutrition, protecting crops through herbicides and pesticides and maintaining their quality through preservatives, could be easily ignored by the New Class. It was mindful only of their supposed dangers.[126]

---

[125] Rael Jean Isaac and Erich Isaac, *The Coercive Utopians*, (Regency Gateway, Inc. 1983), p. 290.
[126] Ibid., p. 291.

These liberal movements were also attractive because they assigned guilt. The villain was the pursuit of profits by corporations, a pursuit intrinsic to the capitalist system. ... The New Class paid no price for berating the corporation for its alleged wickedness. It had the luxury of creating a guilt culture, for which its members bore no guilt—the guilt was all in the producing sector. The presence in every religion of methods by which people can confess and alleviate their sense of guilt for sins they have committed suggests this fills a deep human need. The New Class could confess the collective guilt of society while the actual penalties would be borne by others.[127]

Since the New Class included the communicators and the regulators, it was in a position to perform the work of "the people" (the New Class never spoke in terms of its own interests or values) against the producers. And in the process its members could obtain power for themselves, the power that had so long resided in the "business class", which the New Class felt was in every respect less worthy than itself.

Before the growth of the New Class, the notion that intellectuals could create a base for power among people very much like themselves would have seemed laughable—to intellectuals above all.[128]

---

[127] Ibid., p. 291.
[128] Ibid., p. 293.

EXCERPTS

Glen T. Martin, in his short essay "The Utopian Horizon of Objective Human Values",[129] offers clear definitions (or rationalizations) of some of our utopian **VISION OF THE ANOINTED**:

Our primordial temporality means that we are projecting towards a "potentiality-for-Being" that places the future in ontological priority over the past and present. The future forms for us a "horizon" within which we can authentically actualize our being.[130]

Our temporal horizon is a utopian horizon. And these values (Heidegger asserts) are implicit to the evolving universe itself come to consciousness in us.[131]

Heidegger emphasizes: "What one wills is always ideal. I will what I conceive to be a better state of affairs and of myself than what actually exists." ... "Utopian thought always relates to the future, whether near or far away, and a future quite different from present reality." ... "Denial of utopia mutilates freedom and reason."[132]

And so on.

These courses and concepts are not meant to prepare students for living in the real world. And unless the students can understand

---

[129] *Academia Letters*, December 2020.

[130] Glen T. Martin, "The Utopian Horizon of Objective Human Values", p. 3.

[131] Ibid., p. 4. Heidegger is an example of liberals being so seduced by grand abstractions that they don't notice these grand statements have no identifiable connection to reality—here, the notion that the "evolving universe itself" has implicit values which have "come to consciousness in us".

[132] Ibid., p. 4. If you haven't read thinkers like these, or haven't had such courses in college, don't be impressed. These statements aren't about the real world. They're about, and confined within, the ungrounded imaginative worlds that too many college professors and students have been trained to live within. Remember the Scarecrow's Delusion.

how unrelated they really are to the world that student will need to share with the majority of his or her fellow citizens, these thinkers, professors, colleges and universities will have both betrayed and defrauded the students. In many or most cases, the professors themselves may be incapable of distinguishing between ungrounded intellectualism and grounded reality. This is a betrayal of students, their still-developing character, and our whole society.

The Ruling Class: How they corrupted America and what we can do about it, by Angelo M. Codevilla.[133] He makes other helpful distinctions between the two classes, which he identifies as The Country Class (the First Culture) and The Ruling Class (the Second Culture):

The class's chief pretension is its intellectual superiority: its members claim to know things that the common herd cannot. It confuses its own opinions with "science". Our Ruling Class prays to themselves as saviors of the planet and as shapers of mankind in their own image. While the Ruling Class thinks that Americans are unfit to run their own lives, most Americans have noticed that our Ruling Class has lost every war it has fought, run up an unpayable national debt, and generally made life worse.[134] Without both feet on the ground, Antaeus is just a teetering fool. It's like playing tennis without a ball.

The Country Class is civil society, including both what Max Weber called Gemeinschaft, meaning the network of voluntary organizations that give communities their common element, and Gesellschaft, meaning commercial/professional relationships.[135]

The Country Class also takes part in the US armed forces, body and soul: nearly all the enlisted, non-commissioned officers and officers under flag rank belong to this class in every measurable way. Few vote for the Democratic Party.[136]

---

[133] An *American Spectator* Book, 2010.
[134] *The Ruling Class*, p. xix.
[135] Ibid., p. 53.
[136] Ibid., p. 59.

Our rulers believe it is right for the ruled to shut up and obey, or at most cut little deals for themselves.[137]

The Revolt of the Elites and the Betrayal of Democracy, by Christopher Lasch. Lasch calls the Second Culture the Thinking Classes or The Elites.[138]

Elites, who define the issues, have lost touch with the people.[139]

Theirs is essentially a tourist's view of the world—not a perspective likely to encourage a passionate devotion to democracy.[140]

The thinking classes are fatally removed from the physical side of life. They live in a world of abstractions and images, a simulated world that consists of computerized models of reality, as distinguished from the palpable, immediate, physical reality inhabited by ordinary men and women. The thinking classes have seceded not just from the common world around them but from reality itself.[141]

Robert Reich's category of "symbolic analysts" includes people who live in a world of abstract concepts and symbols, ranging from stock market quotations to the visual images produced by Hollywood and Madison Avenue, and who specialize in the interpretation and deployment of symbolic information. Reich contrasts them with the two other principal categories of labor: "routine production workers", who perform repetitive tasks and exercise little control over the design of production, and "in-person servers", whose work also consists of routine, but "must be provided person-to-person" and therefore cannot be "sold worldwide".

Reich saw these "symbolic analysts" as the best and brightest in American life. Educated at "elite private schools" and "high-quality suburban schools, where they are tracked through advanced courses"

---

[137] Ibid., p. 65.
[138] *The Revolt of the Elites and Betrayal of Democracy*, by Christopher Lasch, 1996.
[139] *Revolt of the Elites*, p. 3.
[140] Ibid., p. 6.
[141] Ibid., p. 20.

they enjoy every advantage their doting parents can provide.[142]
[They get the Wizard's "diplomas" and are accepted as very smart]

Only in a world in which words and images bear less and less re-
semblance to the things they appear to describe would it be possible
for a man like Reich to refer to himself, without irony, as secretary
of labor or to write so glowingly of a society governed by the best
and brightest. The last time the "best and brightest" got control of
the country, they dragged it into a protracted, demoralizing war in
Southeast Asia.[143]

The Coercive Utopians, by Rael and Erich Isaac

The models the utopians have chosen have all been anti-American.
China, once it tried to forge links to the US, rapidly lost credibility
as a utopian model. ... The implausibility, indeed the downright ab-
surdity, of reconstructing the United States on the basis of total consensus does not give pause to the utopians, because they have
learned to believe that *anything* is possible. Intellectuals are by the
nature of their activity drawn toward the building of abstract models. ... There is less difference between the blueprints of today's utopians and conventional Marxism than meets the eye.[144]

Kindly Inquisitors, by Christopher Lasch

Plato, the greatest of all the masters who have advocated centralized
control of knowledge. Maybe the best reason to read Plato is to be
horrified. Read *The Republic*, and you find that once you look past
the glittering facade of Plato's rhetoric you are face to face with the
ethic of the totalitarian regime. Plato's vision is immediately appeal-
ing, and you have to think hard about it to see why it is bad. It holds
out the promise of governance by the enlightened and humane, of
relief from the foolish and unreasonable, of shelter from uncertainty

---

[142] Ibid., pp. 35-36.
[143] Ibid., p. 39.
[144] *The Coercive Utopians*, p. 297.

and change. Today, as ever, it is a magnet drawing millions of people, including many American intellectuals, toward the political regulation of inquiry. (31)

The founding principle is that of absolute individual devotion to, and submission to, the good of the state. The state should control procreation and marriage, for eugenic and population-control purposes, so as to prevent the racial debasement of the ruling (guardian) class. (32)

The state must exercise strict and vigilant control of speech, including poetry. "We must begin, then, it seems, by a censorship over our story-makers" (377c). "We will beg Homer and the other poets not to be angry if we cancel those and all similar passages", says Plato, after citing verses of the kind which "we will expunge" (387b and 386c). Artists and craftsmen must also be controlled. No form of expression is to be untouched by the state's tendrils. The state "must throughout be watchful against innovations in music and gymnastics counter to the established order" (424b). Just so did Stalin and his minions supervise the innovations of Shostakovich. (32-33)

Real, healthy, grounded liberalism holds that knowledge comes only from a public process of critical exchange, in which the wise and unwise alike participate. But Plato believed that knowledge comes from wisdom, and so knowledge belongs especially to the especially wise—to the true philosophers, who are rare indeed (Confucius had earlier called them Princelings). The real philosophers are the people "who are capable of apprehending that which is eternal and unchanging, while those who are incapable of this, but lose themselves and wander amid the multiplicities of multifarious things, are not philosophers" (484b). (33)

Philosophy "is impossible for the multitude", and "the perfect philosopher is a rare growth among men and is found in only a few" (494a and 491b).

Such a person is likely to be laughed at by "the whole rabble". Never mind; here is the man whose spirit and mind are fit to rule. (34)

The fundamentalist social principle: *Those who know the truth should decide who is right.* (100)

One horse-laugh is worth 10 thousand syllogisms. (H.L. Mencken) (111)

As is so often the case with egalitarian activists, they support equality for everybody, except people who don't share their political agenda. (116)

Practically all knowledge of any importance began as a statement that offended someone. "All the durable truths that have come into the world within historic times," said Mencken, "have been opposed as bitterly as if they were so many waves of smallpox." (124) [This is also the history of most *heretics* in religion. Virtually every advance made in every field has come from heretics: those who, when told the choices were closed, said "No, I'm not through choosing."]

People who like authoritarianism always picture themselves running the show. But no one stays on top for long. (143)

Where you find fundamentalist righteousness, there you will find the totalitarian idea. (153)

Intellectuals are losing their nerve or their souls, or both. (154)

Intellectuals and Society, by Thomas Sowell (2011)

> *Intelligence is quickness to apprehend as distinct from ability,*
> *which is capacity to act wisely on the things apprehended.*
> • Alfred North Whitehead (3)

Intelligence minus judgment equals intellect. (4)

Intellectuals, in the restricted sense which largely conforms to general usage, are ultimately unaccountable to the external world. Not only have intellectuals been insulated from material consequences, they have often enjoyed immunity from even a loss of reputation after having been demonstrably wrong. As Eric Hoffer put it:

One of the surprising privileges of intellectuals is that they are free to be scandalously asinine without harming their reputation. (10)

Bertrand Russell, for example, was both a public intellectual and a leading authority within a rigorous field. But the Bertrand Russell who is relevant here is not the author of landmark treatises on mathematics but the Bertrand Russell who advocated "unilateral disarmament" for Britain in the 1930s while Hitler was re-arming Germany. Russell's advocacy of disarmament extended all the way to "disbanding the army and navy and air force"—again, with Hitler re-arming not far away. ... The Edmund Wilson who is relevant is not the highly regarded literary critic but the Edmund Wilson who urged Americans to vote for the Communists in the 1932 elections. In this he was joined by such other intellectual luminaries of the time as John Dos Passos, Sherwood Anderson, Langston Hughes, Lincoln Steffens and many other well-known writers of that era. (13)

The ignorance, prejudices, and groupthink of an educated elite are still ignorance, prejudice, and groupthink—and for those with one percent of the knowledge in a society to be guiding or controlling those with the other 99 percent is as perilous as it is absurd. (20)

Intellect—even intellect that reaches the level of genius—is not the same as wisdom. (488)

Professor Richard A. Posner: "Many public intellectuals are academics of modest distinction fortuitously thrust into the limelight" by their activities as public intellectuals, noting a "tendency of a public intellectual's media celebrity to be inverse to his scholarly renown". (505)

Cultivating Humanity, by Martha Nussbaum (1997)

To be a citizen of the world, one does not, the Stoics stress, need to give up local affiliations, which can frequently be a source of great richness in life. They suggest instead that we think of ourselves as surrounded by a series of concentric circles. The first one is drawn around the self; the next takes in one's immediate family; then follows the extended family; then, in order, one's neighbors or local group, one's fellow city-dwellers, one's fellow countrymen—and we can easily add to this list groups formed on the basis of ethnic, religious, linguistic, historical, professional, and gender identities. Beyond all these circles is the largest one, that of humanity as a whole. Our task as citizens of the world, and as educators who prepare people to be citizens of the world, will be to "draw the circles some- how toward the center", making all human beings like our fellow city-dwellers. In other words, we need not give up our special affec- tions and identifications, whether national or ethnic or religious; but we should work to make all human beings part of our commu- nity of dialogue and concern, showing respect for the human wher- ever it occurs, and allowing that respect to constrain our national or local politics. (60-61)

A favorite exercise toward keeping such accidents of station in their proper place is to imagine that all human beings are limbs of a single body, cooperating for the sake of common purposes. Referring to the fact that it takes only the change of a single letter in Greek to convert the word "limb" (melos) into the word "(detached) part" (meros), he concludes: "If, changing the word, you call yourself merely a (detached) part instead of a limb, you do not yet love your fellow men from the heart, nor derive complete joy from doing good; you will do it merely as a duty, not as doing good to yourself." The organic imagery underscores the Stoic ideal of cooperation. (p. 64)

Like much of the ancient Greek tradition, beginning with Herodo- tus, Stoics suggest that the encounter with other cultures is an es- sential part of an examined life. (p. 83)

"Becoming a citizen of the world is often a lonely business. It is, in effect, a kind of exile—from the comfort of assured truths, from the warm nestling feeling of being surrounded by people who share one's convictions and passions." (83)

The Liberal Mind: The Psychological Causes of Political Mad- ness, by Lyle H. Rossiter, Jr., M.D. (2006)

One of the most striking characteristics of modern liberalism, whether benign or radical, is the actual vagueness of its social poli- cies despite their apparent nobility of purpose. A typical "progres- sive" liberal platform, for example, will announce its goals to be the eradication of hunger, poverty, ignorance, disease, faulty childcare, material inequality and political oppression. The platform will dedicate itself to the provision of adequate jobs, housing, nutrition, education, social harmony, and medical care. But in the real world, attempting to reach even one of these goals is a colossal undertaking, whose difficulties the liberal agenda never adequately spells out for review.

History records the failed objectives and destructive consequences of nearly all programs of these types. African dictators, for example, have gotten very rich on programs to end their country's poverty while the people continue to starve and live or die in squalor. In Chicago the effort to enforce a right to adequate housing for the poor has had such disastrous economic and social effects that the projects had to be torn down. Despite history's negative report card on programs of this type, the true believer in the liberal agenda nevertheless presses ahead with "progressive" programs, ignoring their repeated failures. Meanwhile, the character of all the people, those to whom the state gives and those from whom it takes, is profoundly demeaned. The dignity and sovereignty of the individual are lost in the state's perverse ministrations to the collective social mass. (326)

Over the course of the 20th century, the radical liberal's attempts to create a brave new socialist world have invariably failed. (330)

Considered in its entirety, the liberal's goal of making the state into an ideal parent/family and his method of achieving it by compelling competent people to do his bidding constitute the radical liberal agenda. Above all, the agenda is a blueprint for the use of irresistible government power. (333)

Unfortunately, the utopian world he seeks is completely impossible, given the realities of human nature, human relating and the human condition. (338-339)

The radical liberal has typically consolidated his political beliefs by the time he reaches his mid-twenties. (373)

Unfortunately, the history of radical liberalism's attempts to fulfill this promise has been one of stunning failure. The radical agenda by any other name—communism, socialism, collectivism, progressivism, welfarism—has invariably resulted in large-scale social decline. (373)

Radical liberalism promises economic equality for the general population. The declared goal is to eliminate disparities in wealth by forced transfers of material goods and services from citizens who have more of them to those who have less, but transfers of this type have never improved the long-term economic wellbeing of recipients nor corrected economic inequality in the society. Instead, the most prominent effects of such efforts are gross violations of liberty rights and widespread dependency on government. (378)

Liberals believe that much if not most property should be government owned, because only governments will protect it for the common good. (387)

In its childlike demands, the liberal mind seeks a world of cost-free benefits. (388) [But it's a con job.]

The liberal neurosis undermines the integrity of the individual's relationship to society at all levels. (399)

Radical liberalism does not seek a society of sovereign citizens but fosters instead a society of allegedly victimized dependents under the custodial care of the state. (402)

Unfortunately, however, history records the futility of this wishful thinking. Liberalism's past attempts to realize these fantasies have brought catastrophic damage on millions by empowering governments with the means to dominate their citizens. For all of the reasons noted, the liberal agenda, whether benign or radical, is completely incompatible with rational social order. (403)

CHAPTER FOUR

How to Create the Utopia

THE VISION OF THE ANOINTED

Once you understand why only we liberals can envision the needed utopia, the form of government is obvious, as Plato saw 2,400 years ago: it must be totalitarian. That's the attraction of communism and socialism: both give all power to the leaders (who, in our case, have the wisdom, the diplomas, to construct the utopian heaven on earth). As Plato observed, why let the ignorant masses direct culture when there are "philosopher rulers" available? We must keep the masses from interfering in our utopian schemes. Why? Because this is our *religion*, our calling, our sacred duty, that gives our lives their deepest meaning and noblest purpose. Without it we are, in a deeply religious sense, both lost and damned. Everything that really matters is at stake. We obey our ideology as others obey their gods.

How can we get control of the United States culture and government?

How, realistically, could liberals possibly gain control of the US government and culture? Even the question sounds insane. The percentage of liberals has shrunk over the past five years

(2022 figures), from 34% to 27%. The share of Democrats identifying as liberal dropped from 60% to 55%, while the share of Republicans who said they were conservative increased from 70% to 77%. And Republican voters (32%) are far more likely to identify as "very conservative" than Democrat voters (19%) are to say they're "very liberal".[145] And if the liberal media weren't distorting reality, conservatives would easily number more than 50%.[146]

Even treating these as ballpark figures that may fluctuate from year to year, there are only about two-thirds as many liberals as conservatives. Numbers like these make liberal fantasies of one-party rule sound ungrounded and absolutely insane.

THE 1960s: EVERYTHING COMES APART

The 60s culture was soaked in an existential angst, a loss of love, a feeling of loneliness and despair that had barely been there in the 50s. The US changed in the 1960s in ways that presaged the end of American culture as we had known it. Perhaps this was more vivid for me because I was in the Army from 2 January 1964 to 2 August 1967. Eight days after I returned from being a combat photographer and press officer in Vietnam, I went to Ann Arbor to finish my undergraduate degree in music theory at the University of Michigan. Isolated in the alternate reality of the Army, I completely missed the biggest transformations of US culture in my lifetime.

This is more than just a grand abstraction. Maybe an easy way to feel the profound cultural change is by looking at some

[145] https://morningconsult.com/2022/08/18/america-ideology-less-liberal-but-not-necessarily-more-conservative/
[146] See the Introduction to the book *Left Turn: How Liberal Media Bias Distorts the American Mind*, by Tim Groseclose. (2011)

of the #1 songs from 1963, then look at some #1 hits from 1964-1967 (see below). I played in bands in the late 50s and early 60s, and could have played in the kinds of bands backing up the hits of 1963: Rock 'n' Roll, jazz, dance bands. But starting in 1964—perhaps just starting with the Beatles—I couldn't relate to, or sometimes even understand, much of this new music or the culture creating it. A negative, lonely feeling was present that I didn't remember from 1963. The fact that my Army time corresponds so precisely with the cultural earthquake back home helps explain why, when I arrived in Ann Arbor in mid-August 1967, I could barely recognize this world "back home"—which didn't much feel like home. Being at the University of Michigan magnified the change: partly because, with Berkeley and Columbia, it was one of the three most violently anti-war campuses in the country. It was also the campus where, just five years earlier, Tom Hayden, then-editor of the campus newspaper, *The Michigan Daily*, had written the Port Huron Statement about the aims and desires of the Students for a Democratic Society (SDS). The form of government they really wanted was socialism, not democracy, but Hayden was smart enough to know that, in 1962, "socialism" wasn't a strategic name with which to identify. Hayden declared that the ideology of their little student SDS movement needed to take over the culture and government of the United States in order to have the power to put their utopian vision into practice. These are best understood as secular evangelical *religious* passions: a terribly important point.

In 1962 this sounded insane. There were only about 200 students in the whole SDS movement. But because of some of the chance happenings of the 1960s, by 1968-69 the SDS movement had grown by 200 times to a total of about 40,000.[147] Today, almost 60 years after Hayden's fledgling SDS movement began, his wild dreams look to be coming true.

---

[147] *The Breakdown of Higher Education*, p. 52.

Who could have believed it?

The societal changes were deep and vast. And maybe the simplest place to see these changes is in the pop songs from 1963-1967.[148] Even all these years later, the difference in the feelings behind these songs is simply stunning. Consider just these #1 hit songs from that five-year period.

Some of the #1 hits from 1963:

Go Away Little Girl	Sukiyaki
Walk Right In	Surf City (Two girls for every boy)
Hey Paula (I Want to Marry You)	My Boyfriend's Back
Walk Like A Man	Blue Velvet
Our Day Will Come	Dominique
He's So Fine	There! I've Said It Again (I love you)
It's My Party	

Some of the #1 songs from 1964-1967:

Can't buy me love	Help!
A world without love	Eve of Destruction
A hard day's night	Yesterday
Where did our love go	Get off my cloud
Mr. Lonely	The sounds of Silence
You've lost that lovin' feelin'	These boots are made for walkin'
(She's got a) Ticket to Ride	
I can't get no satisfaction	Ballad of the Green Beret

---

[148] I've picked the years 1963-1967 because 1963 was the year before I entered the Army (on 2 January 1964). That was "my world". I was in the Army from 2 January 1964 to 2 August 1967, when I returned from Vietnam and moved to Ann Arbor to complete my undergraduate degree at the University of Michigan (I was technically released from active duty on 6 August 1967). The #1 songs I've chosen from those years are a reflection of the world that developed while I was away, from the Beatles onward.

Monday Monday	Kind of a Drag
Paint it Black	Love is here and now you're
96 Tears	gone
Last train to Clarksville	Ode to Billie Joe
Poor side of town	The Letter
	Hello, Goodbye

Richard Rorty and Todd Gitlin have dated the fundamental transformation of our culture to August 1964, when the Gulf of Tonkin resolution was passed, effectively starting the Vietnam War, and the Mississippi Freedom Democratic Party was denied seats at the Atlantic City Democratic Convention. That was seven months after I enlisted in the Army. Though few saw it at the time, the 60s rang the death knell for our liberal righteousness and our role as philosopher-kings.

Liberalism changed from a politics grounded in our commonalities to politics without commonality, emphasizing our differences—a kind of micro-politics concerned only with certain identities: black, gay, female, etc. It's Identity Politics, but no longer as part of a larger and healthy whole society, just a kind of tribalism. But don't underestimate that. We are a social species: herd animals. We create and defer to all sorts of Alpha figures, titles, political and religious identities to which we give our allegiance and will sometimes sacrifice our lives, driven by our utterly primitive limbic system and the emotional power of Certainty that can trump facts without even breaking a sweat.

The Rights Movements of the 1960s were fundamentally different than the movements of just a decade earlier. These new activists wanted not only their fair civil rights: they also insisted on speaking for themselves, because being spoken for was seen as—and was—demeaning and infantilizing. The women's movement had its own gifted representatives: women like

Betty Friedan, Gloria Steinem, Camille Paglia, and Germaine Greer. Cesar Chavez headed the Latino movement, and black Americans had MLK Jr., Malcolm X, Jesse Jackson, Stokely Carmichael, and others.

The liberal campuses seemed consumed by the growing drug culture, sexual promiscuity (made possible on a larger scale by the development of the birth control pill in 1960), and grand abstractions about War. These kids were resolute in the certainty that they were right, knew all they needed to know about war—like a man who's certain he knows all about carrying and giving birth to a baby—and trying, this time through bullhorns and arrogant protests, to tell the surrounding society of grown-ups to get in line, and where the line was. Young Princelings, flexing their vocal cords.

Where did all the ignorant arrogance come from? And why this new and deep insecurity among the Princelings that masqueraded as righteous certainty? Just focusing on the impossibility of communication between Vietnam veterans and the self-righteous anti-war protestors, the Two Cultures couldn't have been further apart, less able to communicate—or even interested in communicating. Part of this was because ideological differences and identities were hardening into fundamentalist faiths.

Some other thoughts on changes in the liberal movements of the revolutionary 1960s:

Rorty: "The pre-Sixties reformist Left, insofar as it concerned itself with oppressed minorities, did so by proclaiming that all of us—black, white, and brown—are Americans, and that we should respect one another as such. This strategy gave rise to the 'Platoon' movies, which showed Americans of various ethnic backgrounds fighting and dying side by side. By contrast, the contemporary cultural Left urges that America should not be a melting-pot, because we need to respect one another in our differences. This Left wants to preserve otherness rather than ignore it.[149] Now again, and ironically, race *is* destiny.

"To take pride in being black or gay is an entirely reasonable response to the sadistic humiliation to which one has been subjected. But insofar as this pride prevents someone from also taking pride in being an American citizen, for thinking of his or her country as capable of reform, or from being able to join with straights or whites in reformist initiatives, it is a political disaster."[150]

Other important dates from 1960-1975:

1960 — the birth control pill was introduced in the US. (Margaret Sanger, at age 80, had raised over $150,000 to fund the research that resulted in the pill.)

1963 — the assassination of JFK, which let the nation's draft boards increase their monthly quotas *tenfold* within a week after Kennedy's murder to prepare for the already-planned invasion of Vietnam.

1964 — The Beatles, the British Invasion, the deceptive Gulf of Tonkin resolution, as well as the year the Mississippi Freedom Democratic Party was denied seats at the Democratic Convention in Atlantic City, NJ.

1965 — Supreme Court, in Griswold vs. Connecticut, gave married couples the right to use birth control, ruling that it was protected in the Constitution as a right of *privacy*. But in 1965, 26 states still denied birth control to millions of single women.

1968 — IUDs approved by the FDA.

1972 — Supreme Court legalized birth control for all citizens of the US, married and unmarried.

---

[149] *Achieving our Country: Leftist Thought in Twentieth-Century America*, Richard Rorty (Harvard University Press, 1998), p. 100.
[150] Ibid., quoting Todd Gitlin, p. 100.

1972 — Watergate, resulting in President Nixon's 1974 resignation under the threat of impeachment—the only US President in history to resign from office.

1973 — Roe v. Wade legalized abortion but classified it under a woman's "right to privacy". Note that the baby doesn't exist here, even as a concept: just the women. [But really, there's always also the life of a developing human whose life we want to end without feeling like murderers. To do that with integrity, we will first have to reframe the abortion debate to include the babies.]

1975 — The Vietnam War officially ends April 30, 1975.

On a broad societal level, liberals were losing what we saw as our most important social role: speaking for those we saw as our favorite victims (we abandoned unions and workers in the 1960s—Rorty cites this as the biggest mistake of the Left. It lost contact with the Earth here, like Antaeus). For liberals, this is a loss of the first order. We are losing our role, our *relevance* if we can't find victims to speak for, and ways to influence and define the moral and ethical fiber of our society and its direction. But defining other human beings merely by race, gender, or sexual orientation *creates* rather than *solves* the problems of racism, sexism, and homophobia.

This loss of relevance threatened our life, our meaning, and our purpose. Unless we are sure that our grand abstractions are relevant, we have nothing healthy or necessary to contribute to society. We're sure we are, after all, the middle-class, intellectual, and platonically philosophical Royalty of US culture. You can't overstate how completely devastating and death-dealing the 60s were to us. During that decade, the liberals who made the news mostly made it for being in the drug culture and anti-war movements on campuses—like the University of Michigan, UC Berkeley, Columbia, Wisconsin, Kent State, and others. In the 60s-70s, liberals split into two styles

(Rorty) with two different kinds of focus but one driving and desperate need: to find or claim the authority to make others listen to and *obey* us. One of these paths, technically, was treasonous; the other was insane. (Liberalism would end up betraying and trivializing education, the media, politics, race relations, and religion.)

Chance and Fate

As the ancient Greeks said, even the gods are helpless against these dynamic forces in nature and history. And those powerful but unpredictable forces can work either for or against our hopes, dreams, and plans.

Starting in the 1960s, Chance and Fate began making our liberal dream of controlling the US culture and government more and more plausible. It was an unplanned combination of Chance occurrences. Two of them can be dated to 1962, others to 1964ff.[151]

One 1962 event, noted earlier, was the publication of Rachel Carson's anti-scientific book *The Silent Spring*. Behind the scenes, in another country was the greatest mastermind of the most dangerous and damaging events of the past 60 years, a man almost completely unknown by the vast majority of Americans: Maurice Strong. Watching the immense energy of the fledgling environmental activists in response to Carson's book, he realized that *Activism* could be the vehicle capable of carrying enough passion to help deconstruct the power and government of the United States—the country which was, he

---

[151] As previously mentioned, Todd Gitlin has proposed that the turning point can be dated more precisely to August 1964, which he identifies as marking the break in the leftist students' sense of what their country was like. That was the month in which the Mississippi Freedom Democratic Party was denied seats at the Democratic Convention in Atlantic City, and in which Congress passed the Tonkin Gulf Resolution. See Richard Rorty, *Achieving Our Country* (1998), p. 55.

believed, the principal enemy of his own utopian dream of transforming planet Earth into a one-world Socialist government under the control of the United Nations.[152]

Meanwhile, also in 1962, on the campus of the University of Michigan in Ann Arbor, activist Tom Hayden, editor of *The Michigan Daily* and an active dreamer of the US as a socialist country, was a key thinker and writer in the fledgling movement known as Students for a Democratic Society (SDS), mentioned earlier.

How were they to acquire the power they wanted? Through the universities:

> *"An alliance of students and faculty ... must wrest control of the educational process from the administrative bureaucracy. ... They must import major public issues into the curriculum—research and teaching on problems of war and peace is an outstanding example. ... They must consciously build a base for their assault upon the loci of power."*

Why did they choose the universities as their path to political power? Because, as Hayden saw it, "The university is located in a permanent position of social influence. Its educational function makes it indispensable and automatically makes it a crucial institution in the formation of social attitudes."

They wanted to use the universities preemptively to mold the attitudes of people even younger and more inexperienced than themselves. There is a rather unkind word for this: indoctrination. Their intent was to shape opinion before young students were able to gain sufficient experience and maturity to think for themselves. And so a tiny group of extreme leftists

---

[152] Maurice Strong's revolutionary ideas are in the deep background of not only environmental activism but also what has been called the "manmade" climate change hoax. This deserves a book of its own, and many already exist.

decided that though they could never win at the ballot box, they could still get what they wanted by gaining control over the universities—which they eventually did.[153]

WHAT'S WRONG HERE?

The SDS students, like their current successors controlling our colleges, public education, and media, were not planning to advance democracy but to subvert it. Converting the universities into agencies for political control of the general population is something done by brutal dictatorships, not liberal democracies. Morally, the SDS program was a thoroughly disgraceful one. But nobody took SDS or its plan very seriously.[154]

The SDS was founded at the University of Michigan. The SDS Manifesto, known as The Port Huron Statement, was adopted at their first convention in June 1962, based on an earlier draft by member Tom Hayden. The United Auto Workers (UAW), under Walter Reuther's leadership, covered many expenses and let the student group use the UAW summer retreat in Port Huron. The group sought a way to unite a "raw left" that sought political power of young students and "an awakening community of allies".[155]

By the spring of 1963, there were about 200 delegates at the Annual Convention at Pine Hill, NY, from 32 colleges and universities. Todd Gitlin of Harvard University was made President.

After Lyndon Johnson's landslide victory in 1964 and his dramatic escalation of the Vietnam War, student movements, including the SDS, gained many new members through anti-war marches, opposition to the draft (a bit self-serving, that

---

[153] Ibid., p. 50.
[154] Ibid.
[155] See https://en.wikipedia.org/wiki/Students_for_a_Democratic_Society

one), and teach-ins. By 1966 the campus movements had absorbed more energy around the war, the draft, and a larger issue with the political/social power they were increasingly seeking. Under a 20-foot banner proclaiming "Happiness is Student Power", a speaker announced that they would no longer be patient, that they wanted change and power: *"Students are going to be the revolutionary force in this country. Students are going to make the revolution because we have the will."* They closed by grabbing hands and singing—not "We Shall Overcome", but the chorus to the Beatles' hit "Yellow Submarine".[156]

An October 21, 1967 march on the Pentagon of 100,000 people saw many students arrested and injured. The FBI became active in trying to disrupt, misdirect, and neutralize these raids that displayed a new source of power in the country. On April 18, 1968, about a million students skipped classes—the largest student strike in history. But it was the student shutdown of Columbia University in New York that captivated the national media.[157]

Three Chance Occurrences

SDS and radical liberal utopianism became powerful through several chance coincidences. The first of these was the national unrest over the mishandling of the war in Vietnam by the political class. The second was the sudden massive expansion of the universities at exactly the right, or rather the wrong, time—1965 to 1975. The third was the morphing of the civil rights movement into a powerful regime of identity politics marching under the banner of "diversity".[158]

The radical left always tended to see conspiracies of the rich and powerful against ordinary people. As a result, mem-

---

[156] *The Breakdown of Higher Education.*
[157] https://en.wikipedia.org/wiki/Students_for_a_Democratic_Society
[158] *The Breakdown of Higher Education*, p. 51.

bership in the SDS grew so rapidly that by 1968-69 it was 40,000: two hundred times what it had been in 1962![159]

It was just at this moment that a massive expansion of higher education began. The confluence of these historical events—the Vietnam War, sexual revolution, and drug culture, with their effect on the campus mood, and the dramatic rise in college enrollment—turned out to be astonishingly good luck for the radicals.[160]

State governments saw the baby boomers approaching college age and began to build new campuses at an unprecedented rate.[161]

In 1965 there were 2.97 million college students at American public institutions, but by 1975 that figure had tripled to 8.83 million.[162]

The number of new faculty appointments that were now needed was *greater than the number of all the existing professors in the nation.*[163]

Even in the best of times, this would have meant a drastic lowering of quality. But it came during the serious domestic political unrest over the Vietnam War, and the resulting radicalization of a great many undergraduates and graduate students. So not only were the additional professors academically inferior to existing standards, they were much more radicalized, activist, anti-American, and socialist, convinced that colleges should be producing activists like themselves rather than intellectual academics: action above understanding. It would be hard to imagine a scenario better suited to advance the radical left's plan to control higher education.[164]

---

[159] Ibid., p. 52.
[160] Ibid.
[161] Ibid.
[162] Ibid., p. 53.
[163] Ibid.
[164] Ibid.

This coincidence set in motion the shift from a slight liberal lean in university faculties to the virtual shutout of conservatives that we see today.[165]

We need to check this liberal self-absorption before it carries us and those we influence over the cliff. Here are just a few of the obvious problems:

Liberals have no inherent and unique wisdom. No group does, no group ever has—though democracy has come closer than any tyranny because at its best it can incorporate the different beliefs and certainties of the many different people in the society. Just look at the lives of some of our most arrogant politicians. Look at the lobbyists and corporations who sponsor—or own—them. Look at the Plato-endorsed lies and deceits they routinely play on those they've persuaded to vote for them.

It's worth saying again: if you think the members of Congress work for us, ask why they have their own health care, superior to ours, or why they have passed laws awarding them, after only *one year* in Congress, a full lifelong retirement package. Sure, they're clever enough to con us out of enough money to turn almost all of them into millionaires.

Yes, Plato endorsed everything we're doing. The quotations from his most influential book, *The Republic,* are worth seeing again (and again and again):

> *"Our rulers will have to make considerable use of falsehood and deception for the benefit of their subjects" (459c). A ruler may lie as necessary, but if he "catches anybody else in the city lying ... he will chastise him for introducing a practice as subversive and destructive of a state as it is of a ship" (389d). At the top, ruling overall, is the wise philosopher, whose love of wisdom "is impossible for the multitude"*

---

[165] Ibid., p. 54.

(494a).[166]

The founding principle is that of absolute individual devotion to, and submission to, the good of the state. The state should control procreation and marriage, for eugenic and population-control purposes, so as to prevent the racial debasement of the ruling (guardian) class. "The offspring of the inferior and any of those of the other sort who are born defective" should be "properly disposed of in secret, so that no one will know what has become of them" (460c). The private family should be abolished among the ruling class and children raised collectively, so that "these women shall all be common to all these men, and that none shall cohabit with any privately, and that the children shall be common, and that no parent shall know its own offspring nor any child its parent" (457d). Private property should be abolished among the ruling class as a way to get rid of the very notion of a private or individual interest, "so that we can count on their being free from the dissensions that arise among men from the possession of property, children, and kin" (464e).

The state must exercise strict and vigilant control of speech, including poetry. "We must begin, then, it seems, by a censorship over our story-makers" (377c). "We will beg Homer and the other poets not to be angry if we cancel those and all similar passages," says Plato, after citing verses of the kind which "we will expunge" (387b and 386c). Artists and craftsmen must also be controlled. No form of expression is to be untouched by the state's tendrils. The state "must throughout be watchful against innovations in music and gymnastics counter to the established order" (424b).

But Plato, remember, hated democracy. And with only two major options for a form of government—democracy and one-party rule—Plato and our current liberals chose subjugation,

---

[166] Jonathan Rauch, *Kindly Inquisitors: The New Attacks on Free Thought* (2014), p. 33.

hands down. So the vast majority should be ruled by a few ignorant and deadly narcissists? This is lethal. No one has the wisdom to tell other people how they must live, and the most dangerous people on Earth are those who think they do.

As for the alleged *sources* of our presumed superiority? We're smarter because we have more diplomas. And we're right because those who agree with us constitute the vast majority of university professors and students. It may have been different in the past, but today's college campuses have become embarrassing bastions of willful and arrogant ideological conformity, where those who disagree—the First Culture, who are predominantly conservatives—are shouted down, forbidden to speak, and physically attacked. And what about professors, students, or objective media employees who have actually done research and have found that much of the Certainty of today's liberals is based on myths, lies, and intentional deceptions? These people are silenced and fired, because—as our self-anointed leaders shout—they are now heretics: the damned enemy of our utopian vision. They may not speak and should not be allowed to hold the informed opinions they have. However, diplomas don't make us smart; they simply anoint us as the stylishly articulate and *fashionable* class, even while our pretensions to wisdom mark us as fools and clowns.

And on Groupthink, or the idea that "our kind of people", "those who think as we do", actually have more wisdom than mere individuals? Serious and persuasive experiments have been done to test this, and good books published since 1841.[167] The more a group interacts, the more it behaves like a real crowd, and the less accurate its assessments become. Accordingly, the accuracy of a group's aggregate judgment rests on the participants *not* behaving like a crowd. ... In plain English:

---

[167] *Extraordinary Popular Delusions and The Madness of Crowds*, by Charles MacKay, 1841.

beware the ideologue and the true believer, whether in politics, religion, or finance.[168] This is a well-understood fact, though not a widely-understood one. See more in this footnote.[169]

And then the most undeniable evidence of our discerning wisdom: our *diplomas*! Here, no less an authority than the Wizard of Oz can straighten us out. Sure: you don't need a

---

[168] William J. Bernstein, *The Delusions of Crowds: Why People GO MAD in GROUPS*, p. 12.

[169] Novelists and historians have known for centuries that people do not deploy the powerful human intellect to dispassionately analyze the world, but rather to rationalize how the facts conform to their emotionally derived preconceptions. (Ibid., p. 3) ... the human preference of rationalization over rationality. (Ibid., p. 3)

Four dramatis personae control the narrative of manias: the talented yet unscrupulous promoters of schemes; the gullible public who buys into them; the press that breathlessly fans the excitement; and last, the politicians who simultaneously thrust their hands into the till and avert their eyes from the flaming pyre of corruption. (Ibid., p. 4)

Alas, people greatly prefer stories to data and facts; when faced with such a daunting task, humans default into narrative mode. (Ibid., p. 4)

[Cites a 1906 experiment by (Darwin's cousin) Francis Galton. Amazing experiment! He got a group of about 800 people to purchase tickets for an ox-weighing contest, to guess the dressed weight—minus its head and internal organs. Amazingly, the median guess, 1,207 pounds, was less than one percent off the actual weight, 1,198 pounds. The *average* estimate was 1,197 pounds!] (11)

A few years ago finance professional Joel Greenblatt performed a clever variation on the Galton experiment with a class of Harlem schoolchildren, to whom he showed a jar that contained 1,776 jelly beans. Once again, the average of their guesses, when submitted in silence on index cards, was remarkably accurate: 1,771 jelly beans. Greenblatt then had each student verbalize their guesses, which destroyed the accuracy of their aggregate judgment—the new, "open" estimates averaged out to just 850 jelly beans. (12)

Also see Charles Mackay's 1841 classic book (still in print), *Memoirs of Extraordinary Popular Delusions*.

brain; you don't need to be smart. Just take this diploma. Wave it around, hang it on your wall. It'll fool most everyone, including you! And to this day, tens of millions of college graduates still believe this, and pay billions of dollars for the wall-adorning, ego-deceiving diplomas, sure that somehow, they have now become not only Wise, but are in the company of Plato's famous (and imaginary) "philosopher-kings", those enlightened few who should have the power to rule and dictate to all others. Yet, as more and more studies, tests, employer evaluations, and ignorant academic pronouncements continue to scream, our college students aren't coming out of college much wiser or smarter than when they went in. Our US education has been ranked very poorly among the world's developed countries. Why would we count those students who have been so badly defrauded as being "educated"? Indoctrinated, yes; educated, no longer. The Wizard, again, wasn't a real wizard. And diplomas aren't really signs of wisdom or even being smart. Think of it as the Scarecrow's Delusion—now shared by tens of millions of betrayed young graduates in our culture. The educational system of the US is completely mediocre except when it's worse.[170]

---

[170] From February 15, 2017 US students' academic achievement still lags that of their peers in many other countries—https://www.pewresearch.org/fact-tank/2017/02/15/u-s-students-internationally-math-science/

How do US students compare with their peers around the world? Recently released data from international math and science assessments indicate that *US students continue to rank around the middle of the pack, and behind many other advanced industrial nations.*

One of the biggest cross-national tests is the *Programme for International Student Assessment* (PISA), which every three years measures reading ability, math and science literacy, and other key skills among 15-year-olds in dozens of developed and developing countries. The most recent PISA results, from 2015, placed the US an *unimpressive 38th* out of 71 countries in math and 24th in science. Among the 35 members of the Organization for Economic Cooperation and Development, which sponsors the PISA initiative, the US ranked 30th in math and 19th in science.

Some other studies are even more negative. But no one can put the quality of education in the US in the top 20 of developed nations. This is a fundamental, perhaps long-term, betrayal of our students, our people, our culture, and our government—as well as our media, since journalism majors are part of the liberal arts and humanities education which rank near the bottom.

This reminds me of a scene I observed nearly 50 years ago in Ann Arbor, Michigan. At the time I owned a pricey portrait and wedding photography studio in the city's downtown (as opposed to campus) area. As I was walking along Main Street one afternoon, I heard a soprano saxophone playing. I couldn't see the musician, but he was quite good. As I walked around trying to find the source of the nice music, I noticed a taxi cab parked by a corner. And sitting in the driver's seat was a young man playing a curved soprano saxophone.[171] As I walked over to tell him how much I enjoyed his unexpected music, I noticed something taped to the inside of the cab's back side window. When I got close enough to read it, I discovered that it was the cab driver's Doctorate of Music diploma.

Funny stuff.

Here's a translation for liberal elites who don't understand: *"Ordinary people can be trusted more than lushly credentialed professionals in ivory towers."* In Buckley's mind, a healthy democracy requires that average Joes and Janes—random "phone book people"—contribute to the way things are run.[172] So diplomas can't make us smart or wise, or even

---

Another long-running testing effort is the *National Assessment of Educational Progress*, a project of the federal Education Department. In the most recent NAEP results, from 2015, average math scores for fourth- and eighth graders fell for the first time since 1990.

[171] Soprano saxophones are made in both the curved shape, like tiny alto saxophones, or the straight shape, like brass clarinets.

[172] William F. Buckley's quote, cited near the beginning of the book: "I would rather be governed by the first 2,000 people in the Boston telephone directory than by the 2,000 people on the faculty of Harvard University."

employable. An essay in *The Atlantic* says:

> *The job market for those with advanced degrees is clearly tightening, according to the NSF study, with many more Ph.D.s in all fields reporting no definite job commitments in 2014 compared to 2004. Nearly 40 percent of the Ph.D.s surveyed in 2014 hadn't lined up a job—whether in the private industry or academia—at the time of graduation.*
>
> *It may not be surprising that Ph.D.s in the humanities and social sciences are struggling to find tenure-track faculty jobs. After all, graduate schools produced two new history Ph.D.s for every tenure-track job opening in 2014.*[173]

We have college graduates in their early twenties, as wet behind the ears as the ink on their over-rated diplomas. They beam with the certainty that they are members of an elite "fashionable" class with total superiority to the two-thirds of the country without a diploma: citizens much older than they are to boot. Even the Wizard might laugh.

And also remember: it's the *first* culture that's in touch with reality, not ours. We're seduced by grand abstractions, but look at our college majors: the liberal arts and humanities. In one ranking of the top 30 college majors, Political Science, Education, and English are the very bottom three.[174] The word "Smart" needs to mean "Smart in the details and processes of the world, of life". That's not us. We're not where "Smart" lives. We have clever and well-rehearsed moves, but we're playing tennis without a ball. We share the Scarecrow's Delusion.

---

[173] "The Ever-Tightening Job Market for Ph.D.'s" by Laura McKenna, April 21, 2016, *The Atlantic*.
[174] www.mydegreeguide.com

EXCERPTS

The Coercive Utopians, by Rael Jean and Erich Isaac (1984)

There is every reason to expect the utopians, rejecting the imperfect society that we have, to install something far worse—a coercive one.[175] It's what they do.

The single most important cause of the reemergence of utopianism [which was in disarray from the end of WWII to the 1960s] was probably the civil rights movement of the 1950s. ... The Vietnam War created new legions of converts to the notion of an evil America, again especially among college students feeling personally threatened by the draft. The emerging "New Left" on campus, energized by the war, could now argue that not only was the United States internally unjust, but it was an imperialist, expansionist, militarist state intent on subjugation of liberation movements in faraway lands. The 1972 Watergate scandal became a final proof to many—not only were American institutions unjust, but American leaders were personally corrupt. More important, the Vietnam War and Watergate showed that the government could be defeated. The great imperialist juggernaut of the students' imagination was not invincible after all. It was vulnerable. Few but determined opponents could gather strength and eventually win against it.[176]

The Breakdown of Higher Education, by John M. Ellis (2021)

What do we mean "political radicals"?

1. For radicals, politics is everything, and everything is political.

2. They have no interest in debate, as their minds are already made up. The goal is obvious to them, and so submitting it to discussion

---

[175] *The Coercive Utopians*, p. 298.
[176] Ibid., p. 287.

simply wastes time and energy. Only one thing matters: action to implement the plan.

3. The goal is nothing less than a deep transformation of society. Nothing else really matters to them—certainly not the integrity of universities.[177]

The idea of "diversity" as the ruling doctrine in academia grew out of a genuinely positive step forward, the Civil Rights Act of 1964.[178]

But it led to identity politics being inserted into the life of the campuses. Once it starts, there is no end to the operation of identity politics, which means that its ability to corrupt academia is limitless.[179]

The campus obsession with race and gender seemed to offer a new approach to literary criticism. And so the growing tide of campus radicalism got substantial support from faculty who were not themselves politically motivated but jumped on the race-and-gender bandwagon as a career vehicle.[180]

In the humanities especially, the rule of fads and fashion was another factor that helped the radical left gain control.[181]

The 1978 Supreme Court decision in the case of Alan Bakke, a white man who had been refused admission to the medical school of the University of California at Davis, although his credentials were superior to those of some minority students who were admitted. Four justices ruled that race was an inadmissible factor in college admissions, while another four said that it was acceptable when used to remedy past injustices. The swing vote was that of Justice Lewis Powell, who outlawed racial quotas as an unconstitutional use of race, but in a fateful turn of phrase he ruled that seeking diversity

---

[177] *The Breakdown of Higher Education*, by John M. Ellis (2020), p. 55.
[178] Ibid.
[179] Ibid., p. 56.
[180] Ibid.
[181] Ibid., p. 60.

in the student body was a legitimate and lawful goal.[182] Powell's use of the concept of "diversity" allowed identity politics to seize the moral high ground on campus. Diversity soon became the key value in academic life; the campus obsession with it developed into a mania that swept common sense aside. Administrators could wrap themselves in it and acquire invulnerability. By championing diversity they were on the side of the angels.[183]

The importance of "diversity" in weakening resistance to radical control of the campuses would be difficult to overstate. Fifty years ago, the most overused word was "excellence"; now it became "diversity". Those who used "excellence" were increasingly attacked by the radicals on campus.[184]

[Our] high school teachers themselves are no longer well-educated. And the main reason they are not is that campuses have elevated "diversity" over excellence, in faculty hiring and student admissions and in curriculum.[185]

Though the intent of college admissions preferences is to provide upward mobility for minorities, what they really do is reduce the quality of a college education by promoting a force that cripples it.[186]

A Gallup poll published on August 13, 2018, found that in the Democratic Party a comfortable majority (57%) now have a positive view of socialism, and that they outnumber those with a positive view of capitalism by a full 10%. The percentage for the 18-29 age group (not restricted by party) is now 51%. This climate of opinion is still building: as years go by, a larger and larger percentage of the population will have had a radicalized college education.[187]

Two political scientists, S. Robert Lichter and Stanley Rothman, in 1979 and 1980, interviewed 240 journalists and broadcasters of the

[182] Ibid., p. 62.
[183] Ibid., p. 62.
[184] Ibid., p. 63.
[185] Ibid.
[186] Ibid.
[187] Ibid., p. 113.

most influential media outlets. They found the media elite were markedly to the left of the American electorate as a whole. Over a 16-year period, less than 20% of the media elite had supported any Republican Presidential candidate. Their views on issues were in striking agreement with utopian articles of faith. *Both media and business elites had a similar perception of the power of different groups in society, seeing the media, business and unions as those with the greatest influence. But asked how they would prefer to see power distributed, the media elite put themselves at the top, followed by consumer groups, intellectuals, and blacks. In part, the media elite sympathize with the utopians because they define their role in much the same way. Walter Cronkite is said to have declared that journalists identify with humanity rather than with authority. Julius Duscha, a reporter who became director of the Washington Journalism Center, said, "Reporters are frustrated reformers ... they look upon themselves almost with reverence, like they are protecting the world against the forces of evil".*[188]

---

[188] Ibid., p. 252.

CHAPTER FIVE

Our Betrayal of Education

THE VISION OF THE ANOINTED

"Education is a system of imposed ignorance."[189]

"Give me four years to teach the children," Lenin is famously quoted as saying, "and the seed I have sown will never be uprooted."[190]

"Reporters are frustrated reformers ... they look upon themselves almost with reverence, like they are protecting the world against the forces of evil."[191]

This, in Tom Hayden's SDS plan, is the basis of all the other betrayals. He believed that the only way the socialist SDS students and faculty could take over the culture and government of the US was by taking over the colleges, universities, and, through them all, public education in the country.

The subject really isn't education. It's our secular religion, our legitimate heir to God and Heaven: what we're serving with our lives and our gifts that can give us a fulfilling meaning. After all, what are we serving if not God and Heaven? It's

---

[189] Noam Chomsky, *Manufacturing Consent*.
[190] *Climategate*, p. 14.
[191] *The Breakdown of Higher Education*, p. 252.

a hard hole to fill. Liberals began choosing utopia as the real-world substitute for the eternal—but mythical—Heaven almost two centuries ago. Because of our education—our diplomas—we have a wisdom, an elitism, that lets us envision utopia in ways the masses can't—as Plato saw millennia ago. Only we can do this, which means we must have a form of government that gives us the necessary power, and keeps it away from the ignorant common people who would try to impede the utopia they can't understand. The most honest word for this one-party rule is socialism because socialism, like communism, is a totalitarian government, which we need to fulfill our mission.

When Tom Hayden dreamed of taking over the country back in 1962, it simply sounded insane. But then student anger at the Vietnam War, our government's Gulf of Tonkin resolution in August 1964, America's racism, sexism, the enthusiasm over the sexual revolution, amplified by the emotional highs (and intellectual numbness) of our campus drug culture, the doubling of college enrollment from 1950 to 1964,[192] then the tripling of it from 1965 to 1975, the huge new influx of radical activists into our college faculties, and the revolutionary increase in the ratio of liberal to conservative faculty, administrators and students—all this combined to change our campuses into essentially one-party rule of colleges, a model for our national aspirations. By 1999 or earlier, faculty could begin using political ideology as an important factor in hiring new faculty and administration staff.

Then the fortunate (for liberals) 1978 Supreme Court ruling by Justice Powell endorsing "diversity" as a factor in all things collegiate. This, above all else, let us change the focus and purpose of college from "excellence" to "diversity". Excellence is about personal traits: maturity, work, responsibility,

---

[192] *One Nation, Two Cultures*, by Gertrude Himmelfarb, p. 13.

and the rest of the traits exhibited by successful people of all races and religions. These don't help us toward our utopian dreams. People like Neil deGrasse Tyson, Shelby Steele, Thomas Sowell, Walter Williams, John McWhorter, Condoleezza Rice, Candace Owens, Ben Carson, and other successful black people—what good do *they* do us? How do they help us toward our ultimate religious goal of controlling the government so we can bring our utopia into being? Those individuals are admirable, but it's just their individual excellence. We need to help people at a political, corporate, herd level. We're interested in government solutions (and think the government can solve almost all problems).

And "diversity" gave us the license to do this. Fifty years ago the most popular word in university administration was "excellence". But no longer. Now it's "diversity". Has that improved the "excellence" of our colleges or students? Of course not. Our education, which used to be the best in the world, is nowhere near the top. China is delighted. We don't care. We're not trying to "educate" students or make them question the assumptions we're teaching them. We're trying to indoctrinate and convert them.

This may sound like we have missed the point of college. No, we have *changed* the point of college. Since the SDS gave us our goal and means of controlling education, the media and the government of the US, those among our radical activist leaders who are most aware have focused on two major goals:

1. Taking over the control of our colleges, universities, public education, and through them the culture and laws of the country.

2. Changing the purpose of schools from *education* to *activism*; from understanding to action, from democracy and capitalism to socialism and a massive redistribution of wealth. People can get excited over this, imagining that they will become part of the new ruling class. Of course, that's not true.

Almost all of them are destined to become the obedient under-class drones, equal only in their poverty and misery, as occurs in all other socialist governments. And so part of what we must do in college is help mold their character into the sort of citizens socialism needs: simple, unquestioning, obedient citizens who serve the One Truth—socialism, government control—at the soul of our utopian vision.

So of course we have largely stopped exposing students to powerful thinkers. We don't want them to question; we want them to *follow*. We're not interested in developing individual thinkers or geniuses. We need to turn the students into the sort of people our utopian society needs. This is a direct result of having our educational system controlled no longer by intellectuals and academics, but by *Activists*, who are interested in *action,* not *understanding.* We already have the answers and knowledge needed to fashion the utopian (socialist) society that can serve as the legitimate heir to the mythical eternal Heaven.

How does this serve the students who are paying us to help finish forming their lifelong character? We're good at that too. We have taught them a simple and clear identity for the rest of their lives. They learn the Anointed Vision of our activist ideology. The purpose of life? To learn, embody, and serve that utopian picture as we draw it for them. They don't need to be confused by assaulting them with disturbing ontological and existential questions. What's the point of doing that to them? That's focusing on them as *individuals. We don't care about them as individuals, but only as a group, as a political dimension in our utopian vision.* We see the bigger picture of which they are only tiny parts. But at that political level we can—once we get the power—create the socialist utopia within which these less complicated and confused people can be contented parts of our ideal world: the legitimate heir to God's Heaven, orchestrated by the legitimate heir to God's omniscient wisdom: our own Vision of the Anointed.

So yes, of course we've replaced challenging thinkers with mediocre Politically Correct writers. We're teaching them to become small servants of an ideology. It's a *group* goal, a collective *political* vision, a directed mob activity, not an individual one. And no, we're not teaching them how to question or think analytically. A society like that would just be chaos.

It may look like we have ruined education, but, again, we have changed its purpose: from empowering individuals (if they're willing to work hard, read a lot of hard thinkers, spend 20-30 hours a week studying and competing for the few top spots) to creating and empowering a new political reality in the US: our utopian socialism. Wholesale rather than retail. We have taught tens of millions of students to hate democracy, capitalism, and the US (though we seldom say it that boldly) to live the idea of utopian socialism where the government becomes like their parents, and they follow their leaders.

Is there deception here—lying? Yes, of course. But it's in the service of our this-worldly utopian successor to eternal Heaven. Remember Plato:

> *"Our rulers will have to make considerable use of falsehood and deception for the benefit of their subjects" (459c). A ruler may lie as necessary, but if he "catches anybody else in the city lying ... he will chastise him for introducing a practice as subversive and destructive of a state as it is of a ship" (389d). At the top, ruling over all, is the wise philosopher, whose love of wisdom "is impossible for the multitude" (494a).*

Less dramatically, we know from watching all the "Law & Order" type shows that police are also allowed to deceive suspects to try and get confessions. Same principle.

We have indoctrinated students, teachers, colleges, universities, and now secondary schools all the way down to kindergarten by teaching what radical activists want us to become, and by replacing informed and intelligent thought with mediocre politically correct thought from people in our token victim groups. We have converted several generations of our country's young people and have helped distort and deform their character in ways that will sometimes become permanent character deformities, since character formation continues into our mid-twenties, then is basically fixed.

Yes, this is all true. But again: our historic achievement has been to redefine the *purpose* of education, our colleges and public education. We think education's purpose is to help mold young people into the kind of people our utopian vision needs. Education is just part of the bigger picture that we—but not the masses—can see and feel.[193] And since our SDS/socialist-inspired activists have become our leaders, that picture has changed since our grandparents' time. We don't want citizens who question what they have been taught, or who "love their country"; indeed, we radical activists see the truth that the country doesn't *deserve* love.

By the late 1960s, it was racist, sexist, warmongering, with a corrupt government that needed to be replaced by a far more perfect kind of society, where people play the roles written for them by a government defined and run by people who—as Plato hoped—see Truth and Goodness and Fairness far better than most of them can.

And that's our role. We're sure of it.

WHAT'S WRONG HERE?

Etymology again. The root of the word "educate" is -*duc*, which means *to lead*. To educate means to lead into a bigger

---

[193] And this includes many of the masses within our liberal movement. Remember that, as a social species, we're basically herd animals.

reality by exposing students to the challenging ideas of some of our greatest thinkers and teaching them how to question and think analytically and argue logically. These big ideas will make little people (young students) uncomfortable, and adequate education must teach them that they must earn the *right* to criticize and question ideas with which they disagree. And the only way to do that is by being able to understand and explain the others' beliefs in an informed way that those who hold the beliefs could applaud. Students must learn how to think, to question rather than swallowing whole whatever they are taught in life. There are a lot of con men and women, and a lot of sociopaths out there. Some of them are teaching our students.

Two other *-duc* words suggest the opposite of education. *Reduce* is most straightforward: making things or people *smaller* than they were before you began influencing them. But doing anything other than leading them into a bigger world and life is also *seducing* them: leading them *astray*. And with some minor exceptions, for the past three to five decades, most of our colleges and universities—including almost all of our elite schools—have been seducing our students and leaving them as small as they were when they began overpaying the professors and colleges to indoctrinate them.

The schools have done this because they, as Hayden hoped, are run by radical activists who hate the capitalist and democratic US government and want to turn students into fairly unquestioning and unthinking drones who can become the masses in their dreamed-of socialism. They don't want the students to learn the real history of the US because it is so much more impressive than the history of almost every other nation. So they have largely stopped teaching US history. They don't want students to learn from the best thinkers in our history, just to learn today's politically correct propaganda that can lead to hatred of the US, the destruction of capitalism, and the establishment of a totalitarian socialism: the goal of the entire SDS infection of our colleges and universities. And it's working.

This is the teaching that has turned both faculty and students into unthinking and often screaming crowds who forbid others to write, speak, or even think anything that differs from the ideology of the radical activists. As informed observers like John Ellis, Thomas Sowell, Walter E. Williamson, Jonathan Rauch, Jason L. Riley, Richard Rorty, Todd Gitlin, Jim Sleeper, and others have said, too many of the people working as teachers or administrators in our educational system simply have no business at all in education, and cannot do the job. They would have to be replaced, as the former high standards of actually *educating* our students would have to be reinstated if our education is ever to be restored. The odds don't look good. This is also because the people who work in and run our media were mostly educated under these reduced and seductive standards. So they seldom see—or write about—the betrayal that has destroyed what used to be the best educational system in the world.

The Bias of the Media

The media are strongly biased to the left for two main reasons. First is that journalism majors are among the most left-leaning of collegiate liberal arts and humanities majors. The other is that the self-perception of journalists and others in media news have radically—but for no good reason—changed.

Fifty years ago, Walter Cronkite summed up the media perspective in the 1970s when he said in 1974: "There are always groups in Washington expressing views of alarm over the state of our defenses. We don't carry those stories. The stories we carry are those who want to cut defense spending."[194]

---

[194] Ibid., p. 257.

And remember John M. Ellis: *"Reporters are frustrated re-formers ... they look upon themselves almost with reverence, like they are protecting the world against the forces of evil."*[195]

The suspicion of religion is especially conspicuous among journalists, who are generally liberal in politics and secular in belief. In 1993, a front-page story in the *Washington Post* described the "Gospel lobby" as "poor, uneducated, and easy to command". Protests from readers obliged the *Post* to retract that statement.[196]

Tim Groseclose's *Left Turn: How Liberal Media Bias Distorts the American Mind* helps us understand the dishonest and destructive influence of the media.

For instance, according to surveys, in a typical presidential election Washington correspondents vote about 93-7 for the Democrat, while the rest of America votes about 50-50.[197]

In 2018, Mitchell Langbert published the results of a study focusing on elite liberal arts colleges. He looked at tenure-track faculty in 51 of the top 66 colleges in the *U.S. News and World Report* ranking: "Faculty political affiliations at 39% of the colleges have zero Republicans. Of the remaining 61%, Republicans account for slightly more than zero percent."[198]

New faculty recruitment is deliberately selective for radical leftism, and has been for decades.[199]

Of the $4,681,192.76 in political contributions made by University of California employees in 2017-2018, no less than 97.46% went to Democratic candidates and causes.[200]

What happens when our view of the world is filtered through the eyes, ears, and minds of such a liberal group? The

---

[195] *The Breakdown of Higher Education*, p. 252.

[196] *One Nation, Two Cultures,* by Gertrude Himmelfarb (1999), p. 101.

[197] *Left Turn: How Liberal Media Bias Distorts the American Mind*, by Tim Groseclose (2011), p. vii.

[198] *The Breakdown of Higher Education*, p. 35.

[199] Ibid., p. 36.

[200] Ibid.

filtering prevents us from seeing the world as it actually is. Instead, we see only a distorted version of it. Perhaps worst of all, media bias feeds on itself. That is, the bias makes us more liberal, which makes us less able to detect the bias, which allows the media to get away with more bias, which makes us even more liberal, and so on. This means that the political views that we currently see in Americans are not their natural views. We see only an artificial and distorted version of those views.[201]

What if we could see the average American's political views, *once their political views were no longer distorted by media bias*? The person whom we'd see would be anyone who has a "political quotient" near 25. (In Groseclose's terms, a Political Quotient of 100 is a far-left Democrat; a PQ of 0 is a far-right Republican.)[202]

If we could magically eliminate media bias, American political values would mirror those of present-day regions that include the states of Kansas, Texas, and South Dakota. They also include Orange County, California and Salt Lake County, Utah. To the liberal elite, such places are a nightmare. They are family-friendly, largely suburban, and religiously active.[203]

Almost *every* mainstream national news outlet in the US has a liberal bias. Of the one hundred or so news outlets this author examines, only a handful lean to the right. These include *The Washington Times, The Daily Oklahoman, The Arizona Daily Star* (Tucson), and Fox News *Special Report*. But even these supposedly conservative news outlets are not *far right*. For instance, the conservative bias of *Special Report* is significantly less than the liberal bias of *CBS Evening News*, and it is approximately equal to the liberal bias of *ABC World News Tonight* or *NBC Nightly News*. The *effects* of media bias

---

[201] *Left Turn*, p. vii.
[202] Ibid., p. viii.
[203] Ibid., p. viii.

are real and significant. The liberal media bias aids Democratic candidates by about 8 to 10 percentage points in a typical election. If media bias didn't exist, then John McCain would have defeated Barack Obama 56-42 instead of losing 53-46.[204]

In our current world, as mentioned earlier, where views have been distorted toward the left, news outlets such as *The Washington Times* and Fox News *Special Report* seem conservative. However, if we could remove the left-wing bias of the media as a whole—and thus change the average voter's political quotient to 25 or 30—then *The Washington Times* and *Special Report* would seem slightly left-leaning.[205]

So while our media bias isn't as far to the left as the bias of our college faculties, it still paints an inaccurate—and *dishonest*—picture of who we are, both as individuals and as a country.

Again, the reason the radical activists who control our educational system don't *want* us to have a first-rate educational system is because it will teach students honest history, how to question, how to think, how to develop informed, educated positions, and how to present arguments to convince others—rather than just trying to shout them down, refuse to print their papers and books, and physically attack them. (Maxine Waters comes to mind as a particularly embarrassing example of this low attitude: telling Democrats to attack those who disagree with them.[206] She could have learned that in most of our

---

[204] Ibid., p. ix.

[205] Ibid., p. x.

[206] "You think we're rallying now? You ain't seen nothing yet," Waters said at the event, *according to a HuffPost report.* "Already you have members of your Cabinet that are being booed out of restaurants ... protesters taking up at their house saying, 'no peace, no sleep.' If you see anybody from that Cabinet in a restaurant, in a department store, at a gasoline station, you get out and you create a crowd and you push back on them and you tell

elite colleges today.) The situation is more desperate than we want to believe, partly because confronting it would require a degree of moral courage that has become an endangered—and vigilantly hunted—species.

In graduate school, I was fortunate to experience a few hours in a seminar that has remained for me the paradigm of what good education—or just *education*—requires.

It was a doctoral-level seminar in the philosophy of science, taught by Stephen Toulmin, who had studied with Ludwig Wittgenstein in the 1930s and 1940s, and was his most published and influential student. There were a lot of very bright students in that seminar of about ten, all very well-read, having finished almost all the coursework for their PhD. And they were quite opinionated, quite certain. It would be hard to win an argument against any of them in their area of specialization. Becky was the brightest in the class. She was assertive as hell and maybe the most well-read.

Stephen taught the first couple of two-hour sessions of the class, covering basic books on the philosophy of science, of which he had written a couple of the best. Then he chose some students to take turns teaching a two-hour class. He assigned their topic and their reading list. The rest of the class would just have to read an essay or two on their topic. Becky was assigned the task of teaching us about the 19th-century thinker Herbert Spencer, the one who'd come up with the phrase "survival of the fittest" to describe evolution. Becky absolutely *hated* him, everything about him. Her invective was brilliant and unforgiving. He had screwed up evolution, science, thought, everything he touched. She sounded like a fundamentalist preacher condemning a heretic to hell. Stephen let her go on for an hour before stopping her.

---

them they're not welcome anymore, anywhere," she added. (Vox, by Li Zhou, updated June 28, 2018.)

"No. No, that won't do. You must first earn the *right* to criticize a thinker, especially one who was regarded by some very bright people in his time as one of the greatest thinkers alive. You haven't earned the right to criticize him, so that will be your assignment." He gave her a new reading list of four or five books and a couple of weeks to prepare her class. He said to earn the right to criticize someone, you must first understand their argument well enough to present it in a way that they would accept as informed and fair. Before you have the right to condemn a heretic, you must get inside his or her head and heart, and explain why that way of thinking is the *only* true and correct way of thinking in ways that your opponent would applaud. Then and only then have you earned the right to criticize or attack the thoughts or beliefs of someone with whom you disagree. [207]

That, in brief, is the essence of education, of what it takes to help students become *bigger*, better-informed, and to learn how to put together informed and logical arguments to try and convince others instead of just shouting them down or trying to get enough power to coerce them. Too often today, activists have turned education into a fundamentalist religion where your only option is to agree with the teacher or be attacked and damned as one of the unwashed: the enemy.

It's not hard to understand the appeal of the fundamentalist approach to religion, politics, or ideology. We're a social species and want deeply to feel a part of "our group" whether we define that group as small or large. We're Baptists, Catholics,

---

[207] Here are a few of the books by Stephen E. Toulmin that I've read: *The Uses of Argument, Cosmopolis: The Hidden Agenda of Modernity, Return to Reason, Human Understanding: The Collective Use and Evolution of Concepts, The Architecture of Matter, The Fabric of the Heavens: The Development of Astronomy and Dynamics, An Introduction to Reasoning, Wittgenstein's Vienna, The Abuse of Casuistry: A History of Moral Reasoning, Metaphysical Beliefs, The Discovery of Time, Foresight and Understanding: An Inquiry into the Aims of Science, The Philosophy of Science.*

Jews, Muslims, Buddhists, or the rest. We're Democrats, Republicans, libertarians, communists, or socialists. We're Christian believers or scientific atheists. It's a long list of alternatives. And wherever we take our emotional stand, there are people across from us who are just as smart, just as caring, and just as *certain*. Emotionally, that's hard to grant. If we're right—which we are, of course—then they have to be wrong, dammit!

No genuine religious or intellectual endeavor is possible unless we can grow beyond that kind of ignorant, adolescent narcissism. The greatest harm in the world is done by genuinely sincere people whose certainty is grounded in their emotional need to feel righteous and right. But we should remember that the only way to earn the right to dismiss opinions with which we disagree is by first understanding them broadly and deeply enough to be able to state them in ways that would be applauded by those who are as certain of those opinions as we are of our own. We've mostly lost that.

Becky understood, and two weeks later presented Herbert Spencer's arguments and worldview in a way he might well have applauded. "Good work!" Stephen said. "You have earned the right to criticize him. So now get on with that because he certainly *needs* to be criticized."

I wonder how many high school or college—or graduate—students have experienced some version of that lesson in what is required to earn the right to criticize an opinion that disagrees with your own? Judging from stories we've all seen in the media, very few.

There should be thousands of class-action lawsuits against individual professors, administrators, colleges, universities, and public schools for fraud. They have seduced tens of millions of our young people for the past several decades. We have seen televised episodes of college students—and college faculty—shouting down or attacking those who want to speak opinions that don't agree with the narrow biases of the liberal True Believers who dominate and define almost all our colleges. This is the enemy of education, and our students and their parents have been cheated out of billions of dollars, as our country has been robbed of one or two generations of genuinely educated and informed college graduates who have been taught how to think, question, and craft informed and logical beliefs grounded in the real world.

Here is just one example of the culture and agenda of collegiate education—an example of which very few people, and even fewer parents of students, are aware:

From the University of Delaware's Office of Residence Life Diversity Facilitation Training document (see *www.thefire.org* for whole document):

Students living in the University's housing, roughly 7,000, are taught: *"A racist: A racist is one who is both privileged and socialized on the basis of race by a white supremacist (racist) system. The term applies to all white people (i.e., people of European descent) living in the US, regardless of class, gender, religion, culture or sexuality. By this definition, people of color cannot be racists because as peoples within the US system, they do not have the power to back up their prejudices, hostilities or acts of discrimination."* This gem of wisdom suggests that by virtue of birth alone, not conduct, if you're white, you're a racist.[208]

More: "A non-racist: A non-term. The term was created by whites to deny responsibility for systemic racism, to maintain an aura of innocence in the face of racial oppression, and to shift responsibility for that oppression from whites to people of color (called 'blaming the victim'). Responsibility for perpetuating and legitimizing a

---

[208] *Liberty Versus the Tyranny of Socialism*, by Walter E. Williams, p. 12.

*racist system rests both on those who actively maintain
it, and on those who refuse to challenge it. Silence is consent".*[209]

It's a safe bet the university did not highlight this kind of
learning experience to parents and students in its recruitment
efforts. Nor were generous donors and alumni informed that
they are racists by birth. I'd also guess that this kind of "education" was kept under wraps from the state legislators who
use taxpayer money to fund the university.[210]

The questions of how and why specifically liberals, our liberal ideology, education, and all these betrayals came together
is more complex than most people know, although the several
dimensions of that history are well documented.

Who are the people who have destroyed our universities?

Liberal activists. These represent the evangelical fundamentalists of the new liberal religion of the past century. They
don't need more facts, aren't interested in open and informed
arguments. They are the True Believers. These activists, like
all fundamentalists, are not seeking informed understanding;
they're only seeking *converts*. And if conversion can't work,
they move quickly to its dark but inevitable side: *coercion*.

Radical campus historians keep students ignorant of anything that might show the country in a positive light. But unfortunately, that includes almost all the really distinctive
things in our history—for example, America's decisive part in
WWII, its role in the development of modern life, and the process that led to the writing of its extraordinary constitution:
the things that those over 50 learned, that made them proud

---

[209] Ibid., p. 13.
[210] Ibid., p. 13.

of our flawed but healthy and good country. Also, the decisive role the western Enlightenment has played in helping countries grow beyond slavery and structural racism.

John Stuart Mill (1806-1873) seems quite modern and prescient:

> *"He who knows only his own side of the case, knows little of that."*

> *"Both teachers and learners go to sleep at their post as soon as there is no enemy in the field."*

> *"It is in a great measure the opposition of the other that keeps each within the limits of reason and sanity."*

The crucial point here is that you can't really understand the case for the left until you also understand equally well the case for the right, because each is a necessary part of the definition of the other, of democracy, and of Reality. This means that professors in an all-left department will not even be able to give a competent account of their *own* political views, for as Mill puts the point, "they do not, in any proper sense of the word, know the doctrine which they themselves profess". When everyone around is on the left side of the spectrum, even the teaching of leftist thought will become incoherent. The student must therefore "be able to hear [the arguments] from people who actually believe them, who defend them in earnest, and do their very utmost for them. He must know them in their most plausible and persuasive form". People who want to pack their departments with ideological soulmates are political activists, not academics; genuine professors of politics would know that insulating themselves from their opponents is intellectual suicide.[211]

As I've tried to be clear, I think the best and most accessible

---

[211] *The Breakdown of Higher Education*, p. 37.

single book to read for an overview of the current state of education in the United States is John M. Ellis' 2021 book *The Breakdown of Higher Education*. Under 200 pages, it's worth reading by anyone interested in this important subject. Another excellent and accessible book covering how utopian activism replaced religion for liberals, and the very real danger of utopianism is *The Coercive Utopians*, by husband-and-wife team Rael Jean Isaac and Erich Isaac. This 1983 book is written by sociologists, and their bigger picture helps us back off from seeing the problems only as problems of politics, education, or other subheadings. So yes: I'm pushing a few books for those interested in going deeper into these subjects. I've included some excerpts from them in each chapter and have a more complete list in the Bibliography.

The great weakness in Horace Mann's educational philosophy was the assumption that education takes place only in schools. ["smart" vs. "diploma'd".][212]

Like Mann, we believe that schooling is a cure-all for everything that ails us. If there is one lesson we might have been expected to learn in the 150 years since Horace Mann took charge of the schools of Massachusetts, it is that the schools can't save society.[213] But they may be able to destroy it.

The ideology still controlling the minds and imaginations of a majority of—especially liberal arts and humanities—college professors is still the simplistic anti-American, pro-socialist hysteria of the SDS movement that wrote the Port Huron Statement in 1962. Their impossible dream was to somehow take control of the US, changing its government into the socialism they swooned over, hating much of the spirit of capitalism. It was, and remains, a fundamentalist style of religion in which the believers can't even imagine that they might be

[212] Christopher Lasch, *The Revolt of the Elites and Betrayal of Democracy* (1996), p. 151.
[213] Ibid., p. 160.

wrong. That's still in the soul and spirit of the kind of professors, the cancel culture that has removed courses in American History, sought to remove courses in philosophy, and silence— violently if necessary—thinkers and speakers whose informed arguments expose our orthodoxy as uninformed and shallow.

They seem not to have thought of the deadly depth of their betrayal in 1962, and at the time—with only 200 students in their national SDS movement—nobody else would have taken them seriously. But they gave, now to tens of millions of young and intelligent Americans, a simple-minded and incoherent model of "who we are and how we should live" that has poisoned not only the students—the faculty have been poisoned for decades—but now the larger society, especially the liberal culture and the Democratic Party. The model? Don't think, don't question. Just listen and obey, then go forth to serve this socialist ideology, perhaps for the rest of your life.

Walter E. Williams has put a sharper edge on this in an essay on "Academic Slums":

> American education will never be improved until we address one of the problems seen as too delicate to discuss. That problem is the overall quality of people teaching our children. Students who have chosen education as their major have the lowest SAT scores of any other major. Students who have graduated with an education degree earn lower scores than any other major on graduate school admissions tests such as the GRE, MCAT or LSAT. Schools of education, either graduate or undergraduate, represent the academic slums of most any university. As such, they are home to the least able students and professors with the lowest academic respect. Were we serious about efforts to improve public education, one of the first things we would do is eliminate schools of education.[214]

---

[214] *Liberty Versus the Tyranny of Socialism: Controversial Essays*, by Walter E. Williams (2008), pp. 14-15.

This wouldn't be a quick fix, if it's even possible at this point. Tens of thousands of professors—and administrators, college deans, and presidents—need to be replaced. With whom? Are there enough people left who can even determine this intelligently? Are there enough with the moral courage it would require to take on the activists, the media, and the loudest voices in our failed educational system? It seems unlikely.

How bad is it? Consider a few facts:

Only 18% of liberal arts colleges have an American history course requirement for graduation.[215]

When asked questions taken from a basic high school curriculum, 81% of seniors from the top 55 colleges and universities in the US received a grade of D or F. They could not identify Valley Forge, or words from the Gettysburg Address, or even the basic principles of the US Constitution. This is an extraordinary level of ignorance on the part of students at highly selective institutions—colleges and universities that can recruit the best students and the best faculty in the nation.[216]

In a 2015 ACTA survey, only 53% of college graduates knew the terms of office for US senators and representatives; only 41% knew the process of ratification of an amendment to the Constitution; and only 60% knew that war can be declared only by Congress. If these figures were true of the general population, they would be bad enough, but for college graduates they are disgraceful. A study by the Woodrow Wilson National Fellowship Foundation published on October 3, 2018, found that only one in three Americans could pass a multiple-choice test consisting of items taken from the US Citizenship Test. Half didn't know which countries we fought against in the Second World War, and 57% didn't know how many justices are

---

[215] *The Breakdown of Higher Education*, p. 88.
[216] Ibid., p. 89.

on the US Supreme Court. The main problem is with the more recently educated segment of the population: "Those 65 years and older scored the best, with 74% answering at least six in ten questions correctly. For those under the age of 45, only 19% passed the exam, with 81% scoring at 59% or lower."[217]

The fact that radicals think political problems have simple solutions without unintended consequences is what makes them so dangerous.[218]

Reading assignments were often so minimal that a third of students reported that they had not taken a single course in the prior semester that required at least 40 pages of reading. The plain fact is that developing skill in reasoning is not what these teachers want. Making converts is. Once again, we should note who is standing in the way of black progress here: it is the radicals who profess to champion minority causes.[219]

Is this education, or propagandizing? Is it much more than just baptizing students who have neither been educated nor taught how to think critically into a dangerously simplistic radical liberal ideology?

"It's never been easier to get an A, and it's never required so few hours' study!" Those rising grades have also correlated with greatly reduced knowledge and thinking ability among college graduates, as measured by countless studies. So: the less work that students do and the less they learn, the better their grades? Only on the politicized campus.[220]

And this should be more upsetting and infuriating than it seems to be:

Yet again, black students end up shuttered away from mainstream thought in a place where there is much talk of victimization and racism but a great deal less in the way of

[217] Ibid., p. 90.
[218] Ibid., p. 137.
[219] Ibid., p. 139.
[220] Ibid., p. 140.

genuine thought and analysis. This is yet one more way in which the education of black students is sacrificed to the fantasies of radical activists.[221]

The prospects for the adoption of strengthened rules on campus free speech are, in any case, rather poor. The University of Chicago led the way in 2014 with a fine statement of principles that reasserted traditional ideas on the importance of unfettered debate on campus. The statement emphasized that individuals are not free to make decisions on behalf of the whole community as to what can and cannot be discussed whenever they feel offended. This was obviously a response to a recent rash of shout-downs. The Chicago statement has been adopted by some 50 institutions, which might sound promising until we consider that the number that have refused to do so is in the thousands. It is sobering to reflect on the fact that the Chicago statement did no more than reaffirm understandings about academia that were virtually universal before the explosive growth of radicalism on campus, and yet approximately 99% of colleges and universities want nothing to do with it.[222]

John Ellis believes the root of the problem is the character and temperament of present-day college faculty. *The problem is one of personnel*, not of rules or guidance. Large numbers of people holding professorial titles have neither any real interest in academic work, nor aptitude for it, nor the knowledge that would be required for it. The interests they instead have are completely incompatible with academic work, and fundamentally at odds with the nature of a university. But because the campuses are controlled by the very people who are the source of the problem, they can no longer be reformed from within.[223]

---

[221] Ibid., p. 141.
[222] Ibid., pp. 179-180.
[223] Ibid., p. 182.

Academia cannot be cajoled or persuaded to return to a healthy state. Real change can happen in one way alone: by dismantling, as far as possible, the radical faculty regime. These powerful political clans will have to be broken up and removed. Nothing short of this could possibly restore excellence to higher education. Radical activists have rebuilt the academy so that it serves their political purposes. It will continue to do so until we dismantle what they have constructed. [224]

Ellis and others are right: the institutions that resemble universities no longer are such in the true sense. It has been like the invasion of the body-snatchers. A viral invasion of the mind- and soul-snatchers, turning virtually all our colleges and universities into self-destructive enemies of education.

Naturally, perhaps encouragingly, enrollments have plummeted. Our colleges have become more like boot camps for radical political activism. Also, as Ellis and many others are pointing out, students can now find excellent courses online, and for much less money. They can now study in their own time and pace, getting a genuine education from some of the world's best professors at a tiny fraction of the cost of attending college for four years. [225]

But if online education can provide a broad replacement for the now distinctively anti-intellectual colleges, we would also need to create a socializing substitute for colleges, because we are a social species and must go through a mature and healthy socialization during the years of our character formation—which coincide with the years of our public and collegiate education.

Christopher Lasch adds:

---

[224] Ibid., p. 183.
[225] Ibid., pp. 191-192.

Self-anointed "Elites", who define the issues, have lost touch with the people.[226]

Theirs is essentially a tourist's view of the world—not a perspective likely to encourage a passionate devotion to democracy.[227]

---

[226] *The Revolt of the Elites and Betrayal of Democracy*, Christopher Lasch (1996), p. 3.
[227] Ibid., p. 6.

EXCERPTS

Technology and the Academics: An Essay on Universities and the Scientific Revolution, by Sir Eric Ashby, London Macmillan & Co. Ltd. (1959)

The fault lies in what Whitehead called "a celibacy of the intellect which is divorced from the concrete contemplation of the complete facts". It is a preoccupation with abstractions from reality, an escape from the whole of reality. In 1925 in Science and the Modern World, Whitehead warned us that this would become the great danger of professional education. Each profession, he said, makes progress in its own groove of abstractions, "But there is no groove of abstractions which is adequate for the comprehension of human life". And this is how he summed up the kind of adaptation that a university needs to make in order to assimilate science and technology:

We have to disregard the sentimentalists who say that faculties of technology fill the minds and starve the souls of the young. There is no evidence that the souls of technologists are starved. (85)

Professors of technology need to be persuaded that the pattern of curriculum under which they themselves were trained is inadequate for their students; and professors of arts subjects need to be persuaded that the presence of technology in universities puts them under an obligation to reconsider the emphasis in their own humanistic studies. (87)

Whatever else flows upwards in universities there is no disputing the fact that money flows downwards. ... Here is the Achilles' heel of academic freedom inside the university. (106)

The Breakdown of Higher Education: How it Happened, the Damage it Does, & What Can Be Done, By John M. Ellis (Encounter Books, 2020)

During the last three decades the prestige of colleges and universities has been declining. (2)

In 1999 the political scientist Stanley Rothman & co-authors did a study of the political views of American professors and found that "a sharp shift to the left has taken place among college faculty in recent years." Five left-of-center professors for every right-of-center one. ... The skew of the new faculty hires in 1969-1999 must have been more than 5 to 1, then — at least 6 to 1, and probably more like 7 to 1. ... The left/right ratio in English departments had already become 88 to 3, and in political science it was 81 to 2. These are departments where it is most important to have a range of social and political attitudes, because those attitudes are directly relevant to the substance of the department's work, but this is precisely where the tilt to one side had become so extreme by 1999 that it was already close to a virtual exclusion of the other. (26)

Few people are less intellectually open, flexible, and curious than a radical leftist. (27)

By 1999 it was clear that radicals ... were hellbent on hiring fellow radicals. (27)

James Otteson: "Because politics is so fraught with emotion and tribal loyalties, it is extremely dangerous in the context of higher education. It replaces a loyalty to the process of inquiry with a loyalty to one's tribe. We judge arguments and even people on the extent to which they conform to our prejudices or group identities." (40)

From a 1915 statement by the American Association of University Professors (AAUP):

> "... and he should, above all, remember that his business is not to provide his students with ready-made conclusions, but to train them to think for themselves, and to provide them access to those materials which they need if they are to think intelligently. ... The teacher ought also to be especially on his guard against taking unfair advantage of the student's immaturity by indoctrinating him with the teacher's

*own opinions before the student has had an opportunity
fairly to examine other opinions."* (42)

Radical faculty are making sure that students hear one side only and
pressing them to accept it without hearing any other. This alone
constitutes a stunning collapse of the quality and integrity of higher
education. (42)

Democracy itself is damaged by this abuse of higher education. (42)

All across the country, bachelor's degrees in English literature can
be had without reading Shakespeare, Chaucer, or Milton. ... But J.S.
Mill's essay did not survive because its author was a white male, but
because it represented thinking of the very highest quality on an
issue central to human life. (95)

The shallow modern replacements have not earned that standing.
Heather Mac Donald comments trenchantly on the "relentless de-
termination to reduce the stunning complexity of the past to the
shallow categories of identity and class politics". (95)

"The contemporary academic wants only to study oppression, pref-
erably his own, defined reductively according to gonads and mela-
nin." (96)

If we take all of this together it amounts to a national crisis of vast
proportions. Excellence in higher education was one of the major
reasons for this nation's success, but we are now living off the college education that was received by people who are age 50 and over.
When this older cohort dies off, the nation will be largely without
people who have been college-educated in any real sense. ... The
kind of left-wing radicalism that has destroyed so many countries
could achieve supremacy here too if indoctrination of college students is allowed to continue. We must act to stop this madness now.
(172)

We must face up to the fact that the institutions that resemble universities no longer are such in the true sense. (184)

In the case of those schools where politically correct lunacy has hit
the headlines in recent years, enrollments have plummeted. [They
have become] campuses that in reality are only boot camps for radical political activism. (191)

The Revolt of the Elites and the Betrayal of Democracy, Christopher Lasch (1996)

Democracy works best when men and women do things for themselves, with the help of their friends and neighbors, instead of depending on the state. (7)

Arguments are not won by shouting down opponents. They are won by changing opponents' minds—something that can happen only if we give opposing arguments a respectful hearing and still persuade their advocates that there is something wrong with those arguments. (171)

If we insist on argument as the essence of education, we will defend democracy not as the most efficient but as the most educational form of government, one that extends the circle of debate as widely as possible and thus forces all citizens to articulate their views, to put their views at risk, and to cultivate the virtues of eloquence, clarity of thought and expression, and sound judgment. (171)

Kindly Inquisitors: The New Attacks on Free Thought, by Jonathan Rauch (1993-2013)

"You're not black, or gay, or Hispanic, or whatever; you wouldn't understand." That argument deserves a special place in the hall of shame. It is anti-intellectualism at its most rancid. It is the age-old tribalist notion that, as Popper put it, "we think with our blood", "with our national heritage", or "with our class". ... Accept their credo, and you have a race war or a class war [or outright righteous violence] where liberal inquiry once was. (146)

Races or tribes don't *have* perspectives. [Who would speak for blacks? Shelby Steele? Neil deGrasse Tyson? Al Sharpton? Elija Muhammad?] (146)

No personal authority is allowed, nor any racial authority. Gays or blacks or women or whoever are no more in universal agreement than anyone else. When activists insist on introducing the "gay perspective" or "black perspective", etc. into a curriculum or a discussion, they really mean introducing their *own* particular opinion.

Those minority activists want power and seek it by claiming to speak for a race or a gender or an ethnicity. (147) This is close to socio-pathic.

[The fundamentalist intellectual style eventually kills people. The honest intellectual style, instead, kills hypotheses and opinions. A great advance!] (150)

One Nation, Two Cultures, by Gertrude Himmelfarb (1999)

In *The Wealth of Nations*, Adam Smith described the "two different schemes or systems of morality" that prevail in all civilized societies:

> *The strict or austere, and the liberal, or loose system. The former is generally admired and revered by the common people; the latter is commonly more esteemed and adopted by what are called people of fashion. (3)*

[She adds a third category, a person "of the enlightenment".] (4)

The college population more than doubled between 1950 and 1964. (13)

[It then tripled from 1965-1975.]

Tocqueville's "voluntary associations" have the crucial task of mediating between the individual and the state. In addition, it serves as a corrective to that other democratic flaw identified by Tocqueville: "the tyranny of the majority", the power of the collective mass of the people which may be inimical to the liberty of individuals and minorities. (34-5)

CHAPTER SIX

Liberal Racism—Saving Whites, Sacrificing Blacks

THE VISION OF THE ANOINTED

This is easy. History shows that the best friends minorities can have are liberals. We were against slavery, have fought for every equal rights bill in our history, and have even pushed through provisions for affirmative action, racial preferences, and diversity to help black students be better represented in our colleges than they were 50 years ago.

And we've done this without losing sight of our larger goals. We're still focusing on wholesale, not retail; politics, not individualism; group representation, not individual successes. This is still our utopian plan, and individual successes of blacks or others don't help us. So critics may say that issues like affirmative action, racial preferences and diversity may have increased black presence in colleges, but black graduation rates have actually fallen because the blacks weren't prepared to do academic work at that level since they had been so poorly educated in the public schools, especially the dangerous and low-quality public schools where they are assigned. That's not our concern. If you care about that, put more tax money into the education program. We're not pursuing the little picture.

We're about the big picture. And we're doing a good job in the big picture, especially regarding race relations and minority representation in colleges.

WHAT'S WRONG HERE?

Nearly everything. Let's begin with history.

The enemy of integrating races into one picture of the Human Race has always been liberals—Democrats. The fact that this is unknown by the vast majority of Americans is all the proof we need that the information has been intentionally kept from us. Here are just a few notes from the important book *Wrong on Race: The Democratic Party's Buried Past*, by Bruce Bartlett (2008):

• In the 1850s, Democratic Senator Stephen A. Douglas of Illinois engineered the final breakdown and repeal of the Missouri Compromise, thus allowing the spread of slavery into Kansas and Nebraska. He also persuaded Congress to enact a new Fugitive Slave Law to prevent the collapse of slavery through escape to free states. In effect, the Democratic Party became the party of slavery, fighting to save and protect that institution right down to the Civil War.[228]

• Here's what Thomas Jefferson, founder of the Democratic Party, wrote about black people:

In general, their existence appears to participate more of sensation than reflection. To this must be ascribed their disposition to sleep when abstracted from their diversions, and unemployed in labor. ... Comparing them by their faculties of memory, reason, and imagination, it appears to me, that in memory they are equal to the whites, in reason much inferior, as I think one could scarcely be

---

[228] *Wrong on Race*, p. 4.

found capable of tracing and comprehending the investi-
gations of Euclid; and that in imagination they are dull,
tasteless, and anomalous.[229]

Jefferson considered the possibility that blacks' backwardness resulted from the institution of slavery, rather than biology. But he noted that the ancient Romans treated their slaves
even worse than Americans did, yet Roman slaves often ex-
celled at art and science, and were frequently employed as tu-
tors for the children of slaveholders. Jefferson reasoned that
the critical difference was that Roman slaves were white,
while American slaves were black. "It is not their condition
then, but nature, which has produced the distinction," he
wrote; it is nature that "has been less bountiful to them in the
endowments of the head." Jefferson concluded that blacks "are
inferior to the whites in the endowments both of body and
mind."[230]

As University of Alaska historian Kenneth O'Reilly put it,
"He disliked slavery only in theory."[231]

To understand Jefferson in a historical context, he was
from a slave state and could hardly hope for any kind of future
in politics as an opponent of slavery. When Jefferson was
elected president in 1800, it was mainly on the strength of his
support from slave states. He knew that union was impossible
without the Constitution's explicit support for slavery. And he
also knew that there weren't enough votes in Congress to do
anything about it anyway.[232]

Slaves also represented an important part of Jefferson's
wealth; he could not free them personally nor support abolition of slavery without suffering a huge financial loss that

---

[229] Ibid., p. 5.
[230] Ibid.
[231] Ibid.
[232] Ibid., p. 6.

would have severely crippled his lifestyle. He inherited slaves from both his parents and got many more through marriage. By 1783, he owned more than 200 slaves, making him one of the richest men in Virginia. There is no evidence that he treated them any better or worse than was common at that time.[233]

Later, Jefferson opposed the Missouri Compromise because it restricted slavery in the Louisiana territory. In 1806, he even pushed a law through Congress that embargoed trade with Haiti in order to deny American arms and provisions to the black revolutionaries. As historian Forrest McDonald put it, "the Jeffersonians sentenced the black revolution in St. Domingo to death by starvation".[234]

It was Andrew Jackson who was responsible for building the Democrats into the first modern political party. The glue that held them together was slavery and the exploitation of Indians.[235]

President Martin Van Buren, another Democrat, was also pro-slavery and owned around 50 slaves. He even replaced the White House service staff with slaves and turned its basement into slave quarters.

James Polk, the 11th President (1845-1849), was a Democrat, owned a large cotton plantation with many slaves, and was strongly pro-slavery and in favor of removing the Indians. He brought Texas into the Union as a slave state in 1845.[236]

The slavery/anti-slavery chaos produced the Republican Party which was born on an explicitly antislavery platform.[237]

In 1857, the Supreme Court made the *Dred Scott* decision, which ruled that all blacks, free or slave, were mere property

---

[233] Ibid.
[234] Ibid., p. 7.
[235] Ibid., p. 8.
[236] Ibid., p. 14.
[237] Ibid., p. 18.

and therefore could not become citizens. This meant that they could neither vote nor sue in court. Chief Justice Roger Taney, a Democrat who had been appointed by Andrew Jackson, justified his ruling on the grounds that blacks were "a subordinate and inferior class of beings who had been subjugated by the dominant race".[238]

The Democrats voted to admit Kansas as a slave-owning state. Democratic President Buchanan supported it enthusiastically.[239]

Lincoln ran for Senate in 1858 on a strong anti-slavery platform, strongly opposed to incumbent Democratic Senator Stephen Douglas. They arranged for a series of seven debates, perhaps the most famous debates in US history. In the third debate on September 15, 1858, Douglas said that all men were *not* created equal, that blacks were not equal to whites, and that the Founding Fathers never meant to say any such thing. He explained:

> I hold that a Negro is not and never ought to be a citizen of the United States.

Douglas' approach won the day against Lincoln's principled opposition to slavery. Douglas was reelected to the Senate.[240]

Democrats opposed every civil rights measure proposed by the Republican Congress, supported fellow Democrat Andrew Johnson in his efforts to block legislation that would give rights and dignity to former slaves, and cleverly found ways to keep black people down. The denial of voting rights for blacks was pervasive throughout the South, as were separate

---

[238] Ibid., p. 19.
[239] Ibid., p. 19.
[240] Ibid., p. 21.

rail cars, rest rooms, and drinking fountains, which persisted well into the 1960s. The "Solid South" elected only Democrats for a century after the Civil War. *All* the Jim Crow laws were enacted by Democratic legislatures and signed into law by Democratic governors.[241]

Andrew Johnson was Lincoln's Vice President (it was not unusual for the President and Vice President to belong to different political parties). He said slavery was justified because blacks "were inferior to the white man in point of intellect". Moreover, they were "many degrees lower in the scale of gradation that expresses the relative relation between God and all that he has created than the white man; hence the conclusion against the black man and in favor of the white man". He denounced the idea of allowing free blacks to vote. That would "place every splay-footed, bandy-shanked, hump-backed, thick-lipped, flat-nosed, wooly-headed, ebon-colored Negro in the country upon an equality with the poor white man".[242]

Democrats wrapped their complaints "in racist rhetoric designed to appeal to people's basest fears". And they never offered any alternative to Lincoln's Republican anti-slavery strategy, never once putting a plan on the table other than the Crittenden Compromise of 1860, which would have amended the Constitution to permit slavery forever.[243]

Republicans next passed the Civil Rights Act of 1866, which addressed the systematic denial of basic legal protections to black people in Southern states. It would have guaranteed them the same rights to make contracts, own property, and have that property protected by law. President Johnson vetoed it on March 27, 1866. The Senate overrode Johnson's

---

[241] Ibid., p. 24.
[242] Ibid., p. 25.
[243] Ibid., p. 30.

veto on April 6, 1866, even though every Democrat in that body voted to uphold it. The House followed suit on April 9, with 40 Democrats and one Unionist voting to sustain. The Civil Rights Act thus became law despite the best efforts of Johnson and the Democratic Party to kill it.[244]

• 1854 — The Republican Party was formed as an anti-slavery party.

• Virtually all slave owners were Democrats (use your search engines to check it).

• 1865 — The reaction in the South to the Fifteenth Amendment (guaranteeing the right to vote regardless of race) was the formation of the Ku Klux Klan to suppress the black vote by force. It was the "terrorist arm of the Democratic Party". Columbia University historian Eric Foner calls the KKK "a military force serving the interests of the Democratic Party".[245]

After racist Southerners began making it harder for black people to vote, the Republican Party in the South withered away to virtual nonexistence, and the Democratic Party completely dominated the region for the next one hundred years. Although the Republican Party still had significant strength at the national level—holding the White House for all but 16 years between 1860 and 1932—the Supreme Court's decisions left little executive power with which to redress the racist policies. It was not until the Court's philosophy changed with *Brown v. Board of Education* in 1954 that there was once again an opportunity to pass new civil rights legislation.[246]

• The big reversal of political alliances in the South came with LBJ acknowledging that he had lost the South for Democrats in 1964 by backing the Civil Rights Bill—and this turned out to

[244] Ibid., p. 35.
[245] Ibid., p. 38.
[246] Ibid., p. 40.

be true. It was when Southern Democrats—who were overwhelmingly pro-slavery and against any equal rights for blacks—left the Democratic Party and became Republicans. Not because they agreed with everything in the Republican Party's approach to race and civil rights, but because they were angry at having their historically racist Democratic position betrayed by LBJ.[247] In other words, the Southern Republicans after 1964 were the same people, with the same racist attitudes, who had been Democrats for the previous century.

The main role blacks have played for Democrats since the 1950s is as their primary group of token victims, for whom they can speak and feel righteous for doing so. The only purpose of blacks is to serve the (really *religious*) needs of (primarily white) liberals (and black race-baiters like Rev. Sharpton and the NAACP).

The protests of the 1960s differed from those of the 50s in that blacks (and women and gays) also began demanding the right to speak for themselves. This took away their use to white liberals until the birth of "white guilt" and "black power" actually re-established white authority (as Shelby Steele has clearly shown).[248]

And the claim to care only about "wholesale" plans rather than the (allegedly insignificant) "individual successes" has completely missed the point. Unless blacks are graduating and succeeding at higher levels, nothing that's being done for them—affirmative action, racial preferences, and the rest—is doing them a single bit of good. Rather, it is—as several black authors have been clear—done merely to let white liberals feel virtuous as their efforts to help blacks *fail*.

Our love of grand abstractions that often lack much real-world grounding can let us feel righteous and virtuous, while

---

[247] Ibid., p. 168.
[248] *White Guilt: How Blacks and Whites Together Destroyed the Promise of the Civil Rights Era*, by Shelby Steele (2006).

suggesting to us that (a) we do have the wisdom denied to the masses; and (b) we are indeed using that wisdom—which is, as shown by our actions, our candidate for the legitimate heir to the omniscience of God—to create the utopian society that only we can see. *Diversity* plays into this well. It looks good, very pro-race, pro-integration, to see a diverse population in our schools. Walter E. Williams doesn't agree:

> *Diversity is based on the proposition, without any evidence whatsoever, that having some sort of statistical racial representation is a necessary ingredient to a good education.*[249]

White authors are also able to see the hypocrisy and phoniness of many popular racist slogans and sayings. Jonathan Rauch:

Black unemployment was lower under George W. Bush than at any point during the Obama administration. In addition, the black-white income disparity that widened under Obama actually narrowed in the 1980s under President Ronald Reagan.[250]

Black law-school graduates fail the bar exam at four times the white rate.[251] This is a mark of the liberals' policies' total *failure*, not success.

Candace Owens said:

> *What is happening right now in the black community ... There is an ideological civil war happening. Black people that are focused on their past and shouting about slavery.*

---

[249] *Liberty Versus the Tyranny of Socialism: Controversial Essays* (2008), p. 2.
[250] *Please Stop Helping Us*, by Jason L. Riley (2015), p. 9.
[251] Ibid., p. 160.

*And black people focused on their futures. What you're
seeing is victim mentality versus victor mentality.*[252]

The deeply uncomfortable truth is that we liberals have
thought of black people like pets, tokens, Sambo dolls (in
Shelby Steele's poignant image) for centuries. And no matter
what we *say* we believe (and really do believe, I think), *don't
listen to us, watch us.* And as a range of people including the
brilliant black authors I've cited here have said, our efforts are
to let us feel virtuous at the expense of damaging or destroying
the real possibilities of black people.

Some of this is easy to see. If we actually cared about
whether black people were well-educated, successful, and
prosperous, we would follow the mountains of evidence showing that our public education is among the worst in the world,
while many charter schools are producing very successful
black graduates. Barack Obama repeatedly tried to shut down
a voucher program in Washington D.C. that serves poor minorities and produces significantly higher graduation rates
than both D.C. public schools and the national average.[253]

President Barack Obama expressed his affinity for rappers
like Jay-Z and Lil Wayne, whose lyrics often elevate misogyny,
drug dealing, and gun violence. At the time of the president's
interview, Lil Wayne was imprisoned on gun and drug
charges.[254]

Did Obama's endorsement of people like this help or hurt
healthy black people?

When he ran for president in 2008 and was asked about
school vouchers, Obama said that if he were presented with
evidence that they improve outcomes, he would "not allow my
predispositions to stand in the way of making sure that our

[252] *Blackout: How Black America can Make its Second Escape from the Democrat Plantation,* by Candace Owens. Threshold Editions 2020, p. 152.
[253] *Please Stop Helping Us,* pp. 129-130.
[254] *Please Stop Helping Us,* p. 51.

kids can learn ... you do what works for the kids". In fact, his administration has ignored scholars like Forster to placate teachers' unions and has even sat on evidence of voucher success. [255]

Obama said that he wants to increase reading proficiency and graduation rates for minority students, yet he opposed school voucher programs that are doing both. [256] To the Obama administration, the racial balance of a school is more important than whether anyone is learning. [257]

Obama and other liberals stress the importance of blacks having political presence and power—like a black man in the White House. But how much does politics really affect success? And why did even President Obama act more like a Democrat than like someone really committed to helping black people get a better education? Maybe a reality check will help. As Jason L. Riley reports, most of the five million government employees who work in public education are organized into highly effective unions, which overwhelmingly support Democratic candidates and can easily determine the outcome of close elections. With the help of both black and white Democrats, the unions have built a Berlin Wall that protects the public education system from competition by private and voucher schools, and prevents poor children from escaping from the many bad and dangerous schools where they are trapped in schools and environments which do not and cannot educate them. Politicians know this, but operate on their version of the Pinsky Principle: a moral cowardice that punishes the citizens who have become their victims. [258]

Between 1940 and 1960—that is, before the major civil rights victories, and at a time when black political power was

---

[255] *Please Stop Helping Us*, p. 132.

[256] Ibid., p. 171.

[257] Ibid., p. 132.

[258] Ibid., p. 134.

nearly nonexistent—the black poverty rate fell from 87% to 47%. Yet between 1972 and 2011 it barely declined, from 32% to 28%, and remained three times the white rate, which is about what it was in 1972. By 2013, Mississippi had more black elected officials than any other state, but it also continues to have one of the highest black poverty rates in the nation. Other measures of black well-being also don't seem to have improved along with black political progress over the decades.[259]

And if we really cared about black success, we would acknowledge what black people know: that it's that ghetto-style *culture* in some black areas that almost guarantees their failure in school, business, and society. We're so afraid of being called racists that we have let our liberal racism become allied with unspeakable violence to blacks in America. Almost all liberals will deny that we believe this. But don't listen to us. *Watch us*, and you'll see that we don't care what happens to black people in America.

If we want to understand this, it's worth the time to read essays like Thomas Sowell's "Black Rednecks and White Liberals", which is also the title of his 2005 book that contains this as the lead essay. And we could read the book from which Sowell's essay was derived: *Cracker Culture: Celtic Ways in the Old South* by Grady McWhiney (1988). These are important sources with information essential to any decent understanding of what's happening in the real world. If you've been watching us, you'll know that liberals care about grand abstractions that make a good show. We don't seem to care much about what's happening in the real world. This is another measure of the *Second Culture*, and shows up in colleges, intellectualism, and all areas where our beloved (and wildly overrated) Philosopher Kings and Princelings fancy ourselves

---

[259] *Please Stop Helping Us*, p. 21.

belonging.

We relegate black students to the worst and most violent schools, and our government programs have tended to do more harm than good. The facts here aren't subtle; read much more on this in this chapter's **EXCERPTS** section.

Little Black Sambo

Little Black Sambo may have begun as a children's story in 1899, but the cartoonish character became much more, and that degrading, less-than-fully-human image is still rooted deep in the liberal mind as the image of what black people are really like. As Shelby Steele has put it,

> It is a vision of the Negro as a kind of pet, a figure of sweet and harmless inferiority to whom one gives out of the largesse of one's superiority.[260]

> This points to a sad irony at the core of black-white relations in America. The price blacks pay for the mere illusion of recompense for past injustice always requires them—literally as well as metaphorically—to be "Samboized", to be merchandised to whites as inferiors and victims. The Sambo doll, as an image of grotesque black inferiority sold to whites in homage to their superiority, is an ominous and recurring image. ... Yet, even today, when people argue for diversity and, thus, for racial preferences, black students are effectively Sambo-ized. They are assigned an inferiority so intractable that nothing overcomes it, not even good schools and high family incomes.[261]

And for all his smooth talk, Barack Obama left race rela-

---

[260] *White Guilt*, by Shelby Steele. P. 132.
[261] Ibid., p. 134.

tions worse off than they were when he took office. Jason L. Riley has suggested a possibility that no white person can yet suggest without being called a racist by liberals and the liberal media, when he wonders whether Obama might, after all, be remembered as a triumph of style over substance.[262]

Riley also says that the black civil rights leadership knows that black criminality is, at the root, a black problem that needs to be addressed by black people reassessing black behavior and cultural attitudes. But the civil rights movement has no interest in realistic assessments of black pathology. The NAACP is more interested in keeping whites on the defensive than in addressing self-destructive habits.[263]

Liberals don't help matters by making excuses for counterproductive behavior. Nor do the media by shying away from reporting the truth.[264] This was called, over 40 years ago, the "Pinsky Principle":

> News that could prove embarrassing is often simply not reported. Reed Irvine has christened this "the Pinsky Principle" after North Carolina journalist Walter Pinsky, who described his approach in the Columbia Journalism Review in 1976. "If my research and journalistic instincts tell me one thing, my political instincts another ... I won't fudge it, I won't bend it, but I won't write it."[265]

A more honest diagnosis is simply the abiding moral cowardice of the media, liberal politicians—both black and white—and the deadly liberal ideology that continues to spawn self-serving hypocrisy at every level. We are absolutely desperate to believe that our wisdom really is an improvement on that of the omniscient Biblical God we think we outgrew two

---

[262] *Please Stop Helping Us*, p. 32.
[263] Ibid., p. 81.
[264] Ibid., p. 83.
[265] *The Coercive Utopians*, p. 269.

centuries ago. We're dead wrong, and morally, ontologically, bankrupt.

We have turned underprivileged blacks into playthings for liberal intellectuals and politicians who care more about feeling righteous or winning votes than advocating behaviors and attitudes that have allowed other groups to get ahead.[266]

We have also succeeded in convincing blacks to see themselves first and foremost as victims. Today there is no greater impediment to black advancement than the self-pitying mindset that permeates black culture. White liberals think they are helping blacks by romanticizing miscreants. And black liberals are all too happy to hustle guilty whites.[267]

Much more disturbing is that half a century after the civil rights battles were fought and won, liberalism remains much more interested in making excuses for black Americans than in reevaluating efforts to help them.[268]

Yes, this is all racism. But it's not *white* racism or "white supremacy". It's *liberal* racism, practiced by both whites and blacks. Black race hustlers like Jesse Jackson and Al Sharpton, and black politicians more concerned with their careers than with helping black people routinely treat blacks as victims, second-rate humans who can't be expected to accept any responsibility for their culture or behavior, and the rest. And that's an important distinction: this is *liberal racism*, no matter the race of those who are doing it. And it is very destructive to black people.

We need to confess: with liberals, it's always about us, not blacks. Blacks only exist as token victims to serve us, as several respected black authors have said in several ways. Why would we behave in such inhumane ways? The list is worth repeating:

---

[266] *Please Stop Helping Us*, p. 172.
[267] Ibid., p. 173.
[268] Ibid., p. 174.

a. We outgrew traditional religion

b. But we didn't replace the humane, moral, golden rule parts. We've seldom even learned more integrated and caring behavior from a secular philosophy like Stoicism.

c. We tried to become God, and claimed—through our actions—the wisdom to create utopia for everyone, here and now. Whether they liked it or not. That's narcissistic. There's no humility, no love for others for their sake. It's also sociopathic, as psychiatrist Lyle Rossiter has diagnosed it.[269]

d. Traditional people who kept traditional religion kept a notion of themselves as God's children with a duty to obey God's golden rules, and to try and love others. We don't have that.

e. We are *Godless*, with some of the implications of that. We have failed to find an adequate, legitimate heir to an omniscient God and eternal reward. We have tried to play God, and it is a cruel joke—on us, and on the world around us. Our gods are hollow. As liberals, we have nothing healthy to offer the world. As individuals, we may: we could be honest, loving, good parents or friends, and the rest. But operating out of the liberal ideology, we have nothing healthy to offer the real world.

The hard and painful truth is that in many areas—especially religion, education, and race—we have often become a dangerous and evil presence. This is not a plea to return to supernatural religion or to any particular gods, but to find the humility and grounded compassion for others, which is our duty to offer to the real world. Stoic thinking could do all of this for us, if we knew and applied it.

---

[269] *The Liberal Mind*, p. 21.

EXCERPTS

Please Stop Helping Us: How Liberals Make it Harder for Blacks to Succeed, by Jason L. Riley

The persistently high black jobless rate is more a consequence of unemployability than of discrimination in hiring. The black-white learning gap stems from a dearth of education choices for ghetto kids, not biased tests or a shortage of education funding. And although black civil rights leaders like to point to a supposedly racist criminal justice system to explain why our prisons house so many black men, it's been obvious for decades that the real culprit is black behavior—behavior too often celebrated in black culture. (4)

Again, Black unemployment was lower under George W. Bush than it was at any point during the Obama administration. In addition, the black-white income disparity that widened under Obama actually narrowed in the 1980s under President Ronald Reagan. (9)

Today Asian Americans are the nation's best-educated and highest-earning racial group. A 2013 Pew study reported that 49% of Asians aged 25 and older hold bachelor's degrees, versus 31% of whites and 18% of blacks. The median household income for Asians is $66,000, which is $12,000 more than white households and double that of black households. Yet Asians have little political clout in the US. ... In 2008, Asians were significantly less likely than both blacks and whites to have voted. (22)

"The bottom line: Georgia's black counties overwhelmingly desire dramatic new alternatives to the conventional school systems that have failed them for more than a century", wrote journalist Douglas Blackmon. (31)

Having a black man in the Oval Office is less important than having one in the home. (33)

Today, more than 70% of black children are born to unwed mothers. Only 16% of black households are married couples with children, the lowest of any racial group in the US, while nearly 20% are female-headed with children, which is the highest of any group. (37-38)

In the late 1990s the black residents of Shaker Heights, Ohio, an affluent Cleveland suburb, invited John Ogbu, professor of anthropology at the University of California, Berkeley, to examine the black-white academic achievement gap in their community. ... Black students were receiving 80% of the Ds and Fs. (43)

But what Ogbu found is that this problem transcends class and persists even among the children of affluent, educated black professionals. (44)

He concluded the black culture, more than anything else, explained the academic achievement gap. (44)

Among their black friends, "it was not cool to be successful" or "to work hard or to show you're smart". One female student said that some black students believed "it was cute to be dumb". (44)

But this theory can't explain the performance of other nonwhite students, including black immigrants, who readily adjust to the pedagogic methods of US schools and go on to outperform black Americans. Even black immigrants for whom English as a second language have managed to excel in US schools. (48)

Black cultural attitudes toward work, authority, dress, sex, and violence have also proven counterproductive, inhibiting the development of the kind of human capital that has led to socioeconomic advancement for other groups. ... A culture that takes pride in ignorance and mocks learnedness has a dim future. And those who attempt to make excuses for black social pathology rather than condemning these behaviors in no uncertain terms are part of the problem. (50)

In 2004 Bill Cosby was the featured speaker at an NAACP awards ceremony. [He spoke out strongly against all this self-defeating nonsense.] (53)

In Philadelphia circa 1880, 75% of black families and 73% of white families were comprised of two parents and children. In Philadelphia circa 2007, "married-couple families account for only 34% of African American family households, while white married-couple families account for 68% of white family households". ... Nationwide data from every census taken between 1890 and 1940 show the black marriage rate exceeding the white rate. Liberals want to blame the "legacy" of slavery and racism for the breakdown of the black family and subsequent social pathologies, but the empirical data support Bill Cosby. (54-55)

By retarding or otherwise interfering with black self-development, government programs have tended to do more harm than good. (56)

Heather MacDonald:

> *Blacks committed 66% of all violent crimes in the first half*
> *of 2009. They committed 80% of all shootings in the first*
> *half of 2009. Together, blacks and Hispanics committed*
> *98% of all shootings. Blacks committed nearly 70% of all*
> *robberies. Whites, by contrast, committed 5% of all violent*
> *crimes in the first half of 2009, though they are 35% of the*
> *city's population. They committed 1.8% of all shootings and*
> *less than 5 % of all robberies. The face of violent crime in*
> *New York, in other words, like in every other large American*
> *city, is almost exclusively black and brown. (70-71)*

Some 90% of black murder victims are killed by other blacks. (74)

Liberal elites would have us deny what black ghetto residents know to be the truth. (74)

[On stricter gun laws, etc.] "Rules that make self-defense more difficult would impact blacks the most." (77)

In 2007, 90.2% of black murder victims were murdered by blacks. And poor blacks commit crime against poor blacks. Is it less racist to care about the victims or the criminals? (78)

These days it is mostly charter schools that are closing the achievement gap, which is one reason why they are so popular with black people. Charter schools are tuition-free public schools run by independent organizations outside the control of the local school board. ... Blacks who favor charters outnumber opponents by four to one. (122)

Success Academy Harlem I, which selects students by lottery, shares a building with PS 149, one of the city's better traditional public schools. Both schools serve kids from the same racial and economic background in classes that have about the same number of students. But the similarities end there. In 2009, 29% of students at PS 149 were performing at grade level in reading and 34% were at grade level in math. At Harlem I—liberally across the hall—the corresponding figures were 86% and 94%. 97% of Harlem I's students passed the state exam that year, ranking it in the top one percent of all New York State public schools. (124) [There are many more similar examples.]

In 2009 the nation's 50 largest cities had an average high-school graduation rate of 53%. But in a study published the next year, Wolf found that the DC voucher recipients had graduation rates of 91%, versus 56% for DC public schools and 70% for students who entered the lottery for a voucher but didn't win one. (130)

Blacks as a group, and poor blacks in particular, have performed better in the *absence* of government schemes like affirmative action. (155)

The history of affirmative action in academia since the 1970s is a history of trying to justify holding blacks to lower standards in the name of helping them. (157)

Black law-school graduates fail the bar exam at four times the white rate. (160)

The too-seldom-told story of affirmative action in the University of California system is the black *gains* that have occurred since it was abolished. (161)

Obama said that he wants to increase reading proficiency and graduation rates for minority students, yet he opposes school voucher programs that are doing both. (171)

Liberalism has also succeeded, tragically, in convincing blacks to see themselves first and foremost as victims.

White Guilt: How Blacks and Whites Together Destroyed the Promise of the Civil Rights Era, by Shelby Steele (2006)

[White guilt is] *the vacuum of moral authority* that comes from simply *knowing* that one's race is associated with racism. ... This is why white guilt is quite literally the same thing as black power. (24) ... white guilt has given America a new social morality in which white racism is seen as disgraceful. (27)

The most striking irony of the age of white guilt is that racism suddenly became *valuable* to the people who had suffered it. ... Racism was *evidence* of white wrongdoing and, therefore, evidence of white obligation to blacks. MLK had argued that whites were obligated to morality and democratic principles. But white guilt meant they were obligated to black *people* because they needed the moral authority only black people could bestow. So white guilt made racism into a valuable currency for black Americans—a currency that enmeshed whites (and especially American institutions) in obligation *not to principles* but to black people as a class. [White guilt expanded] the territory of white obligation. (35)

For black leaders in the age of white guilt, the problem was how to seize all they could get from white guilt *without* having to show actual events of racism. *Global racism* was the answer. With it, the smallest racial incident proved the "global truth" of systemic racism. This is why one black man being beaten by police in Los Angeles could trigger a massive riot in which some 60 people were killed. By the terms of global racism one racist incident proved the rule of systemic racism. (36)

And I learned that my group identity as a black was more important than my individuality. ... The new black consciousness I was learning from people like Dick Gregory wanted me to voluntarily, even proudly, do the same thing that racism had done: make my race more important than my individuality. This meant that Dick Gregory and George Wallace ("segregation forever") were saying the same thing: that race was destiny. (47)

Only in being responsible for one's life can one take agency over it. And agency—the sovereignty and will that we have over our individual lives—is what makes us fully human. (48)

Authentic black militancy, of the sort that Malcolm X at times seemed capable of, always embraced responsibility as power itself. ... His was a self-help black militancy that was naturally skeptical about what others would actually do for blacks. (59)

[White America and its institutions could only regain moral authority by taking responsibility for blacks: affirmative action, etc.— things that benefit whites, restoring their moral authority, but do *not* benefit blacks.] (62)

Black achievement in music and sports should never be dismissed; rather, it should point the way to black achievement in all other areas. Here is the self-possession, the assumption of full responsibility, the refusal to trade on one's plight, the engagement with the broader American mainstream, and the insistence on excellence as the currency of advancement—all of which makes blacks utterly irrepressible in these areas. And then, in concert with this, come the hard work, imagination, discipline, sacrifice, relentless effort, and—most important—*openness* to competition with *all* others that gave us our Ellingtons, Ellisons and Kings. (65)

It must be acknowledged that blacks are no longer oppressed in America. (67)

Whites needed responsibility for our problems in order to gain their own moral authority and legitimacy. So they set about—once again—to exploit us, to encourage and even nurture our illusions, to steal responsibility from us, to take advantage of our backwardness just as slave traders had once done on the west coast of Africa. Suddenly, in the age of white guilt, we were gold again—and in service to white need. (68-69)

Double standards *always* stigmatize precisely those they claim to help (116)

To see humanity across racial lines one must see frankly how people of other races live as human beings, not as members of a race. (129)

It is a vision of the Negro as a kind of pet, a figure of sweet and harmless inferiority to whom one gives out of the largesse of one's superiority. (132)

In her column devoted to excoriating Clarence Thomas, Maureen Dowd blurts out a word that chills the souls of all blacks. She says that instead of complaining, Clarence Thomas should show "gratitude" for affirmative action. Here she is trying to "annihilate" him, to put him in his place as an inferior who can advance only through the largesse of superiors like herself. Maureen Dowd, thinking herself quite incapable of racism, effectively calls Justice Thomas a nigger who—given his fundamental inferiority—should show "gratitude" to his white betters. ... Addicted to the easy moral esteem that comes to her from dissociation, Dowd plays the oldest race cards of all—I'm white and you're black, so shut up and be grateful for my magnanimity. It is as though in fighting for her human visibility she is really fighting for her superiority—a superiority that Justice Thomas annihilated and that she now wants back. (147)

There is no better example of the self-destruction that dissociation brings to institutions than the American public schools. Those who would take power by making things easier have all but destroyed what was once the greatest public education system in the world. In more liberal states like California, where dissociation has been an orthodoxy, if not a religion, the schools are even worse than elsewhere. (163)

A 70% illegitimacy rate among all blacks (90% in certain inner cities) pretty much makes the point that there is a responsibility problem. (173)

I had become terrified of the Faustian bargain waiting for me at the doorway to the left: we'll throw you a bone like affirmative action if you'll just let us reduce you to your race so we can take moral authority for "helping" you. (174)

Dogmatic Wisdom, by Russell Jacoby (1995)

In higher education as a whole black enrollment grew from about 150,000 in 1960 to over a million today. (84) In the early 1950s, only 1% of the blacks in higher education attended predominantly white institutions; by the late 1970s this figure jumped to 50 percent. (85)

More immigrants entered the US between 1900-1910 than in any decade before or since, about 8.8 million. In the peak year of 1907, 1.3 million arrived. The country's population in 1900 was about 75 million. (151) In the 1980s, about 7.3 million immigrated, including 2 million illegal aliens who were given legal permanent residence. (The country's population was about 225 million, three times as high as in 1900.) (151)

One Nation, Two Cultures, by Gertrude Himmelfarb (1999)

The Welfare State. Welfare dependency is not the primary cause of our social pathology, but it is an important factor in it. This system of relief was less than two years old when its initiator, FDR, cautioned Americans against an excessive reliance upon it: "Continued dependence upon relief induces a spiritual and moral disintegration fundamentally destructive to the national fiber. To dole out relief in this way is to administer a narcotic, a subtle destroyer of the human spirit." Roosevelt's relief program was, in fact, modest. But LBJ's "Great Society" and "War Against Poverty" were not. It took another liberal, RFK to point out that this new mode of welfare degraded those it meant to help. In 1966 he discovered what many liberals were to take much longer to learn:

> *Opponents of welfare have always said that welfare is degrading, both to the giver and the recipient. They have said that it destroys self-respect, that it lowers incentives, and that it is contrary to American ideals.*
>
> *Most of us deprecated and disregarded these criticisms. People were in need; obviously, we felt, to help people in trouble was the right thing to do. But in our urge to help, we also disregarded elementary facts. For the criticisms of welfare*

do have a center of truth, and they are confirmed by the ev-
idence.

Recent studies have shown, for example, that higher welfare
payments often encourage students to drop out of school,
that they encourage families to disintegrate, and that they
often lead to lifelong dependency. (71)

Liberty Versus the Tyranny of Socialism: Controversial Essays,
by Walter E. Williams (2008)

Academic Cesspools II. From the Univ. of Delaware's Office of
Residence Life Diversity Facilitation Training document (see
www.thefire.org for whole document):

Students living in the University's housing, roughly 7,000, are
taught: *"A racist: A racist is one who is both privileged and socialized*
on the basis of race by a white supremacist (racist) system. The term
applies to all white people (i.e., people of European descent) living in
the US, regardless of class, gender, religion, culture or sexuality. By
this definition, people of color cannot be racists, because as peoples
within the US system, they do not have the power to back up their
prejudices, hostilities or acts of discrimination." This gem of wisdom
suggests that by virtue of birth alone, not conduct, if you're white,
you're a racist. (12) It is as fundamental definition of racism as
you're likely to find.

More: *"A non-racist: A non-term. The term was created by whites to*
deny responsibility for systemic racism, to maintain an aura of in-
nocence in the face of racial oppression, and to shift responsibility
for that oppression from whites to people of color (called 'blaming
the victim'). Responsibility for perpetuating and legitimizing a racist
system rests both on those who actively maintain it, and on those
who refuse to challenge it. Silence is consent." (13)

It's a safe bet the university did not highlight this kind of learning
experience to parents and students in its recruitment efforts. Nor
were generous donors and alumni informed that they are racists by
birth. I'd also guess that this kind of "education" was kept under

wraps from the state legislators who use taxpayer money to fund the university. (13)

Insulting Blacks. "I don't feel no ways tired. I come too far from where I started from. Nobody told me that the road would be easy. I don't believe He brought me this far," drawled presidential aspirant Hillary Clinton, mimicking black voice to a black audience, at the First Baptist Church of Selma, Alabama. I'm wondering if Mrs. Clinton visits an Indian reservation she might cozy up to them saying, "How! Me not tired. Me come heap long way. Road might rough. Sky Spirit no bring me this far." Or, seeking the Asian vote she might say, "I no wray tired. Come too far I started flum. Road berry clooked. Number one Dragon King take me far." (322)

CHAPTER SEVEN

Some Distinctions

1. Our sloughing off God let us fall into narcissism, sociopathy, and evil

Liberal psychiatrist Dr. Lyle H. Rossiter Jr. has diagnosed the liberal mind as narcissistic and sociopathic and has blamed it on childhood trauma. The diagnosis seems right, but not the etiology. Liberals don't have categorically worse childhoods than conservatives or others. I want to suggest a deeper and older link between these maladaptive character traits.

In her 2006 book, *The Sociopath Next Door,* Harvard psychologist Martha Stout reported strong data showing that about 4% of the US population is sociopathic. Much of the data came from the Minnesota Multiphasic Personality Inventory, a test that has been used since 1943. The test is used with young people from age 14 through college age and has always had sections in it designed to identify sociopathic patterns and tendencies, making it the most widely used and trusted instrument for the diagnosis of some mental disorders, including sociopathy.

Other data estimate that about 5% of the US population has narcissistic personality disorder, the deepest and most destructive variety of narcissism. However, since most sociopaths are also narcissists, the total for the two psychological aberrations would probably be in the 5% range rather than the 9% range. So, it's relatively rare, meaning that when a psychiatrist like Dr. Rossiter diagnoses "the liberal mind" as narcissistic and sociopathic, it is a diagnosis to be taken seriously. It describes what we call the "far left" or socialist liberal mind, a relatively small but extremely dangerous segment of humanity. These figures aren't for all people on Earth, but specifically those in the US. For an embarrassing comparison, the figure of 4% sociopaths is *one hundred times larger* than the .04% figure for Asian cultures. We are creating and training sociopaths here in the US and are reaping what we have sown.

Liberals aren't more likely than conservatives to have had troubled or abusive childhoods, however. The cause is much deeper and older. The modern liberal lust for a totalitarian socialist utopia goes back two centuries, to the time when liberals began sloughing off the supernatural omniscient loving God of the Bible. Our problem isn't just psychological; it's *religious* and *ontological* all the way down. Understanding how and why that is is the most important thing to understand about us.

The cause of this pathological self-absorption of narcissism and its darker sociopathic sibling goes far deeper than childhood experiences. The evidence is clear and strong that its real origin is the loss of belief in any kind of a significant, loving God.

William J. Murray's 2016 book, *Utopian Road to Hell: Enslaving America and the World with Central Planning,* is helpful here, as he identifies two things that come together as a dangerous pair throughout history: atheism, and tyranny. He considers tyrants from Sparta's Lycurgus of the 9th century BC, through modern tyrants including Marx, Lenin, Stalin, Mussolini, Hitler, Mao Tse-tung, Pol Pot, et al., and finds a "Satanic Influence in Utopian Tyrannies" (the title of his Chapter 1). One thing all these deadly tyrants had in common was their atheism. They had all sloughed off God—Lycurgus also did, a millennia before Christianity and without knowing anything about the Hebrew God Yahweh. They all denied any authority categorically bigger than themselves. All tyrants hate God because they want to replace him. But history—and the murder of over 170 million of their own citizens during the last 100 years—shows they didn't have the wisdom, only the narcissistic lust for power. We don't have the wisdom, either.[270] This, mixed with their narcissism and sociopathy, made them feel responsible for providing the plan for how all others should live and finding the authority to rule: always a totalitarian, one-party, tyrannical rule.

Dr. Rossiter describes the form of government liberals want—and are instituting—as a *Parental Government*, where we intend to be the parents. We are the substitute for parents, for a heavenly Father, for God. We want to take all power (and property, eventually) away from others and tell them that their government will provide everything they need (and that if the government doesn't supply it, they probably don't need it). We will give single mothers Welfare, making the fathers irrelevant—the government will play the role of Parent, as we imagine it should be played. And we're succeeding. About 70% of black children now grow up in a home without a father. And the results of this have been measured for decades. You can check online sources and find that growing up without a father has predictable effects, which we can expect in 70% of black children because of our welfare system that lets us assume the Parent role for them:

---

[270] Saying that we don't have the wisdom of God (or "God") is meant to be like saying we don't have the artistic gifts of Rembrandt or Picasso, don't have the musical genius of a Bach, Mozart, Beethoven, Stravinsky, the legendary instrumentalists and singers, the scientific brilliance of Einstein, Hawking, etc. The word "God" is not to be understood as a literal kind of Being, an existence with awareness and intelligence. That is, as Origen named it 1,800 years ago, at the simplistic level of religion for children.

- The children are more likely to be aggressive,
- more likely to be depressed,
- more likely to have low self-esteem,
- more likely to do poorly in school,
- more likely to be incarcerated and commit suicide,
- less likely to trust others,
- sadder and more hopeless,
- and more likely to use drugs.

Lack of a healthy father figure helps determine the children's social and psychological growth, whether good or bad. A study done by the University of Wisconsin-Madison[271] found that children of divorce have a higher likelihood of being arrested for a violent crime. The children of single mothers are more likely to commit suicide, abuse drugs, be depressed, get pregnant as teenagers, and get divorced themselves. In addition, there is evidence that suggests the psychological effects of no father figure in life will make children have a higher chance of committing crimes or being involved in gang-related activities. Intact families have far more health and real-world wisdom than top-down governments can, if only because they're grounded in realities rather than abstractions. Growing up without an adequate god can also have deep and lasting effects. The esteemed American writer David Foster Wallace was channeling Ecclesiastes when he observed the following:

> *In the day-to-day trenches of adult life, there is really no such thing as atheism. There is no such thing as not worshiping. Everybody worships. ... And an outstanding reason for choosing some sort of God or spiritual-type thing to worship ... is that pretty much anything else you worship will eat you alive. If you worship money and things—*

---

[271] https://www.irp.wisc.edu/resource/involved-fathers-play-an-important-role-in-childrens-lives/

if they are where you tap real meaning in life—then you will never have enough. Never feel you have enough. It's the truth. Worship your own body and beauty and sexual allure and you will always feel ugly, and when time and age start showing, you will die a million deaths before they finally plant you. ... Worship power—you will feel weak and afraid, and you will need ever more power over others to keep the fear at bay. Worship your intellect, being seen as smart—you will end up feeling stupid, a fraud, always on the verge of being found out.

The question is not whether we yearn for or pursue meaning and purpose. The question is: Where are we looking to find it? What are we depending on to make our life worth living?[272]

The link between atheism, narcissism, sociopathy, tyranny, and evil is seldom mentioned but is terribly important to understand.

2. We are a social species: herd animals. This is the real source of our humanistic, compassionate, empathetic, and loving behaviors—not the gods we have created as projections and personifications of them.

Atheism, by itself, is not necessarily bad, as Stoicism and Buddhism have demonstrated for many centuries. Rejecting a literal understanding of God as a Guy in the Sky is a mark of outgrowing childish notions that can't serve our adult needs. The damage is done when we think the term "God" is *only* meant as a literal Guy in the Sky. As Origen sketched so well 1,800 years ago, the grown-up and religious understandings of that term are far deeper, richer, and more essential for

---

[272] https://www.goodreads.com/quotes/100888-because-here-s-something-else-that-s-weird-but-true-in-the

becoming a full and complete human. The word "God" is a sound we make when we're trying to say that we sense, believe in, and need a far larger and deeper frame for living than merely our own biased and transient opinions. Some things, we need to believe, are permanent and essential, and need to command us: the command to do unto others as we would have them do unto us, to love our neighbor, to be compassionate and caring presences in our world, good friends, honest and courageous when honesty and moral courage are necessary. The notion of a God who holds these characteristics and commands us, his "children", to obey them and grow into their forms, is essential not only for a full and commendable humanity, but also for a healthy and safe culture and society. When liberals slough off the childlike picture of the Biblical God as just a Guy "up there", without finding a linguistic and conceptual way of keeping the deeper and more valuable messages of the necessity of the Golden Rule or being a loving and compassionate presence rather than a self-absorbed tyrannical presence, then we have opened the door to evil and begged it to enter our lives and poison our world.

The role played by the symbol and metaphor of God is to caution us that we don't have the wisdom to tell others how they must live. That would take "godly" wisdom, which we will never have, any more than we will have the gifts of the greatest artists, musicians, scientists, or others. All we have are our various beliefs, orthodoxies, political ideologies, and so on. Each of them is, by definition, just partial and incomplete. Only by combining and merging all the various perspectives on life, politics, religion, and the rest could we hope to have a perspective adequate to rule without destroying others, society, etc. And no humans are ever likely to do that. We need some kind of symbols, metaphors, and images to remind us of this in a powerful enough way to feel like existential commands. That's something that God-language can simply do linguistically.

Without at least an acknowledgment of the category higher than our own, we have nothing adequate to bind back to that's able to make us more fully human, or to help us create more adequate humans. This is a terrifying—and currently very real—possibility.

It's ironic, because we have an innate sense of these things, and show spontaneous love of them when we see loving, friendly, compassionate, and empathetic behavior in our pets and many other animals that are members of a social species, as we are also members of a social species.

Social species: herd animals, with two levels to their identity. The first is their individual identity, the selfish identity, the individual style we see in children, pets, and other social animals—maybe it survives from 75 million years ago, when we were still members of reptilian species, before social species evolved. This is the primitive identity we mean when we speak of being "true to ourselves", being our "best" selves, and so on. It's important but not sufficient. And by itself, it reduces us to narcissism, sociopathy, tyranny, and the rest. We sometimes even call such behavior "reptilian", which is more deeply accurate than we realize.

As social animals, our second identity, our broader and larger one, is our identity as members of our social species. The Stoics have a couple of good visual metaphors for this. They say we should think of ourselves as limbs on the body of humanity, and as the smallest circle in the center of a large number of bigger concentric circles of which we are also organic parts: our family, our partners, children, relatives, friends, fellow soldiers, fellow professionals (doctors, lawyers, engineers, police, etc.), communities, nations, world, and history. We'll each be a slightly different size in this picture, some with more circles, some with fewer. But growing outward from our individual (reptilian) selves into our far bigger *social* identities is one of our most important challenges as a human.

And our best ethical, spiritual, and moral teachings come from this social world: the Golden Rule, the command to love our neighbors, even our enemies, and the rest. Without these, we cannot and will not become fully human. Someone who lives only by their reptilian self is properly (and sometimes actually) called *subhuman*. We'll deal with this in the third part, below.

But for atheists, it's especially important that they become aware of this deeper social identity. And it's very easy to do, realizing how much we have in common with other social animals, how deep and ancient our need for love, fairness, compassion, and the rest really go. Think of how many times you have heard people say that dogs offer "unconditional love"— something almost every dog owner will smile and agree with. We recognize, love, and need that rare quality of unconditional love. We often attribute it to parents, our partners, and our closest friends. These deep loving—*social*—behaviors are the reservoir from which the concepts of our best gods have grown.

Personally, I've always admired the wisdom in the ancient Greek gods, especially their 12-13 Olympic gods. These gods are projections of natural, personal, and psychological powers and traits. So Poseidon represented the powers of the deep oceans. But he also represented the power that can lie deep in our character: our anger, fury, and destructive capacity. Or consider wonderful, invisible Hestia. One of the original 12 Olympian deities (six males and six females), she was the only one who was almost never drawn or sculpted. She didn't exist as a creature, but as a *presence*. She was a spirit. In Hestia's case, she was called Goddess of the Hearth. So her presence was the difference between a House and a Home. It was also the difference between a "church" service and a "worship" service. A couple thousand years ago, the Greeks removed her from the Olympic Dozen and replaced her with the drunk party god Dionysus. But all the Olympic deities offer a good place to start understanding how we created our gods to evoke the deeper—sometimes positive, sometimes negative—dimensions of ourselves and of Nature. And there are many good books on these deities. Liberals should, it seems, love them. So privately, in adult study groups, high school or college classes, or in adult study groups in (probably liberal) churches, I recommend starting with the Olympic 13: Zeus, Hera, Poseidon, Demeter, Athena, Apollo, Artemis, Ares, Hephaestus, Aphrodite, Hermes, and either Hestia or Dionysus. But be able to talk about the different *levels* represented by each god, for there are many levels. And the genius of the ancient Greeks is baked into all of our Western cultures, as the wisdom of Confucius is baked into Asian cultures.

But learn it. If you've sloughed off or outgrown the literal God as presented in the Bible, you need a way to be opened to, and made subservient to, these larger meanings of what it means to become more fully human.

Besides the many gods we have created, we can go much farther back in history by observing the deep similarities we share with social animals. There are, luckily, many videos available in this area on YouTube and elsewhere. I recommend starting with the wonderful scientific experiment "Monkeys and Fairness". Just look it up online. It's under three minutes, has become a classic experiment, replicated with several other species, and may be the funniest scientific experiment you're likely to find. The experiment was designed by Sarah Brosnan while doing some post-doctoral work under ethologist Frans de Waal at the Yerkes National Primate Research Center at Emory University in Atlanta. De Waal asked Sarah to devise an experiment that could show whether a sense of fairness was *innate* in Capuchin monkeys. They had two large cages of Capuchin monkeys there, in addition to huge enclosures of rhesus monkeys, and a large yard of chimpanzees.[273]

[273] I visited Frans de Waal and met Sarah during a visit to the National Primate Research Center around 2006.

But there are hundreds, maybe thousands, of good short videos showing the kinds of behaviors we recognize, identify with, and admire in many other social species. Some can warm your heart or bring you to tears. Watching these makes it easier to understand where we got the ideas for the many gods we have created to embody and command loving, compassionate, and other social behaviors; to help us become more complete humans.

3. Homo sapiens vs. Humans

It's worth understanding this word "human" as a qualitative and honorific adjective to describe the presence of decency, compassion, and moral courage—the *social* qualities—that we respect and should aspire to. *Homo sapiens,* the designation of our species, is biological. We all share that DNA. But it represents only the *possibility* of humanity. All the best religions and philosophies have existed to try and point us, tweak us, get us beyond our smallness and toward building ourselves into more complete humans.

We're all *Homo sapiens*: Hitler, Pol Pot, Ted Bundy, Mother Teresa, MLK, all serial rapists and killers, saints, the best and worst people you can imagine. We all have the same DNA, all evolved from over 20 varieties of *hominid* species: *Neanderthal, Australopithecus, Atlanthropus, Ardipithecus, Denisovans, Homo sapiens*, etc. But that's not what we mean by the word *humans*. Being a *Homo sapiens* is just the basic potential for becoming human. It's like the difference between caterpillars and butterflies, or tadpoles and frogs. Both pairs share the same DNA, but are dramatically different creatures. And notice, we are much fonder of butterflies and frogs than caterpillars and tadpoles. It's worth making the distinction between *Homo sapiens* and Humans and realizing we are much fonder of Humans, and have a chance and obligation to grow from mere *Homo sapiens* into fully human beings.

With an intelligent use of the symbol "God", God symbolized the wholeness that's always beyond us. When we don't know that, we exalt our idols, our ideologies and theologies, etc. If we don't grow beyond our reptilian narcissism, we do not develop into what, throughout our history and in almost all cultures, we have recognized as what it means to be fully human. That would make us, by definition, subhuman. We seldom see this distinction made in this way, but it's important and clear.

The "human"

Think of other words showing that we are aware of this distinction: inhumane, dehumanizing, subhuman, sociopathic, psychopath ("sick soul"). Or humble, humility, sharing the same root as human. We can't be fully human without them. Or think of the ways in which we use a word like *subhuman*. What do we mean by it? What qualities of character do we think are missing in a *Homo sapiens* member we would describe as subhuman? The point here is that being considered a good example of a Human involves incorporating the deeper and more loving and empathetic *social species* qualities that are needed to become a more full and complete person, a memorable example of humanity, a good Human. Some of the most important and memorable experiences in our lives are those that opened doors to this deeper and higher quality of human existence.

Some free associations here:

I often think of the New Testament class I took as a college sophomore, taught by that very liberal Jesuit. He said the key words and concepts in the Bible were best understood as symbols and metaphors of far deeper and more existentially constructive traits and behaviors: loving your neighbor as yourself, the Golden Rule, and so forth. That was the first time in my life I had heard religion, or the Bible, taught that way, and it was one of the seeds that grew into my own eventual graduate education in religion, and 23 years as a liberal minister.

I'm forever grateful for my 43 months in the Army, when I learned how it felt to be serving something larger than myself and my private world. I'm convinced that we would have a much healthier country if there were a universal draft for both men and women. It could be in the military, or something like the old Peace Corps and Vista, or two years of working with inner-city challenges, and so on.

Another memorable and powerful experience came many years later while finishing my doctoral studies at the University of Chicago. It was that seminar with Stephen Toulmin, who had been Wittgenstein's most influential student, and the first megamind genius I had met. Stephen taught us that in order to earn the right to criticize someone with whom we disagree, we must first be able to present their case with an understanding, depth, and breadth that they would *applaud*. Only then have we earned the right to criticize them. I thought then, and still think, that this was the paradigm of a liberal education—or just an *education*.

You will be thinking of some of the reading, experiences, and mentors in your life that opened these doors for you. It's a different set for each person. But, as you also know, it's an essential set, as finding a way to open these doors to an appropriately humbling re-evaluation of ourselves and the larger world around us is what's involved in becoming more fully human.

CLOSING ARGUMENT

"Becoming a citizen of the world is often a lonely business. It is,
in effect, a kind of exile — from the comfort of assured truths, from the
warm nestling feeling of being surrounded by people who share one's
convictions and passions."[274]

If only the world were as pure and holy as I am, it could be perfect![275]

Don't worry about what other people think. Most of them don't.[276]

I've called this a Closing Argument because I want you to view it as the closing argument in a criminal trial, in which the arguments of the case are summarized. I believe our liberal betrayal of education, the media, politics, human/race relations, and religion is absolutely criminal. Understand that I'm not attacking liberals (most of my friends are liberals, as I am) but the *ideology* of liberalism: the beliefs, not the believers. I want to recap the evidence presented, bring it together into a summary argument, and let you decide, as a jury member would, about the guilt or innocence of the "betrayers" as well as the nature and severity of damage done by the betrayals.

Throughout this book, I've argued that the several facets of the behavior of liberalism are all parts of our *religion*—the secular religion that liberals adopted as our successor to the

---

[274] *Cultivating Humanity*, by Martha Nussbaum, p. 83.

[275] Silently believed by too many anonymous people to count.

[276] This follows from the previous footnote.

omniscient Biblical God and the supernatural reward of an eternal Heaven for those whose behaviors qualified them for "salvation". Traditionally, that word has been interpreted supernaturally: our eternal presence in Heaven with God, the angels, and all of our favorite people. Many liberals outgrew or denied any such notion of "eternal". The kind of "salvation" we hope for is a salvation based more on the shared root with the word "salve"—a healthy kind of wholeness here, now, and in the memory of those who knew us or were touched by our character and our actions.

We need, more desperately than we admit, a convincing assurance that we will have this. The most important way in which we pursue this goal is through the utopianism to which liberals have been drawn for two centuries (though the spirit of utopian fantasy goes back to Plato and, before him, to Lycurgus and Sparta). As William J. Murray has written:

> Utopians running for office promise a perfect and equal life for all. Rather than simply promising equal opportunity, however, they guarantee the unobtainable goal of an equal outcome for everyone. Once utopians are in power, their inability to deliver an equal outcome leads very quickly to totalitarianism because their utopian vision requires central control of all resources.[277]
>
> THE DYSTOPIAN REALITY. Thomas More's Utopia inspired many future thinkers and science fiction writers to create their own versions of utopian—or dystopian—societies. Contriving idealized and perfect societies in fiction is harmless, but the evil results become clearly evident when a utopian zealot attempts the creation of such a society in real time in a real world. What inevitably ensues

---

[277] William J. Murray. *Utopian Road to Hell: Enslaving America and the World with Central Planning.* WND Books, 2016, p. 7.

is a hideous Dystopia, not a Utopia. People die, produc-
tivity is killed, and human freedom is extinguished, often
for decades or longer.[278]

Liberals reject checks and balances and any other re-
strictions in the Constitution designed to protect Ameri-
cans from a despotic government, particularly those pro-
vided to the states and the people. In Progressive elitist
thinking, most Americans are too stupid to self-govern
and need an army of bureaucrats and social engineers to
herd them like sheep to do whatever the statists think is
good for them.[279]

A second way, shallow though also destructive, is through
the Politically Correct categories involving our group's ideas
of racism, sexism, and "white supremacy" detailed in Chapter
Two. The important realization is that none of these is an accurate description of today's culture in the real world, and all
are being intentionally and cynically used to destroy healthy
social bonds and help weaken our society for the planned socialist take-over that's already in progress, at both national
and international levels.

Building a utopia rather than a dystopia would require the
omniscience of a God. We don't believe in such a thing, so instead of God's wisdom, we have substituted our *own*. We believe that only *we* can bring about this utopia, which would
also mark our "salvation" at a high level. Of course, all socialisms have failed miserably. And, of course, we liberals don't
have the wisdom needed. No one ever has, and history shows
that the closest we're likely to come to an ideal government is
democracy, combined with some form of capitalism that recognizes and rewards differences in individual abilities, ambitions, and efforts. Even China, still a totalitarian socialist

---

[278] Ibid., p. 38.
[279] Ibid., p. 236.

government, has abandoned socialism's failed top-down controlled economy and embraced broad and successful varieties of capitalism.

At the bottom, most of us really know there is no utopia coming. Thomas More coined the word for the title of his 1516 book. He made the word out of Greek word parts: *topos,* meaning *place,* and the prefix *U,* which means *no* or *not:* in a word, utopia means *nowhere,* and most of us know that's the case. More honestly (and obviously), our striving for a socialist, totalitarian society is really a striving for the political power to rule over both the liberal and conservative ignorant masses, to whom we love comparing ourselves. Historically, socialism is always and only about power, not utopia. The utopian promises are just bait to entrap the gullible masses, the naïve herd. It is our duty to rule. Plato believed this, and our actions show that we do too.

But religions, including our secular liberal religion, must be judged by the quality of the ideals that believers have served, and the effect of their actions in the real world. Healthy and admirable education, the media, politics, human/race relations, and religion must always and only be defined by the very highest ideals: *realistic* ideals, not just in the Second Culture, but ungrounded ideas and ideologies we've exalted in our love of abstractions. Both of Antaeus' feet must be grounded: both the First and Second Cultures. This is also a good definition of democracy.

The lower the ideals and principles, the farther from "ideal" and closer to "abysmal" or miserable the endeavor will be judged by those forced to live in it or looking back at it. Virtually *everything* is at stake for believers depending on their beliefs to lead them to salvation—whether that's considered supernaturally or existentially. And trying to play God has always made us look like fools, demons, and clowns.

However, and this is a central point, there are *two* distinct categories of belief, action, and result to be considered:

1. The quality of the *endeavors*: the education, media, politics, human/race relations, and religion we have created and what serving low values has done to them.

2. More deeply and permanently, we must consider the quality of the *humans* we have helped to create. We are acting out these values in all five areas, during the first 25 years of our young people's lives, while their *character* is being formed and fixed. Good education, religion, and the rest can help create good, healthy people: admirable, full humans. Over half of our character—our deep and permanent *style* of being and doing—is genetic, but the remainder is forged by our education, religion, mentors, and experiences in the first quarter-century of our lives. This includes the most influential experiences, thinkers, and positive and negative memories and mentors of our first two dozen years. In other words, many of the most powerful things that shape and harden the character of our young people come through their *education*. Considering the damage we liberals have done to American education—K-12 and the vast majority of our colleges and universities—that should terrify all of us.

Scientists and medical doctors know that our ability to do symbolic and metaphorical thinking, and to understand it, is done in the hippocampus and the right pre-frontal neocortex of our brain. They also know that around our mid-twenties, the prefrontal cortex *myelinates* or becomes enclosed and no longer open to formative influences as it had been earlier.

Our character becomes essentially fixed by our mid-twenties.
Now how important do you think our education is?

And looking back on the utter breakdown of our education since being taken over and redefined by liberal activists, starting in the late 60s and becoming widespread and dominant in the 80s and 90s, what do you think it has done to our future generations? The student (and faculty) shout-downs of speakers whose ideas, research, and conclusions threaten activism's simple-minded delusions are done by people who are showing their *character*, their *essence*, which is not likely to change—ever.

What miserable humans we have helped to create.

Chris Hedges believes "the liberal class" really ended over a century ago, with World War I.[280]

By the time Cold War liberalism shifted into a liberal embrace of globalization, imperial expansion, and unfettered capitalism, the ideals that were part of classical liberalism no longer characterized the liberal class.[281]

Perhaps the worst offender within the liberal class is the Democratic Party. The party consciously sold out the working class for corporate money.[282]

The liberal class has become a useless and despised appendage of corporate power.[283]

Hedges describes how liberals no longer include enough iconoclasts with the necessary moral courage to reform the class, how they stripped away the country's manufacturing base, disempowering the workers, how corporations have 35 thousand lobbyists in Washington and thousands more in state capitals that use corporate money to buy our political system and write legislation that favors the corporations. It's a good book for those interested in this subject.

---

[280] Chris Hedges, *Death of the Liberal Class*. Nation Books, 2010, p. 7.
[281] Ibid., p. 8.
[282] Ibid., pp. 10-11.
[283] Ibid., p. 12.

So: Let's look at the consequences of our betrayal of these five key endeavors during the past 50-200 years.

Education

"Education is a system of imposed ignorance." [284]

Here, decades of mindless activism's destruction of most of the highest ideals of education is a life-altering betrayal whose cost we're just starting to realize. We trust education to lead our young people into bigger identities and lives than they might have had without it. Instead, the radical liberal activists in Tom Hayden's SDS planted seeds that grew into the anti-educational activism that has changed our universities from educational institutions into anti-intellectual places to turn students into activists, programming them to become obedient little socialist drones with no significant education, taught to hate the US and endorse the shallowest and most destructive and self-serving sort of liberal racism and sexism I've seen in my lifetime. More independent and uninfected thinkers who see beyond their shallow activist drivel are attacked, shouted down like modern heretics, and forbidden even to *think* healthy, informed, or realistic thoughts.

In his recent essay "The New Segregationists of the Left", professor Thomas DiLorenzo offers these insights:

"Having been a university economics professor for 41 years, I am sometimes asked how college students—and the university world in general—has changed over the years. One response that I give is that when I started out I noticed that the campus Marxists—who had become academics not because they wanted lives as intellectuals but as political activists in tenured jobs—would capture or corral about say, five or ten percent of the incoming students and convince

---

[284] Noam Chomsky, *Manufacturing Consent.*

*them to become left-wing campus rabble rousers instead of
spending their time educating themselves. Uneducated,
sanctimonious, loud-mouthed spouters of leftist platitudes,
in other words, just like their Marxist professors. Today, I
would say that a strong majority of college students would
fit into that category, not just five or ten percent.*

*"The reason for this is that cultural Marxism has in-
fested the lower levels of education, beginning with elemen-
tary school. Today, most college freshmen have already been
relentlessly subjected to the constant repetition of Marxist
platitudes for 12 years. I have had students who just could
not comprehend the simplest, most basic concepts in economics, but could give a two-hour oration about global
warming, how 'diversity is our strength', or virtually any
other left-wing fad. They have been taught that to reject the
platitudes of the Left makes one an enemy of society and, of
course, a racist. If you're wondering why so many college
students claim that they prefer socialism to economic freedom, this is it. This, and the fact that they were never taught
a single thing about socialist reality in particular and economics in general".*[285]

It's not said often enough that this has stunted and deformed the character of tens of millions of students: the generations constituting our future, a significant percentage of
college graduates under the age of 50, including most journalists. The destructive power of this cannot be overstated.

Education, in Tom Hayden's SDS plan, is the basis of all
the other betrayals and disasters. He believed that the only
way the SDS students and faculty could take over the culture
and government of the US was by taking over the colleges,
universities, then all public education in the country. And in
the six decades since then, the radical liberal activists he

---

[285] "The New Segregationists of the Left" by Thomas DiLorenzo, July 21,
2021. https://www.lewrockwell.com/2021/07/thomas-dilorenzo/the-new-
segregationists-of-the-left/

sanctioned have done it, replacing education with indoctrination and replacing understanding with ignorant but energetic activism. Again, we have betrayed the high ideals of education and replaced them with their enemies.

The subject really isn't education. It's liberalism's new religion, our replacement for God and Heaven: what we're serving with our lives and our gifts that can give us a fulfilling meaning. After all, what are we serving if not God and Heaven? It's a huge vacuum to try and fill. We chose a socialist utopia here and now almost two centuries ago as the real-world substitute for the eternal but mythical Heaven. Because of our education—our diplomas and our self-anointed elitism as Plato's philosopher-rulers (Confucius's Princelings)—we have an arrogance that lets us envision utopia in ways the masses can't—as Plato saw 2,400 years ago. Only we can do this, which means we must have a form of government that gives us the necessary power, and keeps it away from the ignorant common people (again, both liberal and conservative) who would try to impede the utopia they can't understand. The established words for this one-party rule are socialism, communism, and totalitarianism. It's the only reason liberals are pushing and propagandizing the socialism that has failed miserably and murderously everywhere it has been tried. We're sure that we are smarter than all the people who have failed so disastrously over the past century. Amazing.

And when *education* is replaced by *reduction and seduction* during the first 25 years or so when our character is being formed and fixed for the rest of our lives, it's not the teachers or administrators who suffer—unless they really had high ideals they just didn't act on. No, the victims are young people whose fraudulent education leaves them—perhaps for life—uneducated, small, unable to question or think well, incapable of seeing shallow ideologies and narcissistic solipsism for the terminally trivializing and dehumanizing values that they are.

Low and irresponsible education can turn them into fools and clowns, embarrassments to themselves, their society, and the only race we should be identifying people as parts of: the *human* race.

These are sins and crimes against humanity that should be seen as unforgivable. They must be corrected, or our culture is doomed.

We have destroyed education in America. Doing so has almost certainly guaranteed that China, not the USA, will become the next world superpower—and probably by 2035, the year they have already set for it. Studies of our colleges like that done by John Ellis in *The Breakdown of Higher Education*[286] are very depressing and suggest that the *majority* of both professors and college administrators are too incompetent and cowardly to educate anyone, and would have to be replaced else we keep defrauding and sabotaging the education and the character of our future generations: a recipe for cultural suicide. I can't see any realistic and hopeful possibilities here. The teachers' union owns the political parties (especially Democratic), and they would fight to the death for a continuation of the status quo (and their own job security).

The Media

Journalism majors are among the humanities and liberal arts majors who have been the most eagerly seduced by our liberal utopian activists. Their simple-minded depictions of reality and utopia sound exciting! It can mean that journalists who serve as bullhorns for the Left are, like their leaders, genuine Messiahs, saviors of the race, the nation, the world, and the planet itself! Wow! It can also make great stories that attract

---

[286] Ellis, John M. *The Breakdown of Higher Education: How It Happened, the Damage It Does, and What Can Be Done.* Encounter Books (August 10, 2021).

new readers and please advertisers. As such, the media have mostly become those bullhorns (pun intended) for the radical activist propaganda which has caused so much destruction in our society and the world. For decades, journalists have fancied themselves not merely as "reporters", but as active agents in saving America from conservatives and converting our masses to the utopian one-party rule which alone, they've been trained to believe, can turn our country into the legitimate heir to the mythical Heaven of the non-existent God.

Golly!

Victor Davis Hanson at Stanford University's Hoover Institution has written a short piece on this point titled "The Lethal Wages of Trump Derangement Madness" (June 6, 2021). (If the title made you instantly angry, you have it.) He says of liberal politicians, writers, and the media, *"in their uncontrolled aversion and detestation, they suspended all the rules of empiricism, logic, and rationality—and people died as a result. ... The result of such knee-jerk revulsion was a great deal of damage to the country in general and unnecessary deaths of Americans in particular."* Specifically, he cites the almost universal attacks by liberal politicians and media on the drug hydroxychloroquine as a very inexpensive, safe, proven treatment for Covid-19 simply because Trump recommended it. But now a new study conducted at the Saint Barnabas Medical Center in New Jersey has found "that when the dosages of hydroxychloroquine were calibrated and adjusted by patient weight, and fortified by the antibiotic azithromycin, there was a more than 100 percent increase in survival rates among Covid-19 patients—without any correlation to heart arrhythmias". Dr. Stephen Smith, of the nonprofit Smith Center for Infectious Diseases and Urban Health, recently argued that "perhaps 100,000 lives might have been saved had the medical guild not demonized the drug and utterly dismissed it". The drug had formerly been hailed by the United Nations as an essential medicine, especially in poor countries, for its dirt-cheap cost, effectiveness, and general safety. This is the "Trump derangement syndrome" infecting the media, politics, and politically-linked medical authorities (like Dr. Fauci) at the possible cost of 100,000 American lives. None of these groups was acting under the high standards of their field. All had betrayed those in order to preach hatred of a politician and President who accused them (rightly, in many cases) of creating "fake news".[287] Since we're talking about the *religion* of liberals in all areas here, it's easy to see the deep threat such an accusation carries. If our news is fake, we are fake, our religion is fake, our delusion of serving noble or holy ideals is fake, and the notion that our lives are pursuing a decent, honest, and healthy purpose—all this is fake.

As a more empirical corrective to journalists' delusion that they are rooted in reality rather than merely ideology, remember the studies cited in *Left Turn*:

> In at least one important way journalists are very different from the rest of us—they are more liberal. For instance, according to surveys, in a typical presidential election Washington correspondents vote about 93-7 for the Democrat, while the rest of America votes about 50-50.[288]

> As my results show, if we could magically eliminate media bias, then American political values would mirror those of the states of Kansas, Texas, and South Dakota. They also include Orange County, California, and Salt Lake County, Utah.[289]

> My results suggest that media bias aids Democratic candidates by about eight to 10 percentage points in a typical

[287] Victor Davis Hanson, "The Lethal Wages of Trump Derangement Madness", June 6, 2021, in FedUpPAC.org, June 8, 2021 or VDH's Blade of Perseus (https://victorhanson.com)
[288] *Left Turn*, p. vii.
[289] Ibid., p. viii.

election. I find, for instance, that if media bias didn't exist, then John McCain would have defeated Barack Obama 56-42 instead of losing 53-46. [290]

Politics

We should start by remembering that neither liberals nor conservatives are right. They're just liberals and conservatives, limited by the blinders on their partial and inadequate ideologies. J.S. Mill put it well a century and a half ago, as he did with so many things:

"He who knows only his own side of the case, knows little of that." [291]

"Both teachers and learners go to sleep at their post as soon as there is no enemy in the field." The student must therefore "be able to hear [the arguments] from people who actually believe them, who defend them in earnest, and do their very utmost for them. He must know them in their most plausible and persuasive form."

"It is in a great measure the opposition of the other that keeps each within the limits of reason and sanity." Where there are no right-of-center voices to keep the left healthy, the result will inevitably be a much more extreme and self-indulgent political culture. [292]

Mill spoke of the need for a culture of "order and stability" (what C.P. Snow has called the First Culture) and a culture of "progress and reform" (the Second Culture) and believed that those must balance and complement each other in order to have a healthy and stable society (or a healthy and stable *character*).

---

[290] Ibid., p. ix.
[291] John Ellis, *The Breakdown of Higher Education* (2020), p. 36.
[292] Ibid., pp. 37-38.

Like the two feet of Antaeus, both parties must be well-grounded. Both parties must be judged primarily on how they treat each other and what they accomplish working together: "Love even your enemies". It's not about dictating to those whose certainties differ from ours; it's about learning to see and treat them as our moral and human equals. It's about humility, about what kind of world—and what kind of humans—we are helping to create.

Don't underestimate the effects of an education no longer ranked anywhere near the top quarter in the world, which is concerned not with education but with the conversion of students to what, in retrospect, is little more than hollow liberal activism, preparing them to become obedient servants in a socialist dystopia. Anything that challenges or disproves those simple beliefs is treated as religions have for centuries treated *heresy*.[293]

These "heretics"—in all times and places—aren't just considered wrong by the orthodox, but *evil* as well. They must be stopped, one way or another. Again, suffer through the widely criticized invective of Maxine Waters, who directed Democrats to openly attack their Republican opponents:

> *"You think we're rallying now? You ain't seen nothing yet," Waters said at the event, "Already you have members of your Cabinet that are being booed out of restaurants—protesters taking up at their house saying 'no peace, no sleep.' If you see anybody from that Cabinet in a restaurant, in a department store, at a gasoline station,*

---

[293] Remember, heretics aren't necessarily bad or wrong. They have just chosen options outside the box of choices approved by the dominant orthodoxy: the Church, Democrats, Republicans, pacifists, Nazis, and all the rest. Also remember that every advance in every field has been made by the people who wouldn't be limited by the choices of those around them. Without our heretics, we would still believe what Neanderthals did 40 thousand years ago.

you get out and you create a crowd and you push back on them and you tell them they're not welcome anymore, anywhere."[294]

Perhaps surprisingly, the downright rude treatment of conservatives by Maxine Waters, and nearly hysterical and physically dangerous treatment by liberal college students and professors, liberal ministers, and the liberal Antifa and BLM rioters toward anyone who says the liberals are wrong—this seems to go back nearly two centuries. To what extent might this be due to the fact that when liberals lost belief in a God who loved them, and who considered *all* people to be His children, they lost the essential humanity and humility needed to be healthy and constructive parts of human society?

History shows a great and categorical difference between some liberals and conservatives who don't agree. Some conservatives may consider their opponents to be good people holding wrong beliefs. But others—the liberals, the activists, the anointed—condemn and damn the people and their opinions. When Malthus attacked a popular vision of his time, exemplified in the writings of William Godwin and Condorcet, he said: *"I cannot doubt the talents of such men as Godwin and Condorcet. I am unwilling to doubt their candor."* Yet Godwin's response was quite different. He called Malthus "malignant", questioned "the humanity of the man", and said, "I profess myself at a loss to conceive of what earth the man was made".[295] This fits well with our treating these anointed visions as our religion, and as the successor to God.

This asymmetry in arguments reflected an asymmetry in visions that has persisted for centuries. When Friedrich Hayek's *The Road to Serfdom* attacked the welfare state and

---

[294] https://www.vox.com/2018/6/25/17501450/maxine-waters-trump-pelosi-civility-sarah-sanders. Article by Li Zhou, updated June 28, 2018.
[295] *The Vision of the Anointed*, p. 3.

socialism in 1944, he characterized his adversaries as "single-minded idealists" and "authors whose sincerity and disinterestedness are above suspicion", but his own book was treated as something immoral, which some American publishers refused to publish.[296] A contemporary writer has summarized the differences between those with the vision of the anointed—the Left—and others this way:

> Disagree with someone on the right and he is likely to think you obtuse, wrong, foolish, a dope. Disagree with someone on the left and he is more likely to think you selfish, a sell-out, insensitive, possibly evil.[297] (Again, this is describing a religion, not just a political view. It's what we replaced Biblical religion with two centuries ago.) But why then do we sound so desperate? Is it because our replacements for God have never let us feel loved, worthwhile, essential?

Problems exist because others are not as wise or as virtuous as the anointed.[298]

Thomas Sowell points to the self-endorsed moral exaltation of the anointed above others, who are to have their very different views nullified and superseded by the views of the anointed, imposed via the power of government.[299]

I'll repeat an insightful list from Dr. Rossiter's critique of the ungrounded nature of so many of liberalism's "wise" prescriptions for society. Liberals can be so easily seduced by grand abstractions—ending hunger, for example—that they forget, or don't care, that without the knowledge and ability to

[296] Ibid., pp. 3-4.
[297] Ibid., p. 4, quoting Joseph Epstein, "True Virtue," *New York Times Magazine*, November 24, 1985, p. 95.
[298] *Vision of the Anointed*, p. 5.
[299] Ibid.

change dozens of real-world situations, their grand abstractions are just rainless little cloudbursts:

One of the most striking characteristics of modern liberalism, whether benign or radical, is the actual vagueness of its social policies despite their apparent nobility of purpose. A typical "progressive" liberal platform, for example, will announce its goals to be the eradication of hunger, poverty, ignorance, disease, faulty childcare, material inequality and political oppression. The platform will dedicate itself to the provision of adequate jobs, housing, nutrition, education, social harmony and medical care. But in the real world, attempting to reach even one of these goals is a colossal undertaking, whose difficulties the liberal agenda never adequately spells out for review. Consider, for example, the announcement of a program whose intent is to end starvation in a single third world country.

Questions of the following type must be answered with verifiable facts and proven or at least plausible strategies if the program is to succeed:

1. *What is the history of the problem? When and for what reasons did the starvation begin?*
2. *Has the country ever been able to feed itself? How?*
3. *How do weather factors affect the problem?*
4. *What has made the problem better or worse?*
5. *What are the economic, social, political, religious, legal and ethnic factors affecting the problem and any realistic attempts at solving it?*
6. *What are the logistical problems in providing food to the population?*
7. *Who will provide the food? Who will grow it, collect it, preserve it, record its type and amount, ship it?*
8. *Who will ensure that the food is preserved and edible when it arrives for consumption?*

9. *How and by whom, and at what cost will it be received and distributed to those in need?*

10. *Who will administer the program? How will corruption and graft be prevented?*

11. *How and by whom will all phases of the program be funded, and how much will it cost?*

12. *How will providing food to the target population affect them socially, psychologically, politically?*

13. *What are the attitudes of the people toward the program?*

14. *Will anyone, especially politically positioned persons, object to the program?*

15. *Will anyone attempt to thwart it? Assist with it?*

16. *Who will benefit financially and politically from the program? How much?*

17. *Who will be harmed by the program?*

18. *How long is the program to continue?*

19. *Does the program incorporate a plan to make the population self-sufficient? What is it?*

20. *What are the medical consequences of the starvation to date?*

21. *What are the developmental consequences of the starvation?*

22. *What will be the incentive and disincentive effects of the program?*

23. *Toward what better uses, if any, could the funds, efforts and resources for the program be allocated?*

24. *What exit strategy will terminate the program?*

Verifiable facts and proven or plausible strategies to answer most of these questions will not be offered by anyone proposing a program of this type, and any such proposal is therefore meaningless for practical purposes.[300]

---

[300] *The Liberal Mind*, pp. 324-325.

So no, without the ability to answer these very grounded "First Culture" sorts of questions, the grand liberal abstraction of "ending starvation in a single third-world country" is no more than "moral narcissism"—which was its only real purpose anyway.

History records the failed objectives and destructive consequences of nearly all programs of these types. African dictators, for example, have gotten very rich on programs to end their country's poverty while the people continue to starve and live or die in squalor. In Chicago, the effort to enforce a right to adequate housing for the poor has had such disastrous economic and social effects that the projects had to be torn down. Despite history's negative report card on programs of this type, the true believer in the liberal agenda nevertheless presses ahead with "progressive" programs, ignoring their repeated failures. Meanwhile, the character of all the people— those to whom the state gives and those from whom it takes— is profoundly demeaned. The dignity and sovereignty of the individual are lost in the state's perverse ministrations to the collective social mass.[301]

Another brief summary will help in highlighting the essentially childlike nature of the liberal agenda. Through drastic government action, the radical liberal seeks the following:

- A powerful parental government to provide everyone with a good life and a caring presence;

- An elite corps of surrogate parents that will manage the lives of the people through approximately equal distributions of goods and services, just as real parents provide equally for the needs of their children;

- A guarantee of material security from the state, similar to that which a child extracts from his parents;

[301] Ibid., p. 326.

- A form of parental social justice that cures or mitigates all states of deprivation, inequality, suffering, and disadvantage;

- A guarantee that negative rights for the protection of individual liberty will yield to positive rights that reduce or eliminate inequalities of wealth, social status, and power, just as good parents would balance benefits to their children;

- Government laws that will punish the "haves" for their excesses and compensate the "have-nots" for the pangs of envy, just as good parents would do for their children;

- Government directives from wise and caring officials that channel the citizen's initiative and industry through social programs and tax incentives, just as wise parents determine the directions of the family's labors;

- Government policy that instructs the people in how to relate to each other politically, just as good parents instruct their children in how to conduct themselves properly;

- Permissive laws passed by sympathetic legislators that lower the obligations of contracts, ease codes of acceptable conduct, and relax the burdens of established institutions such as marriage and adoption procedures, just as indulgent parents would do;

- Government welfare programs that free the citizen-child from the duties of altruism, just as parents do;

- An international caring agenda that will enhance the family of nations by understanding everyone's hardships, tolerating destructive actions by others, and empathizing with aggressors to bring them to the negotiating table, just as good parents do in resolving family disputes. (331-332)

These and other goals dear to the modern liberal heart are remarkable for the childhood needs they address and the adult needs they ignore. What the radical liberal mind really longs for, as revealed in his political goals, is a child's relationship to a loving family whose caretaking compensates him for the injuries he suffered in his early years. He seeks all of this in the contemporary political arena. The major problem he faces is that a substantial portion of the population is still competent: it is a population that deeply reveres individual liberty, readily accepts its responsibilities, and passionately opposes its destruction. It is not about to yield to the liberal's mad dream.[302]

The great wisdom of democracy is that it is an acknowledgment that there is no utopia. There is no final truth here, and the most dangerous, arrogant, narcissistic people are those who think that they have the answers that should be made to rule everyone. The best we can do, as history has shown over and again, is a moving, sliding set of "operating instructions" for today, moderated by the changing, evolving opinions of many millions of people who are as smart, as decent, and as certain as we are. This is the genius of democracy: the word means rule by the *demos—the people.*

Those who think they alone have the answers that everyone should have to live by—our liberal utopians, for example— are really the ignorant masses who don't get it, and whose arrogance is one of the most dangerous and deadly certainties on Earth. This, in broad strokes, describes today's liberals. The irony, like the danger, could hardly be greater.

The high values of politics are about how citizens who will never agree on the best way to do things can treat each other so we can have a peaceful and efficient government: our

---

[302] Ibid., p. 332.

democracy—much like a healthy relationship or marriage, which also suffers terminally under authoritarian rule. The old Stoic idea of seeing ourselves as limbs on the much larger body of humanity is pointing in the right direction. So is our adoration of the caring and empathetic behaviors of so many other species of social animals, and the way we especially cherish dogs for their unconditional love.

Yet in place of this, we liberals have wanted—for about two centuries—communism or socialism. Both are totalitarian forms of government, which is our real desire. Plato wanted philosophers to rule because he seemed to think government was run by Truth, which he thought only philosophers had in abundance. Really, politics is run by *power*, and diplomas don't make us smart, just more articulate and—in some circles—fashionable. But the power, we insist, should go only to those who can see the truths that can help us create a here-and-now utopia. And that's us, we're sure: not the ignorant masses. (But remember the Wizard of Oz.) The original SDS students of the 1960s and their successors have not taught students about historical socialisms, because almost all of them have failed, and the few still hanging on—Cuba, Venezuela, Nicaragua, and North Korea—are some of the most miserable countries in the world. No one has the wisdom to design a utopia. Nor is utopia ever really the goal. Rather, our real goal is always the totalitarian control of all others. The goal is always power, disguised in whatever way might best fool the liberal and conservative masses.

Betraying the highest ideals in any area is dangerous, immoral, unethical, and possibly deadly. In religion, substituting ideology for ontology means that no religion is even *possible* in that atmosphere. In politics, trying to convert the US democratic form of government to socialism is a dangerous and deadly act of *treason*. The goal, always, is to gain power through convincing—then coercing—others to surrender their power to us. And we're doing it. But it's a con, and the most aware among our liberals have known it all along.

Alexandria Ocasio-Cortez's former chief of staff, Saikat Chakrabarti, has admitted that "the Green New Deal is not about climate change ... the true motivation is to overhaul the entire economy".[303] It would cost an estimated $93 trillion over ten years, guaranteeing our government's control and enslavement of all our formerly free citizens. Again, this totalitarian rule is always the goal, and has been since before Tom Hayden stated it explicitly in the *Port Huron Statement* of his SDC group in 1962 at the University of Michigan.

Liberal Racism

When liberal racists disguise their racism as its opposite, when we define others by their race rather than their humanity—because doing so provides us with token victims who let us feel virtuous for speaking for and pretending to care about them—the racists don't suffer. We get our virtuous feelings and are sure we're a blessing to the larger world around us. But by defining the others by their differences, by their race, and by using unproductive policies like affirmative action and racial preferences, we have defined these minorities as second-rate humans, inherently and permanently inferior to us, making their race their destiny, and making it terribly hard for them ever to feel the sense of worth and self-respect without which any real personal or professional success will be highly unlikely.[304]

---

[303] By Jack Crowe, July 12, 2019, in *National Review*.
[304] Again, see some of the works by bright, informed, reasonable and logical black authors like Shelby Steele, Thomas Sowell, Walter E. Williams, Jason L. Riley, John McWhorter, Candace Owens, Justice Clarence Thomas, and others.

Remember the most important questions for all religions and life-guiding philosophies:

Who, at my best, am I?

How should I live, so that when I look back, I can be glad I lived that way? [305]

Our choice of ideology, belief, and behavior demands an awareness of and obedience to those ultimate questions.

The self-serving hypocrisy of liberal racism is that it champions political rather than individual approaches to race which have done deep and lasting harm to black people—while letting liberals feel virtuous (like the activists). We approach racism as we approach education: with political rather than individual concerns. All this fits with our religious mission to gain power over the country and, we dream, the world.

To overstate it a bit, liberals must simply be removed from any significant positions of power and influence over others in these important areas. We are so desperate for a feeling of virtuous righteousness that we seem certain to keep following our sociopathic activists, defining minorities by their *differences* from us: race, sex, gender orientation, and the rest. We have been deeply dehumanizing racists since the days when virtually all slave owners were Democrats, and the days when Southern Democrats formed the KKK as an angry militant group determined to use violence to keep black people from voting.[306] Our liberal racism still views blacks as things to use: as pets and Sambo dolls, in Shelby Steele's painful but de-

---

[305] I have reduced the key existential questions to these two. It's my wording, but it's true in all the religions I know of.

[306] For example, see *Wrong on Race: The Democratic Party's Buried Past*, by Bruce Bartlett (MacMillan 2008).

scriptive analogies.[307]

The fact that educated white people—liberal *ministers*, no less!—have declared the use of intelligent reason and logic forbidden because we believe black people can't keep abreast is one of the most depressing and despicable examples of dehumanizing and infantilizing racism I've ever heard.[308] The answer, as religions at their best know, is to define all people by our *similarities*, not our differences. There is only one race to which we all belong: the *human* race. Succeeding in any field requires what it always has: commitment, some intelligence, reason, talent, and hard work. Look at the successes of black athletes, musicians, and actors for examples. The standards are the same for everyone. Our eagerness to adopt black people as our token victims and little pets or Sambo dolls and define them by much lower expectations shows, I'm afraid, not only our paltry ideology but also our paltry character. We are not to be trusted.

Remember that we're a social species: herd animals. We follow the leaders of our kind of people, our herd, because—well, who could be more trustworthy than people like us? This makes us easy marks for con men, sociopathic women, politicians, advertisers, mobs of preachers, teachers, and all activists.

So yes, you play a role in this, and there are no neutral roles. You are either part of the solution, or you're part of the

---

[307] *White Guilt*, p. 134.

[308] This is painful to me because, while I never identified as a "Unitarian Universalist", I served churches affiliated with that denomination for 23 years. I did guest preaching at many other "UU" churches, was featured theme speaker for summer camps, and contributed some essays to the denomination's then-monthly (now quarterly) magazine. I wasn't aware at the time of this subculture, which has now—500 ministers?—apparently become the dominant culture.

problem. Naturally, we self-anointed liberals hope you're part of the *problem*, because it makes you part of our *solution*. It's the same way we hope you are seduced by ungrounded grand abstractions like Truth, Justice, White Supremacy, and all the rest, without ever checking with the real world to see how hollow, ungrounded, and destructive our Second Culture slogans usually are.[309]

Religion

Religion must embody the highest standards of all, because they will be—for better and worse—the values we "bind back to" for the rest of our lives. "Sin" comes from an ancient Hebrew archery term that meant "to miss the mark". Merely ideological religious values can miss the whole target. All serious religions must make their best effort to outline an ontology: their picture of how we can become our best version, and how we should live so that when we look back, we can be glad we lived that way. The focus is on our self-image, on how to be true to our best selves, and on how to behave toward others so that we might be a kind of blessing to them—or at least no worse than an indifferent presence. To take this seriously will always require significant moral courage, because many people in our herd—including most of the loudest voices—won't aim that high. This is about our "salvation"—our healthy wholeness—which we will either find here and now or nowhere and never. Could there be higher stakes?

When bad preachers and teachers hawk religions grounded in ideological or social fads rather than demanding notions of ontology, they still get their whole paychecks. The victims are

---

[309] See again Dr. Rossiter's list of real-world questions that must be answered in order to let grand abstractions like "feeding the hungry" have any grounded meaning at all.

in the pews and the families of people who trusted religion to give something of the highest caliber to help guide them. Instead, they were fed shallow values, simple-minded and faddish ideologies, incapable of grounding any full or noble life. Can you imagine going to church and being told by your minister that only white supremacists value logic and reason because black people aren't capable of them? That's what they have bound back to? That's beyond sad. It's tragic. It's also clownish.

LAUGHING THE CLOWNS OFF THE STAGE: THE STRATEGIC USE OF RIDICULE

One horselaugh is worth ten thousand syllogisms.[310]
Orwell long ago showed the way to one of the most potent methods of doing away with moral narcissism—unrestrained ridicule.[311]

The folly of our liberal betrayals would just be ridiculous if the betrayals weren't so destructive. But in figuring out how to diffuse them, it's worth remembering that they *are* ridiculous. These clowns need to be laughed off the stage, and the very best method of doing this may well be *ridicule,* as Mencken's line above suggests. Or consider this from Dr. Rossiter:

> Instead of promoting a rational society of competent adults who solve the problems of living through voluntary cooperation, the modern liberal agenda creates an irrational society of child-like adults who depend upon governments to take care of them. The liberal agenda undermines the character traits essential for individual liberty, material security, voluntary cooperation and social

[310] H. L. Mencken.
[311] George Orwell, *Animal Farm.* In Roger L. Simon's *I Know Best*, p. 182.

order.[312]

For all its avowed good intentions, the agenda's political operations are essentially sociopathic.[313]

Our betrayal of education and our youth should be slapped with thousands and thousands of class-action lawsuits targeting professors, colleges, and administrations. While just one or two such lawsuits would be ignored by the courts, a few thousand would have to be allowed to proceed, and might change the face of our education from inane to academic and intellectual again.[314]

Dealing with more specific areas of the farce can be done in more focused and fun ways. This is already happening.

Two professional ridiculers were Peter Boghossian and James Lindsay who, in 2017, published a paper in the academic journal "Cogent Social Science". Their peer-reviewed paper was titled "The Conceptual Penis as a Social Construct", which proposed that:

"The penis vis-à-vis maleness is an incoherent construct. We argue that the conceptual penis is better understood not as an anatomical organ but as a gender performative, highly fluid social construct."[315]

The only problem was that it was a hoax carried out by these two academics. Once the authors admitted to their hoax, the journal in question unpublished the piece. But the culprits have successfully repeated the exercise with other academic

---

[312] *The Liberal Mind: The Psychological Causes of Political Madness*, by Lyle H. Rossiter, Jr., M.D. (2006), p. 12.

[313] Ibid., p. 21.

[314] This may be unrealistically hopeful. What do you think?

[315] *The Madness of Crowds: Gender, Race, and Identity*, by Douglas Murray (2019) p. 61.

journals in the years since.[316]

In 2018, with the addition of Helen Pluckrose, the same academics managed to get a paper published in a journal of "feminist geography" titled "Human Reactions to Rape Culture and Queer Performativity at Urban Dog Parks in Portland, Oregon". This paper claimed that dog-humping in Portland parks was further evidence of the "rape culture" that many academics and students had by then begun to claim was the most perceptive lens through which to see our societies. Another paper published in a journal of "feminist social work" was titled "Our Struggle is My Struggle". There, the spoofers successfully managed to meld together passages from *Mein Kampf* and pastiches of feminist social-justice theory jargon and pass it off as an academic study.[317]

What makes our liberal culture silly enough to be laughed off the stage through informed and clever ridicule? Well, just consider some of this:

If you search on Google Images for "Gay couple", you will get row after row of photos of happy gay couples. They are handsome, gay people. Search for "Straight couple" by contrast and at least one to two images in each line of five images will be of a lesbian couple or a couple of gay men. Within just a couple of rows of images for "Straight couple" there are actually more photographs of gay couples than there are of straight men, even though "Straight couple" is what the searcher has asked for. The plural throws up an even odder set of results. The first photo for "Straight couples" is a heterosexual black couple, the second is a lesbian couple with a child, the fourth a black gay couple, and the fifth a lesbian couple. And that is just the first line. By the third line of "Straight couples" the results are solely gay. Then we have "Straight couples can learn from gay couples". Then a gay

---

[316] Ibid., p. 62.
[317] Ibid.

male couple with an adopted baby. And then just a photograph of a cute gay male couple from the gay luxury lifestyle magazine *Winq*. Why—just three lines down of images requested for "Straight couples"—is everyone gay?

Search for "Black family" and you will see smiling black families all the way down, without even a mixed-race family in sight. Type in "White family", on the other hand, and three out of the five images in the first line alone are either of a black or mixed-race family. Soon it is black family after black family. In the interests of weeding out human biases, humans have laced an entire system with biases using artificial intelligence programmed by biased humans.[318]

Then there's this: studies have shown that gay men and lesbian women consistently earn more on average than their heterosexual counterparts. There are a variety of possible reasons, not least the fact that most of them won't have children and can put in the extra hours at the office, which benefits both them and their employer. Is this a gay advantage? At what stage can heterosexuals claim that they are unfairly disadvantaged in the workplace? Should there be a "stepping back" by gay people to allow their straight contemporaries a better run at work opportunities?[319] Should this be attacked, maybe by shouting mobs of faculty, students, and religious liberals, as "Gay Supremacy"?

When liberal ideologues have invaded the real world with inanities and insanities like these, with student and faculty shout-downs of anyone who threatens to expose their childish delusions, when 500 people posing as ministers take self-righteous pride in excommunicating a minister who exposed

---

[318] Ibid., p. 119.
[319] Ibid., p. 242.

as racist and dehumanizing their prescribed denominational belief that

> "We recognize that a zealous commitment to 'logic' and 'reason' over all other forms of knowing is one of the foundational stones of White Supremacy Culture."[320]

It's too late for intelligent or informed arguments to register. The stage is filled with clowns who have declared that they own it. It's time for intelligent, creative, and grown-up people to come to the rescue, and the first step is laughing the clowns off the stage.

Okay, the ridicule was appropriate, necessary, and fun in a snarky way. But it doesn't bring us together, and thus doesn't solve the problem of what we can do together as a society seeking the best kind of government for people who will never agree on many of our basic values: religious or political.

SUGGESTIONS

I wanted to title this section **ANSWERS** or **SOLUTIONS**— maybe because, like many liberals, (a) I am easily seduced by, and really like, grand abstractions, and (b) Like many others, I'm often sure that I'm right, and that I see solutions most people miss. Yes, I like Plato, too (though I think "First Culture" Aristotle is a much better balanced and more trustworthy mega-mind).

---

[320] *The Gadfly Affair*, by Todd Eklof, p. 21. I keep mentioning this example partly because its racism is so clownish, and partly because I can hardly believe it.

But along the way in my life, I have also had experiences, mentors, and have learned skills that aren't grand or abstract but are grounded in the real world. I've learned to treasure these. Primarily, I credit the US Army for teaching me real-world leadership and strong bonding and identification with "my people". I learned that being an officer didn't make me a superior person—just like getting diplomas doesn't make us smart. It gave me a different job: to serve the larger mission while also serving and caring for the enlisted men (in 1964-67, it was men). There are officers who are so narcissistic they act like their rank—even the low rank of Lieutenant—makes them *superior* to those under their command. These are the officers—they're few but disgustingly memorable—who bark out orders and demand obedience just because they outrank their men. Here, they're like college graduates or academics who think their empty platitudes should be obeyed because they have diplomas. The technical term for this is *Bullshit*. Those are bad officers, poor leaders, and ungrounded academics.

The most fundamental mistake of history, and of our present political reality and culture, is the foolish and destructive belief that the ungrounded intellectuals—the Thinking Class, the Anointed, the Elites, the Best and Brightest, the Ruling Class, Tourists—are the rightful rulers of societies. Plato thought so because he was one of the greatest abstract thinkers, and because he hated democracy. But as brilliant and important as that great ancient Greek thinker has been, he was wrong on at least two fundamental points:

1. Plato thought philosophers should rule because they were smarter and wiser than "the masses"—the working people, like the roughly 70% of Americans who don't have college diplomas. History and common sense show that our diploma'd thinking classes have no such wisdom, and the fact that they are so

easily and often seduced by ungrounded grand abstractions screams that they/we should *not* be followed. A look at their own lives shows that—like the rest of us—they can almost never even put together one ideal life for themselves, and so should never be given the power to tell others how they must live.

2. Plato also thought that governments were ruled by wisdom (and he thought that philosophers *had* wisdom). But no, governments are ruled by power (and philosophers don't necessarily have or deserve any more power than anyone else).

But no one has the wisdom to construct a utopia. And giving people the power to do it will be deadly and miserable, never utopian. The best we can do is give the decisive gate-keeping power to the grounded *First Culture*, not the thinking class *Second Culture*. Thinkers do have an important role. We liberals can offer imaginative suggestions. These must make sense in the real world. And those judgments can only be made by the most grounded and wise people in the First Culture.

But boy, we liberals will fight like hell to keep our power and our pretense that we really *are* superior: the ordained, anointed holders of Wisdom and your rightful rulers! Any hope of moving toward a realistic successor to the impossible utopias begins with removing power from the Second Culture—liberalism—and placing it with the grounded people and sciences of the First Culture. We're betting you can't do it.

As a lifelong liberal, it hurts to say this, but for goodness' sake—and your own—*Don't vote for us. Don't give us power.* You see what we do with power, and we have no other choice. Maybe it would be different if we could believe things like "God loves us", "We're all children of God", and so on. But we mostly don't, and we haven't found an adequate or life-giving way to plug these holes. So, denied any divine love, respect, or sanction, we seek power and control. Our myth of a healthy and sustainable socialism will, we believe, fool enough of you to let us destroy the healthy bonds of the US society, and bankrupt it by taking away the power that keeps America afloat: nuclear, fossil fuel, everything that actually works. Estimates of the actual efficiency of solar and wind power have said that, *combined*, they can't produce more than about 3% of our power requirements—so that you will be utterly dependent on your Parental Government: on *us*.[321] [322] Then we will have a kind of forced respect that we desperately hope will make up for the loss of God, believing that He loves us and considers all of us His children. History says socialism won't work since it has never worked, and the roughly twenty socialisms have murdered an estimated 170 million of their own citizens. We don't care; we know we're smarter and wiser than everyone else who has constructed the socialist governments that have all failed so miserably and murderously. Don't underestimate our narcissism, and what liberal psychiatrist Lyle H. Rossiter diagnoses as our sociopathy.[323]

---

[321] For example, "Germany's investment in solar power makes no sense. Although they get the same amount of sunlight as Alaska, 800 hours a year, they have installed 50% of the global solar photovoltaic capacity. At a cost of eight billion euros a year, Germany is generating only 3% of its electricity via solar panels." Incredible. (*Roosters of the Apocalypse*, Rael Jean Isaac, 2013. p. 74.)

[322] "Fossil fuels (petroleum, natural gas, and coal) represent almost 82% of all energy used in America. Nuclear power provides 9% and hydroelectric power represents 2.5%. Of the renewable energy sources preferred by environmentalists, biofuels such as ethanol in gasoline represent 5%, wind power is 2%, and solar energy is only 0.5% of our energy total. Over 92% of the energy used for transportation is provided by petroleum. Natural gas and coal generate 64% of our electricity." *The Mythology of Global Warming*, p. 137. (There are many more such sources.)

[323] *The Liberal Mind*, p. 21.

CAN THERE BE AN ANSWER?

What *is* a realistic and healthy successor to utopia? Maybe just add one letter: **EUTOPIA**. The prefix EU means "good": so, not a perfect place (which is no place), but a "good place". Besides shifting the gatekeeper power to representatives of the First Culture,[324] what else should we be doing? Here are my suggestions, open to and inviting informed comments and criticisms:

TOWARD BUILDING A EUTOPIA

Government of the people, by the people, for the people,
shall not perish from the Earth.

You cannot escape the responsibility of tomorrow
by evading it today.

I am a firm believer in the people. If given the truth, they can be
depended upon to meet any national crisis. The great point
is to bring them the real facts.

We the people are the rightful masters of both Congress and
the courts, not to overthrow the Constitution but to overthrow
the men who pervert the Constitution.[325]

Remember this prescient statement about the duty of a teacher from the American Association of University Professors (AAUP) 1915 Declaration of Principles:

---

[324] No, I don't personally know how this could best be done. Do you? It's clear that it would have to involve informed and honest—non-political—input from experts covering the whole spectrum.
[325] All quotes from Abraham Lincoln.

"... and he should, above all, remember that his business is not to provide his students with ready-made conclusions, but to train them to think for themselves, and to provide them access to those materials which they need if they are to think intelligently. ... The teacher ought also to be especially on his guard against taking unfair advantage of the student's immaturity by indoctrinating him with the teacher's own opinions before the student has had an opportunity fairly to examine other opinions." [326]

People from both cultures can contribute facts and grounded data from the First Culture; ideas, imagination, and possibilities from the Second. HOWEVER: the decisions on what to use and adopt must come from the First Culture, not the Second. In other words, Imagination, fantasy, and ungrounded, untested ideas are not the ally of stability, health, and progress, but its enemy. Hollywood relies on them—democracy, not so much. This is the biggest and deepest change from the way our history has traditionally gone. Traditional education has exalted the liberal arts and humanities. But since the birth and growth of sciences in the past two centuries, the second culture has become less realistic, less relevant, less helpful, and much less optimistic.

Remember the flagrantly anti-American and anti-educational activism of Tom Hayden's SDS movement, which planted the seeds that have grown into such cannibalistic and treasonous anti-intelligent infestations of our colleges, universities, administrations, and public schools. Remember that their socialism is always and only about a play for power, and that neither these activists nor anyone else have the wisdom to plan any healthy or stable utopia. Remember that college faculties have been hiring ideological True Believers for four

---

[326] *The Breakdown of Higher Education,* p. 42.

decades now, along with mediocre thinkers and uncourageous administrators. The poison is broad and deep.

This would mean the loss of thousands of jobs for teachers and administrators. So it would be strongly opposed by their unions, which exercise immense political control. But we have reached the point where replacing them has become a healthy necessity.

We're a social species, and our education must include healthy socialization. Here too we need to consider a revolutionary restructuring of our education. We want the form and style of our education to model the kind of culture we want. What should we want?

A culture that recognizes only one race: the human race. Anything that defines people by their race is the very definition of racism and is profoundly dehumanizing.

A culture in which all people are morally and "humanly" equal. Yes, they will be wildly *unequal* in their gifts, abilities, interests, and the rest. Natural competition will sort them out as it does in sports, entertainment, business, and other parts of the real world. However, education should try to give them competence in whatever fields Nature/God/Chance has steered them toward.

But how to socialize our youth? Can they go through a continuing rotation of hands-on, healthy help to the larger society during, and as an essential part of, their education? Think of the Peace Corps, Vista, inner-city work, maybe in hospitals, etc.: *human* work, not partisan *political* work. During their education, they also learn to serve something bigger than they are: the healthy parts of a healthy society. The helpful and broad metaphors are the Stoic picture of us as limbs on the body of humanity, and of us in the middle of a lot of concentric circles.

But it's important that the social communities in which

students grow are microcosms of the EUTOPIA we can agree is grounded, realistic, and broadly desirable. It must be a community of optimism, competence, respect, challenge, and compassion, in which members are proud of who they are as a society: virtually the opposite of the hateful and negative images today's education has been teaching students for over four decades. Workers, thinkers, artists, athletes, and the rest should all be represented as unequally endowed human equals in the pool of classmates and friends throughout our education. With the thinking class in charge as it has been for centuries, a false and nonproductive hierarchy has been the rule, where the virtue-signaling thinkers are taught to see themselves as superior to the others. They're not. Remember John Stuart Mill's insights of over a century ago, worth repeating again and again:

> "He who knows only his own side of the case, knows little of that."[327]

> "Both teachers and learners go to sleep at their post as soon as there is no enemy in the field." The student must therefore "be able to hear [the arguments] from people who actually believe them, who defend them in earnest, and do their very utmost for them. He must know them in their most plausible and persuasive form."

> "It is in a great measure the opposition of the other that keeps each within the limits of reason and sanity." Where there are no right-of-center voices to keep the left healthy, the result will inevitably be a much more extreme and self-indulgent political culture.[328]

It is also critical that all students be made uncomfortable by being presented with ideas and beliefs contrary to their

---

[327] John Ellis, *The Breakdown of Higher Education* (2020), p. 36.
[328] Ibid., pp. 37-38.

own, and that they learn how to earn the right to criticize opinions with which they don't agree: again, the opposite of today's cancel cultures where unwelcome opinions are shouted down, forbidden, and the speakers are attacked.[329]

Student educations should be blended: college, trade school, apprenticeships, OJT, etc., mixed as they will be in society. They must also learn about the prevailing ideologies of the time. In other words, get rid of the activists and let education again rise above all ideologies and give students an informed overview. And against the background of betrayal of our education for the past two generations, it has become important to educate students about deceptions like con games, sociopaths, and toxic narcissists in education, politics, the media, human/race relations, and religion. We have invited many narcissists, activists, and sociopaths into all of our important endeavors. It's time to disinvite them and teach students the difference between healthy humanity and the selfish, willfully ignorant, narcissistic, and baldly sociopathic viruses always looking for ways to infect healthy bodies politic.

Students must be taught *honest* history of the US, not the hate-filled one. The US has been and remains a government admired and envied by most people on Earth. It has a tremendous amount of which to be justly proud. The faddish anti-American activism defining our collegiate and public education makes ignorant, nearly insane, accusations of Americans as inherently racist because a tiny percent of them—all Democrats—once owned slaves (virtually all slave-owners were Democrats). The ignorance here is breathtaking. Our country

---

[329] Again, see the comments Edward Luce made in *Financial Times* about how the current practice of "safetyism" in colleges, protecting students from any opinions that might upset them, does fundamental harm: *"Students are treated like candles, which can be extinguished by a puff of wind. The goal of a Socratic education should be to turn them into fires, which thrive on the wind. Instead, they are sheltered from anything that could cause offense...."*

was one of the countries embodying the Enlightenment values which *stopped* slavery around the world. And if blame is to be assigned for capturing and selling black Africans to many foreign countries as slaves for a thousand years, why not blame the people who captured and sold them: other black Africans? This liberal racism defines black people by their race and treats them as permanently inferior.[330] We need better informed and more honest education. Students must also be taught about the honest history and nature of socialism, communism, totalitarianism, and democracy. We embody the Enlightenment values. We are a great and justly proud country. Liberal racism, like the rest of the activist/socialist propaganda so prominent in education today, seems to let liberals feel virtuous at the expense of black people and others.[331]

Part of education is learning—in ordinary language an 18-year-old can understand—to respect and love all others. This does not need God-language, though these are traditionally religious teachings. But they can be expressed in ordinary language, and images like the Stoic metaphors. Churches can reinforce the lessons in their own vocabulary, as can secular groups, families, etc. But everyone must learn these religious, spiritual, ethical attitudes and behaviors as essential parts of becoming more fully human. Belief in gods is not necessary, and atheism doesn't excuse nonbelievers from this social and moral responsibility toward others.

The same high standards must be applied to everyone because that's the only way that success (and self-respect) can happen. This can also help form a country of equals. Not token equals. Human equals. This means education must be equal, safe, etc. (private schools, charter schools, and online education currently look most promising). The style of education

---

[330] See Shelby Steele's *White Guilt*, pages 39, 47, 56, 60 for example.
[331] As in the title of Jason L. Riley's *Please Stop Helping Us: How Liberals Make it Hard for Black People to Succeed*.

cannot be controlled by the teachers' unions.[332] No, we won't have equal *outcomes*. We are differently gifted.

We need a secular version of teaching our youth that we're all God's children, we're all products of Life's longing for itself, all children of the Earth, and so on. We have, at our best, souls that touch the universe and carry forward a sense of being in a community of equals, all beloved by the life forces that have brought us forth and will reclaim us in the end.

It's important to blend students of all kinds of education: laborers, nurses, craftsmen, thinkers, doctors, lawyers, police, firemen, etc. Let them learn what the others do and why their contributions are important. Let them learn healthy humility. They are all parts of the body of humanity and need to learn how to function as a body: workers, thinkers, artists, and the rest are all parts of the body and need to grow up in that context and model.

Some Closing Thoughts on Religion

I've tried to be clear that what's responsible for the destructive betrayal of so many dimensions of our society is our secular liberal *religion*. As a society, we have gradually but dramatically outgrown the narrowest interpretations of the supernatural Biblical religions that have been the spiritual spine of Western civilization for two thousand years. Granted that if everyone could see that, as my old Jesuit professor so memorably put it, "You *do* know these are *myths*, don't you?"—then our culture might simply have outgrown what Origen saw as the religion only meant for children, and grown into more adult and intelligent understandings of the deeper symbolic, ontological, ethical, moral, and spiritual dimensions of religion.

But that didn't happen. Speaking broadly, many con-

---

[332] *The Breakdown of Higher Education*, p. 122.

servatives in the First Culture did not—and were not taught how to—outgrow the literalism and see that these stories of gods, saviors, heavens, and hells are symbolic and mythic. That could free them from the stunted understandings of childhood and let the profound religious myths become windows into their heads and hearts throughout their lives.

And too many liberals, ironically, correctly saw them as myths, but ignorantly believed that "myths" were just false stories and lies that no smart person should take seriously at all, because only sciences—which few liberals understand very deeply—can tell us everything we need to know. Wittgenstein was closer to the truth when he said that when all scientific questions have been answered, they won't have touched life's human questions much at all. The irony is that these smart Second Culture liberals, like many First Culture conservatives, completely missed the essential, ontological depth of religion because—like Origen's "children"—they couldn't see beyond mere literalism.

For liberals, it meant they had lost—outgrown, or been too simplistic to see the existential and ontological depth of—a religion, a god, and any emotionally or intellectually convincing and comforting sense of salvation: healthy wholeness. That's what we have been—unsuccessfully—trying to replace for two centuries. Our actions have shown that we believe *we*—our intelligence, our diplomas, our special liberal wisdom—are the legitimate heir to God. No, we're not.

The grand abstractions that so easily seduce us—thinking our sacred duty is to serve Truth, Justice, Fairness, Compassion, and the rest (as only we understand them)—are illusions because we can't make them fit into the real world. Besides the varieties of liberal racism dealt with earlier, consider just two more ungrounded and dishonest grand abstractions that have done far more harm than good: "Open borders" and "Affirmative action".

"Open Borders". You know the argument: we should let everyone coming across our border from Mexico, Cuba, or South American countries enter the United States, give them education, medical care (through emergency rooms), and so on. This is hypocritical but also mindless. Hypocritical because the reason we are arguing for it is that once these illegal aliens come over, we believe they will feel obligated to vote for Democrats. And since liberals constitute only around 24% of the country while conservatives make up about 37%, we need all the votes we can get, however we can get them. No high ideals are being served here.

But if we were serious about the grand abstraction of open borders, then shouldn't we be advertising to all people of the world that they're welcome here, can get educated, get health care, and be able to vote (Democratic, of course. Otherwise, we'll call them traitors to their race, as we call black Republicans)? Why not bring in about four billion poor and hungry people and let our citizens pay for all this? The hypocrisy should embarrass us.

"Affirmative Action". Many black students are not adequately educated in our public schools to meet the academic admission requirements of our colleges. There are two major reasons for this. One is that a far higher percentage of black schools are offering very poor quality education and are far less safe. The other reason, as many have noted, is the self-destructive nature of "black culture". We mean by that the black ghetto culture, with its poor English, proud aversion to education, avoidance of work and ambition, and easy attraction to violence. This is terribly important. Thomas Sowell has written a very informative essay on this, which he titled "Black Rednecks and White Liberals", which is also the title of his 2005 book that contains this as the lead essay. Sowell's essay was derived from the 1988 book, *Cracker Culture: Celtic Ways* *in the Old South,* by Grady McWhiney. The tremendous irony here is that this culture did not begin in the black communities at all. It was a culture of many of the white Celtic immigrants from Northern Ireland who populated our South. Their slaves learned the language and the self-destructive culture from these whites, who eventually mostly outgrew it. But the black former slaves brought this way of talking and acting with them when they moved to our northern cities to find work. Unless we make black schools safe and their education high quality, and unless the self-destructive "Cracker Culture" of many ghetto blacks can be changed, there is no serious hope of giving our black citizens the quality of education that all our citizens deserve.

Affirmative action doesn't address or solve any of these problems. It is done to treat black people like our token victims, letting liberals feel virtuous for speaking up for them—while doing virtually nothing to help them.[333]

These liberal ideas aren't just stupid. They're also destructive and ungrounded. They're good examples of why these unrealistic Second Culture misunderstandings, like the Scarecrow's Delusion, do so much harm, and why the gatekeepers must come from people in the First Culture who, like Antaeus, have their feet on the ground in the real world.

The problem isn't limited to liberals. The problem is that, for the reasons already shown, we have mostly lost the ability to center ourselves or our culture around healthy ontological values and have degraded ourselves and our world into merely ideological squawkers. But to become only a Democrat, Christian, atheist, Republican, etc., is even cheaper than worshiping golden calves. To "bind back to" shallow and cheap ideals degrades us. It's a kind of theological *treason.*

---

[333] This is the point of Jason L. Riley's book *Please Stop Helping Us: How Liberals Make It Harder for Blacks to Succee*d, cited earlier.

DAVIDSON LOEHR

Society will continue to become more secular (etymology again: "secular" refers to this world). Church attendance has been estimated at under 20% for decades and will keep falling. If your religion has something applicable to people who will never believe your theology or ideology, figure out how to translate your religion's teaching into plain talk that is important and relevant regardless of individuals' beliefs.

Those still in a traditional Biblical, Koranic, Buddhist, Hindu, et al. religion have a great advantage because their books and their traditions have supplied them with a rich collection of stories and examples and metaphors, symbols, etc. that can appeal to children—at least until adolescence, when kids seem like slaves to the whims of their hormones, and are beginning to learn enough about the sciences to begin questioning and mostly rejecting the old stories that seem to have coherence only in a child's fantasy world.

There are many good theologians, however, who—like Origen 1,800 years ago—can help reframe the children's stories in terms of their symbols and metaphors, making it easy to relate them to life, and our increasingly scientific view of the universe.

Ordinary Language. I think this must be the trump suit. The challenge for traditional religion in a secular society is explaining what insights into life your religion offers that transcend God-talk. If people must believe your theology, your God, your salvation formula, then you'll continue to lose members, influence, and significance. If you can't translate it, then neither your religion nor your God is any bigger than that language game, that way of talking. That trivializes everything you think is holy: again, it is theological *treason*.

Atheists, "Scientism" devotees. Don't reject simplistic literal religion as though that's what religion is really about.

Intellectualism, scientism describes humans in too-simple ways. Origen again, or the Jesuit professor from 1961: "You *do* know these are *myths*, don't you?"

One Last Warning from Nature: The Liberal Death Spiral

The "Ant Death Spiral", first observed in 1910,[334] is a bizarre phenomenon that occurs when **one ant in the group loses the scent path;** in other words, loses its way. The result sees the other ants follow the ant that has become the leader, moving one after the other in a continuous, endless spiral, a vortex created by the trail of smell. *The death spiral is an example of what happens when the swarm gets misdirected. It is a convenient metaphor illustrating the perils of follow-the-leader behavior in any society.* When the scent of the last ant gets lost, the ant before that ant gets confused and cut off from the main pack. The ants then look this way and that, following the wrong trail which makes them walk in a never-ending spiral. Because they aren't aware that they are walking this spiral, they keep walking thinking that they are reaching their destination. This leads to them walking until they eventually die.

In our species, we observe a similar tragicomedy: *Ideo-*

---

[334] First observed in 1910 by the scientist W.M. Wheeler in his laboratory. He wrote: "I have never seen a more astonishing exhibition of the limitations of instinct. For nearly two whole days these blind creatures, so dependent on the contact-odor sense of their antennae, kept palpating their uniformly smooth, odoriferous trail and the advancing bodies of the ants immediately preceding them, without perceiving that they were making no progress but only wasting their energies, till the spell was finally broken by some more venturesome members of the colony." See https://www.bing.com/search?q=W.M.+Wheeler%2C+ant+death+spiral&form=QBLH&sp=-1&pq=w.m.+wheeler%2C+ant+death+spiral&sc=5-30&qs=n&sk=&cvid=22B2D2AEC10E4033B48551B96BFE6A30

logical death spirals. The tragic and murderous history of all but the barely surviving four socialisms of the past hundred years is a perfect example. An estimated 170 million of their own citizens were murdered while following blind but certain narcissistic and sociopathic leaders in circles of death, ending in death.

Conclusion

Why bother writing this book? Neither the available evidence nor a basic understanding of the "herd animal" nature of all social species—including our own—offer any compelling signs that the kind of ideological infections documented here can be removed from the body politic, after 40-60 (or 200) years.

To be blunt, there are two major conclusions to this book, one from each side of the "We" argument here.

First, I believe offering this confession is the responsible thing for me to do. No, I have no power in education, the media, politics, human/race relations, or religion that could force such a change in consciousness. But "We"—meaning the badly misguided ideology of current liberalism—have done deep and brutal harm to these institutions, our society, and our responsibility to help form the highest quality of new humans to replace us. Anyone who is aware must do *something*! I'm 80 now (born April 29, 1942), so these really aren't my problems, but the problems of the younger generations. Still, to remain silent felt treasonous at every level.

So much for my personal sense of decency and responsibility. No, I no longer agree with the leftist/socialist ideology that has done such deep harm to individuals and our culture. Most of the offenders count among the "ignorant masses" of the left. The overwhelming majority of us are among the ignorant masses of many groups. The small percentage of people who are shaping and teaching this ideology which Dr. Lyle

Rossiter has helpfully diagnosed as both narcissistic and sociopathic, however, are *not* innocent. And the self-serving harm they're doing is a mark of their own defective character. It's hard to get more serious or more criminal and treasonous.

But even if they understand this, they don't care, because they're quite sure that they are closer to victory than at any time in the past two centuries. Their goal is always and only power, and they believe they have an almost divine right to do whatever is required to get and keep the power to tell the rest of us how we must believe and live: the agenda of all socialisms, communisms, and totalitarianisms.

I'll give "them" the last word. They're certain they're right, as they are certain there isn't a damned thing you will do about any of this. It's gone on too long, has roots too deep, and has deformed many in the past two generations into unquestioning, unthinking, obedient herd animals. Much as I'd like to dream, they're positive that two facts are finally clear:

We've won, and—for at least the next generation—***you're screwed***.[335]

---

[335] For a short, well-researched, pessimistic and somewhat terrifying view of our current situation, see *Final Battle: The Next Election Could Be the Last*, by David Horowitz. Humanix Books, 2022.

BIBLIOGRAPHY

Arendt, Hannah. *The Origins of Totalitarianism*. A Harvest Book, 1968.

Ball, Tim. *The Deliberate Corruption of Climate Science*. Stairway Press, 2014.

Bartlett, Bruce. *Wrong on Race: The Democratic Party's Buried Past*. Macmillan, 2008.

Bastardi, Joe. *The Climate Chronicles: Inconvenient Revelations You Won't Hear from Al Gore—and Others*. Relentless Thunder Press, 2018.

Bastiat, Frederick. *The Law*. Creative Commons, 2013 (Originally published in 1850).

Bell, Larry. *Climate of Corruption: Politics and Power Behind the Global Warming Hoax*. Greenleaf Book Group Press, 2011.

Belzer, Richard and Wayne, David. *Dead Wrong: Straight Facts on the Country's Most Controversial Cover-ups*. Skyhorse Publishing, 2013.

Bernays, Edward. *Propaganda*. 1928.

Bernstein, William J. *The Delusions of Crowds: Why People GO MAD in GROUPS*. Atlantic Monthly Press, 2021.

_____. *Masters of the Word: How Media Shaped History from the Alphabet to the Internet*. Grove Press, 2013.

Brick, Howard and Parker, Gregory, Editors. A New Insurgency: The Port Huron Statement and Its Times. Maize Books, 2018.

Bryce, Robert. *Power Hungry: The Myths of "Green" Energy and the Real Fuels of the Future*. Perseus Books Group, 2011.

Bunker, Bruce C. *The Mythology of Global Warming: Climate Change Fiction vs. Scientific Facts*. Moonshine Cove Publishing, 2018.

Callenbach, Ernest. *Ecotopia*. Banyan Tree Books, 2014.

Chaffetz, Jason. *The Deep State: How an Army of Bureaucrats Protected Barack Obama and Is Working to Destroy the Trump Agenda*. Harper Collins, 2018.

Chomsky, Noam. *Profits over People: Neoliberalism and Global Order*. 7 Stories Press, 1999.

Codevilla, Angelo M. *The Ruling Class: How They Corrupted America and What We Can Do About It*. Beaufort Books, 2010.

Delingpole, James. *Watermelons: The Green Movement's True Colors*. Publius Books, 2011.

DiLorenzo, Thomas J. *The Problem with Socialism*. Regnery Publishing, 2016.

Driessen, Paul. *Eco-Imperialism: Green Power, Black Death*. The Free Enterprise Press, 2003-2004.

Dyson, Freeman J. *A Many-Colored Glass: Reflections on the Place of Life in the Universe*. University of Virginia Press, 2007.

Ellis, Bret Easton. *White*. Alfred A. Knopf, 2019.

Ellis, John M. *The Breakdown of Higher Education: How It Happened, the Damage It Does, and What Can Be Done*. Encounter Books (August 10, 2021).

Fray, Calvin. *Climate Change Reality Check: Basic Facts that Quickly Prove the Global Warming Crusade is Wrong and Dangerous*. Calvin Fray, 2016.

Friedrichs, Rebecca. *Standing up to Goliath: Battling State and National Teachers' Unions for the Heart and Soul of Our Kids and Country*. Post Hill Press, 2018.

Gibelyou, Cameron and Northrop, Douglas. *Big Ideas: A Guide to the History of Everything*. Oxford University Press, 2021

Goreham, Steve. *Climatism: Science, Common Sense, and the 21st Century's Hottest Topic*. New Lenox Books, 2010.

_____. *The Mad, Mad, Mad World of Climatism: Mankind and Climate Change Mania*. New Lenox Books, 2012.

Graeber, David and Wengrow, David. *The Dawn of Everything: A New History of Humanity*. Farrar, Straus and Giroux, 2021.

Groseclose, Tim. *Left Turn: How Liberal Media Bias Distorts the American Mind.* St. Martin's Griffin, 2011.

Guyenot, Laurent. *JFK-9/11: 50 Years of Deep State.* Progressive Press, 2014.

Halpern, S. William. *Germany Tried Democracy: A Political History of the Reich from 1918 to 1933.* W.W. Norton & Co., 1974.

Hayek, F.A. *The Road to Serfdom (The Definitive Edition).* University of Chicago Press, 2007.

Hedges, Chris. *Death of the Liberal Class.* Nation Books, 2010.

Herland, Hanne Nabintu. *New Left Tyranny: The Authoritarian Destruction of Our Way of Life.* Christian Publishing House, Cambridge, Ohio, 2020.

Himmelfarb, Gertrude. *One Nation, Two Cultures.* Alfred A. Knopf, 1999.

Isaac, Rael Jean and Erich. *The Coercive Utopians.* Regnery Gateway, 1984.

Isaac, Rael Jean. *Roosters of the Apocalypse: How the Junk Science of Global Warming is Bankrupting the Western World (New, Revised and Expanded Edition).* CreateSpace Independent Publishing Platform, November 25, 2013.

Jamail, Dahr. *The End of Ice: Bearing Witness and Finding Meaning in the Path of Climate Disruption.* The New Press, 2019.

King, M.S. *Proofs of the New World Order: Quotes from Famous People Confirming the One-World Government Conspiracy.* Tomato Bubble, 2018.

Kingsnorth, Paul. *Confessions of a Recovering Environmentalist and Other Essays.* Faber & Faber Ltd., London, 2017.

Krauthammer, Charles. *Things That Matter: Three Decades of Passions, Pastimes and Politics.* Crown Forum, 2015.

Laframboise, Donna. *Into the Dustbin: Rajendra Pachauri, the Climate Report & the Nobel Peace Prize.* Ivy Avenue Press, 2013.

_____. *The Delinquent Teenager Who Was Mistaken for the World's Top Climate Expert.* Ivy Avenue Press, 2011.

Landes, Richard. *Heaven and Earth: The Varieties of the Millennial Experience.* Oxford University Press, 2011.

Lasch, Christopher. *The Revolt of the Elites and Betrayal of Democracy.* W.W. Norton & Co., 1996.

_____. *The Culture of Narcissism: American Life in an Age of Diminishing Expectations.* W.W. Norton & Co., 1979.

Le Bon, Gustave. *The Crowd: A Study of the Popular Mind.* Dover, 2002 (Original edition 1895).

Levin, Mark R. *Unfreedom of the Press.* Threshold Editions, 2019.

Lord, Jeffrey. *Swamp Wars: Donald Trump and the New American Populism vs. The Old Order.* Bombardier Books, 2019.

Lukianoff, Greg and Haidt, Jonathan. *The Coddling of the American Mind: How Good Intentions and Bad Ideas are Setting Up a Generation for Failure.* Penguin Press, 2018.4

MacDonald, Heather. *The Diversity Delusion: How Race and Gender Pandering Corrupt the University and Undermine Our Culture.* St. Martin's Griffin, 2018.

MacKay, Charles. *Extraordinary Popular Delusions and the Madness of Crowds.* Pantianos Classice, 1841.

McWhiney, Grady. *Cracker Culture: Celtic Ways in the Old South.* University of Alabama Press, 1988.

McWhorter, John. *WOKE Racism: How a New Religion Has Betrayed Black America.* Penguin, 2021.

Michaels, Patrick J. and Knappenberger, Paul C. *Lukewarming: The New Climate Science that Changes Everything.* The Cato Institute, 2016.

Montford, A.W. *The Hockey Stick Illusion: Climategate and the Corruption of Science.* Stacey International, 2010.

Morano, Marc. *The Politically Incorrect Guide to Climate Change.* Regnery Publishing, 2018.

Moriarty, Patrick and Honnery, Damon. *Green Energy and Technology: Rise and Fall of the Carbon Civilisation: Resolving Global Environmental and Resource Problems.* Springer-Verlag, 2011.

Murray, Douglas. *The Madness of Crowds: Gender, Race and Identity.* Bloomsbury Continuum, 2019.

_____. *The Strange Death of Europe: Immigration, Identity, Islam.* Bloomsbury Publishing, 2017.

Murray, William J. *Utopian Road to Hell: Enslaving America and the World with Central Planning.* WND Books, 2016.

Newman, Lawrence. *The Climate Change Hoax: Pathway to Socialism.* Silver Millennium Publications, Inc., 2021.

Nunes, Devin. *Countdown to Socialism.* Encounter Broadside, 2020.

Owens, Candace. *Blackout: How Black America can Make its Second Escape from the Democrat Plantation.* Threshold Editions, 2020.

Plato. *The Republic (Translated by Benjamin Jowett).* Logos Books, 2021 (Originally published in 1892).

_____. *Republic (Translated by G.M.A. Grube).* Hacket Publishing Co., 1992. (This is thought to have been written in 380 BC).

_____. *Dialogues on the Trial & Death of Socrates: Euthyphro, Apology, Crito, Phaedo.* Translated by Benjamin Jowett.

Plimer, Ian. *Heaven and Earth: global warming, the missing science.* Taylor Trade,2009.

_____. *Climate change delusion and the great electricity rip-off.* Connor Court Publishing Pty Ltd., 2017.

Prager, Dennis, Joseph, Mark, Editors. *No Safe Spaces.* Regnery Publishing, 2019.

Rauch, Jonathan. *Kindly Inquisitors: The New Attacks on Free Thought.* The University of Chicago Press, 2013.

Reilly, Wilfred. *Taboo: 10 Facts You Can't Talk About.* Regnery Publishing, 2020.

Riley, Jason L. *Please Stop Helping Us: How Liberals Make it Harder for Blacks to Succeed.* Encounter Books, 2014-2015.

_____. *The Black Boom.* Templeton Press, 2022.

Roberts, Donald and Tren, Richard. *The Excellent Powder: DDT's Political and Scientific History.* Dog Ear Publishing, 2010.

Rossiter, Jr., Lyle H. *The Liberal Mind: The Psychological Causes of Political Madness*. Free World Books, 2006.

Ryun, Ned. *Restoring Our Republic: The Making of the Republic and How We Reclaim It Before It's Too Late*. Ned Ryun, 2019.

Sayet, Evan. *The WOKE Supremacy: An Anti-Socialist Manifesto*. Evan Sayet, no date.

Schneider, Anne Larason. *A Self-Confessed White Supremacy Culture: The Emergence of an Illiberal Left in Unitarian Universalism*. Anne Larason Schneider, 2019.

Schweitzer, Peter. *Profiles in Corruption: Abuse of Power by America's Progressive Elite*. HarperCollins Publishers, 2020.

Siegel, Fred. *The Revolt Against the Masses: How Liberalism has Undermined the Middle Class*. Encounter Books, 2015.

Simon, Roger L. *I Know Best: How Moral Narcissism is Destroying Our Republic, If It Hasn't Already*. Encounter Books, 2020.

Singer, S. Fred and Avery, Dennis T. *Unstoppable (Every 1,500 Years) Global Warming*. Rowman and Littlefield Publishers, Inc., 2008.

Skousen, Paul B. *The Naked Socialist*. Ensign Publishing Co., 2014.

Sowell, Thomas. *A Conflict of Visions: Ideological Origins of Political Struggles*. Basic Books, 2007.

_____. *Black Rednecks and White Liberals*. Encounter Books, 2005.

_____. *The Vision of the Anointed: Self-Congratulation as a Basis for Social Policy*. Basic Books, 1995.

_____. *The Dismantling of America*. Basic Books, 2010.

_____. *Discrimination and Disparities*. Basic Books, 2019.

_____. *Intellectuals and Race*. Basic Books, 2013.

_____. *Intellectuals and Society (Revised and Enlarged Edition)*. Basic Books, 2011.

_____. *Knowledge and Decisions*. Basic Books, 1980.

Spencer, Roy. *Climate Confusion: How Global Warming Hysteria Leads to Bad Science, Pandering Politicians and Misguided Policies that Hurt the Poor*. Encounter Books, 2009.

_____. *The Great Global Warming Blunder: How Mother Nature Fooled the World's Top Climate Scientists*. Encounter Books, 2013.

Starkes, Taleeb. *Black Lies Matter: Why Lies Matter to the Race Grievance Industry*. Taleeb Starkes, 2016.

Steele, Shelby. *A Dream Deferred: The Second Betrayal of Black Freedom in America*. Harper Perenniel, 1998.

_____. *White Guilt: How Blacks and Whites Together Destroyed the Promise of the Civil Rights Era*. Harper Perennial, 2006.

Stout, Martha. *The Myth of Sanity: Divided Consciousness and the Promise of Awareness. Tales of multiple personality in everyday life*. Penguin Books, 2002.

Strong, Maurice. *Where on Earth are We Going?* Texere LLC, 2000.

Sussman, Brian. *Climategate: A Veteran Meteorologist Exposes the Global Warming Scam*. WND Books, 2010.

Tren, Richard and Bate, Roger. *Malaria and the DDT Story*. Institute of Economic Affairs, 2001.

Williams, Walter E. *Liberty Versus the Tyranny of Socialism: Controversial Essays*. Hoover Institution Press, 2008.

_____. *American Contempt for Liberty*. Hoover Institution Press, 2015.

Wrightstone, Gregory. *Inconvenient Facts: The Science that Al Gore Doesn't Want You To Know*. Silver Crown Productions, 2017.

Yadav, Nitish. "Plato's Theory of the Philosopher King". https://www.academia.edu/37809734/Platos_Theory_Of_Philosopher_King

VIDEOS

Gibbs, Jeff. *Planet of the Humans*. Executive Producer Michael Moore. 2020.

About Atmosphere Press

Atmosphere Press is an independent, full-service publisher for excellent books in all genres and for all audiences. Learn more about what we do at atmospherepress.com.

We encourage you to check out some of Atmosphere's latest releases, which are available at Amazon.com and via order from your local bookstore:

ABOUT THE AUTHOR

Davidson Loehr is a Renaissance Man—or just someone who never grew up. A professional musician from ages 16 – 21, playing clarinet, alto and tenor saxophone in rock 'n roll combos, Dixieland, jazz, and dance bands, before enlisting in the Army at 21. He wanted the best and most challenging experiences he could get, and all of his jobs during that 43 months came from arranging interviews with Colonels, convincing them that the Army could get more of its money's worth out of him doing it his way. It worked every time.

While in Germany, he attended the 7th Army NCO Academy in Bad Tolz, which was the Army's best, held in the building that had been General Patton's WWII headquarters. Then after nine months in Germany, back to the States for six months in Artillery Officer Candidate School: another excellent and challenging experience. After OCS, nine months as Assistant Brigade Adjutant for a 4,500 man training brigade. Sent to Vietnam, another interview, which made him the Vietnam Entertainment Officer, with the small office that handled all USO shows that toured the country except the Bob Hope show (which was so big it had its own office), working with some childhood heroes, like Roy Rogers, Dale Evans, Martha Raye, Jennifer Jones, Arthur Godfrey, and Jimmy Boyd. But after a few months, when an OCS classmate was awarded the Purple Heart and Silver Star, his cocky little world came crashing down. Now he saw war as an archetypal event, this as his only chance to experience it, and felt that if he returned home without having experienced war, he wouldn't want to live with himself. So after the next arranged interview, he served his final seven months as combat photographer and press officer with the 11th Armored Cavalry Regiment in Xuan Loc. He also got to know Co Rentmeester, LIFE Magazine's Vietnam War photographer, and convinced him to shoot a photographic feature on the Black Horse Regiment (11th Armored Cavalry—in the June 2, 1967 issue). Those seven months remain sacred for him; the first five months, merely a whole lot of fun.

In August 1967, after returning from Vietnam, like many vets, he was a little lost for about a dozen years. He completed his degree in music theory at the University of Michigan, then did Master's work at North Texas University to learn jazz arranging. But for him, music wouldn't be a fulfilling career. So he spent time studying with half a dozen of the best people-photographers in the country, then owned a high-priced portrait and wedding photography studio in Ann Arbor.* But that also got boring, so he sold the studio and learned carpentry and woodworking until he decided woodworking made a better hobby than profession.

What, then? Surely not religion! He was through with religion at age six, when he decided it was a dishonest and irrelevant subject. But thirty years later, he grew to realize that if it could be done honestly, it could be challenging enough to fill a lifetime. He still wanted the best—and so, an M.A. in "Methods of Studying Religion" and a Ph.D. in theology, philosophy of religion, philosophy

---

* See his 2022 book, *STORIES OF LIFE: The Nature, Formation, and Consequences of Character* for some outstanding portraits and stories.

of science, and Wittgenstein's "language philosophy" from the University of Chicago, then a year as a staff hospital chaplan and 23 years as a Unitarian minister, retiring in 2009. He has been a Fellow in the liberal Jesus Seminar since 1992. And in 2014, he joined a new group, the International Big History Association (IBHA), where he has presented papers and written a chapter for their 2022 book, *Science, Religion, and Deep Time.* Davidson's chapter is on "The Nature of Humans, Science, and Religion."